WALKING PALESTINE

25 Journeys into the West Bank

STEFAN SZEPESI

Signal

Oxford

This book is dedicated to you

First published in 2012 by
Signal Books Limited
36 Minster Road
Oxford OX4 1LY
United Kingdom
www.signalbooks.co.uk

This edition converted and created in 2017 by
Andrews UK Limited
www.andrewsuk.com

General Editor: Michel S. Moushabeck
Assistant Editors: Ramon Elinevsky, Leyla Moushabeck
Proofreaders: Sara Rauch, Shannon Laurel Barnsley
Production: Pam Fontes-May
Cartography: Stefan Szepesi and Issa Zboun
Cover photo: Rolf Bos
Book Design: James McDonald / The Impress Group
Photo Credits: Ahmad al-Bazz: 84; Andrea Krogmann: 15, 19, 96, 108, 141, 148, 150, 234, 236-237, 238, 239, 240, 260; Angela Goerlach: 201, 216-217, 218; Carla Benelli: 220; Benjamin Goerlach: 167, 204; Dima Khoury: 241; Erik van Houwelingen: 158-159, 160, 166, 261; Ilse van Heusden: 140; Imad al-Atrash: 30, 40, 41, 85; Italian Cooperation Office: 248-249, 252; Joris van Winckel: 27, 90, 92, 100; Kirsten Asmus: 57, 112, 251; Mamoun Abufarha: 66, 265; Moenes Qatami: 42; Mujahed Abu al-Rob: 60; Natacha Mathy: 145, 151; Peder Larsson: 257; Philipp Meissner: 7, 56, 64, 138, 173; Rolf Bos: 102, 206-207; Rüdiger Hamann: 35, 81, 101, 102, 155, 262; Sander van Hoorn: 20, 39, 76, 89, 94-95, 98, 99, 114, 117, 120, 127, 144, 152, 153, 165, 177, 182, 193, 226, 229, 235, 245; Sandra de Waele: 109; Stefan Szepesi: 25, 46, 47, 51, 52, 54-55, 61, 62, 65, 67, 68, 69, 72, 74, 75, 78-79, 80, 91, 103, 113, 121, 123, 125, 128, 129, 130, 131, 135, 136, 149, 154, 162, 163, 164, 170, 172, 174, 175, 176, 180, 183, 184, 186, 187, 191, 192, 194, 197, 198, 199, 200, 205, 212, 213, 215, 219, 221, 225, 227, 228, 232, 244, 253, 255, 256, 258, 268

Word of Thanks

The idea for this book would not have occurred to me if it was not for the generosity of the people I met on and off the trail in the past years. *Shukran ala husn ildiyafaa* to all those who I encountered while walking: farmers, shepherds, Bedouin, picnicking or olive picking families, shopkeepers, taxi drivers, priests, and the list goes on. *Walking Palestine* was an immersion into the meaning of hospitality for me, and I've never regretted accepting any of the invitations for coffee in the middle of nowhere which allowed me to become familiar with a Palestine behind the headlines.

In Jerusalem, I am grateful to Tony Blair and to the many friends and colleagues at the Office of the Quartet Representative, the European Union Representation Office, and to a wide range of Palestinian and Israeli individuals in government, business and civil society who I have been working with in the last five years. Their stubborn dedication to keep working for peace in the face of countless obstacles has provided much of the inspiration for this book.

The list of people I owe gratitude to for invaluable advice on exploring specific areas in this book, for practical assistance in its completion, or simply for the creative brainwaves they caused, is long. At risk of inadvertently missing a few, my thanks goes out to Adel Yahya, Avner Goren, Awad Duaibes, Basil Ayish, Carla Benelli, Clemens Messerschmid, David Landis, Elias Tabban, Fadi Jueejat, Firas Raad, Fuad Bateh, George Mashriqi, George Rishmawi, Gerhard Schlaudraff, Gidon Blomberg, Giovanni Antonelli Fontana, Hassan Muamer, Hijazi Eid, Ibrahim Odeh, Imad al-Atrash, Jad Abu Said, John Deverell, John Edwards, Lubna Ghneim, Maria Khoury, Mazen Iwais, Michel Awad, Michel Massad, Mohammed Atari, Nasser Abu Farha, Nassim Nour, Nick Robson, Nidal Kanzou, Omar Abu Harthiyeh, Osama Hamdan, Patricia Selwick, Raed Saadeh, Raja Shehadeh, Rami Duaibes, Rianne Franken, Samer Haddad, Samia Botmeh, Sari Ghazel, Shadi Kiwan, Shireen Ibrahim, Suheib Houareh, and Zaghloul Samhaan.

I am especially grateful to Michel Moushabeck at Interlink Publishing for taking on this rather unusual book in his collection. As a Palestinian who has walked some of the most challenging trails on the globe, I hope these pages inspire him to make his first return trip in 45 years and walk Palestine. Thanks also to James McDonald and Ramon Elinevsky for their dedication and care in designing and editing this book.

Further thanks to Issa Zboun at the Alternative Research Institute of Jerusalem (ARIJ) for doing an excellent job on mapping the trails in this book; to Tarek Atrissi and Paul Klok for designing the logo and helping me create an inspiring face of Walking Palestine's virtual community online; and to my good friends back home: Bas Banning,

Freek Roset and Victor Wollaert for their critical armchair reading of the manuscript.

The Walking Palestine group that started loosely with a few early enthusiasts in 2008 and eventually grew to over 200 foreign and Palestinian walkers has been vital to the writing of this book. Group members willingly served as "dummies" in testing walking routes and their energy, feedback, and enthusiasm have been a constant inspiration for me.

For many images in this book, I have gratefully relied on the photography virtues of fellow walkers: thanks to Andrea Krogmann, Angela and Benjamin Goerlach, Dima Khoury, Erik van Houwelingen, Ilse van Heusden, Joris van Winckel, Kirsten Asmus, Natacha Mathy, Peder Larsson, Philipp Meissner, Rolf Bos, Rüdiger Hamann, Sander van Hoorn, and Sandra de Waele. Special thanks to Imad al-Atrash of the Palestinian Wildlife Society who generously shared his image database of Palestinian flora and fauna and to Alaa Ashkar for joining hands with me in organizing the Palestine Outdoors Photo Competition for young photographers. I'm very excited some of the work made by the winner, Moenes Qatami, and some of the other competitors, Ahmad al-Bazz, Ma'amoen Abu Farha, and Mujahed Abu al-Rob, is used in this book and on the website.

For leading countless test walks across the West Bank throughout 2010 and 2011 and for providing detailed feedback on logistics and trail descriptions, I am immensely indebted to Sander van Hoorn, Yvette Szepesi, and Helen Winterton. They walked it all and dealt bravely with their many adversaries such as the summer heat, uncertain road directions, a fear of heights, and most impressively, a strong inborn reluctance to get up early in the weekend. For providing extensive critical feedback on early drafts, helping with map design, test walking various trails twice, and for a lot of other things, I owe about a dozen other thanks to Sander. And he owes me at least one for being in so much better shape than he was two years ago. Yvette provided a true home away from home on my monthly visits back to Jerusalem. She still is my favorite sister, even if she is the only one I have.

This book would not exist without the one person who stood through the writing of it all from nearby and, so much harder, from afar. My love to Kirsten for always walking with me, every step of the way.

Walk good.

—*Stefan Szepesi*

Map Legend

 start and end of trail

 end of trail on non-circular trails

 trail (marked or unmarked)

 nr corresponding to direction in text

 Palestinian village

 wadi

 elevation in meters

 spring or cistern

 large road

 main road

 small road

 dirt road

 road number

 pretty neat view

 point of interest

 mosque

 church or monastery

 archeological heritage

 restaurant

 uncultivated land, forest, wild vegetation

 cultivated land

 division areas a,b and c

 Israeli settlement

 Israeli millitary base

 seperation barrier

Green Line (1949 Armistice Line)

 attention to route (directions may not be obvious)

and flowering shrubs. Summer provides the opportunity to enjoy the starkness of the arid landscape with its large variety of limestone rocks with their contrasting hues.

With all this beauty, mostly, the Palestinian landscape described in this book is never dazzling, hardly ever dramatic. It is just lovely. And yet with all the unique pleasures awaiting walkers, Palestine continues to be an area that has been neglected by walkers. This is not only because of the devastating effect of the politics but also because the infrastructure of walking, the ordnance maps, the walkers' guide, the marked trails are, on the whole, absent. Newcomers to the area would not know how to go about planning their walks. This is why *Walking Palestine: 25 Walks into the West Bank* is indispensible for anyone wanting to walk in Palestine or simply interested in reading about what this important region of the world has to offer.

This book offers walkers sound advice on how to plan for the walks, what to look out for and what to expect. Each walk becomes an occasion to take excursions in Palestinian anthropology, archeology and social history. And he ends each excursion with suggestions of a place for rest and a cup of tea or a meal and experiencing Palestinian hospitality. Each of the walks Stefan has chosen to write about is carefully described with good accompanying maps and GPS positioning for those using modern technology. While filling an important gap in the available literature, this book will no doubt be treasured and used by all those who have wanted to walk in Palestine but didn't know how to go about it. It is a guide to enjoy and to trust. So read along, put on your boots and start walking. And be prepared for experiences that will surely be memorable.

—*Raja Shehadeh*

Jersualem wilderness, to one of the first instances of terrace agriculture in Battir, to the throne village in Ras Karkar where an Ottoman period citadel has recently been renovated, to the town of Taybeh where Palestinian beer is produced, to the lush spring of Wadi Auja near Jericho and to the beautiful hills around Ramallah. Each walk serves not only as an occasion to encounter a different terrain but to comment on the various facets of Palestinian life and history. Stefan also attempts to explain some of the more Kafkaesque political arrangements and land designations of the period after the Oslo Accords.

Not too long ago, Palestinian villagers moved from village to village using dirt tracks along the hills and in the wadis. Some of these are ancient trails that go back many hundreds of years. They are marked on old British mandate-era ordnance maps. With the changes that have occurred in the region few of these have survived. Most of what remains are paths created by the shepherds. The evocative sight of flocks of goats and sheep grazing on West Bank hills is not uncommon. It is often accompanied by another encounter with the beautiful sound of the *nay* (reed flute) music played by the shepherds, reverberating in the hills.

Much of the landscape in the West Bank is rapidly being destroyed by road works, expansion of existing cities and the fast unprecedented increase in the Jewish settlements being established there in violation of international law. These are specifically designed to confiscate as large an area of Palestinian land as possible in the shortest period of time. It is as though the Israeli authorities responsible for this illegal activity are engaged in a race to claim as much of the land in the West Bank as they possibly can in their continuing attempt at creating new political facts which they hope would prejudice the political future of the land in favor of an expanded Israeli state. As a result, many areas of outstanding beauty have been destroyed by the hastily built Jewish settlements that stand out as artificial impositions on the delicate features and contours of this ancient land.

Yet despite the massive devastation that has blighted this land there still remain areas which have been untouched by the effect of recent developments. Some of these possess a unique beauty that cannot be found anywhere else in the world. Every season provides its own special pleasures. Autumn, with its moderate weather when the sun is shielded by the clouds that begin to gather in this season, provides ideal conditions for taking a walk. Winter is the time when the dust of summer has been washed away and the air has become fresh and clear. It is also the time when the cyclamen, crocus and other early bulbs begin to sprout, when the almond trees blossom and the grass begins to cover the hills. Spring is lush and green. It is the time when the hills are covered by a great variety of wild flowers

Spring in Turmus'ayya

Foreword

The best way to know a place is to walk it. It is no exaggeration to say that Palestine is a walker's paradise. The weather is temperate and the landscape has much to offer all year round. Yet in recent years Palestine's West Bank—the central highlands—has acquired an uneasy reputation. But as Stefan Szepesi writes in the introduction to this splendid book: "Simply put, there is another Palestine from the one filling our television screens." In the course of the four years when he lived there, he came to know and love that other Palestine and this book is a testament of his appreciation of this precious land and an invitation to others to experience it for themselves.

The twenty five walks described here provide an excellent guide to the small but varied area of the West Bank: the desert, the plain, the hills, the wadis. These walks take you to the Roman stadium in historical Sebastia, to the springs of Wadi Bidan near Nablus, to the plains of Jenin, to the desert monasteries in Wadi Qelt and the

Contents

Introduction

The Walks

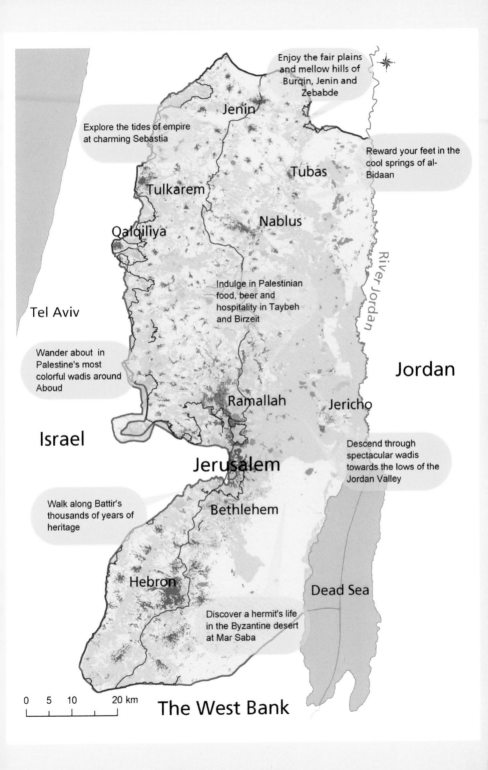

The Unfortunate Timing of Mark Twain

Of all the lands there are for dismal scenery, Palestine must be the prince.
— *Mark Twain,* The Innocents Abroad

Amidst the piles of travel literature about Palestine, Mark Twain's account of his journey in 1867 is legendary. I started reading *The Innocents Abroad* when I took up walking across the West Bank, geographically a small part of the Palestine that Twain had visited; yet subject to a large share of his writing. I was eager to read what had become Twain's most successful book during his lifetime. *The Innocents Abroad* sold three times as many copies in its first year of publication as *The Adventures of Tom Sawyer*. But more important, 140 years after it first appeared *Innocents* remains a classic of travel literature. Its passages quoted today often concern Twain's scorn of Palestine as an unappealing place, unworthy of a visit. Indeed, there is little nuance in Twain's words as at various points in his book he describes the land as desolate and unlovely, monotonous and uninviting.

I enjoyed reading *Innocents*, especially Twain's constant mockery of the circus around holy sites, the evangelical zeal of guidebooks, the shameful vandalism of his fellow American pilgrims and the occasional self-ridicule of the writer. Yet his judgment on the appeal of Palestine became more and more of a puzzle to me as I walked across the West Bank, at times literally in his footsteps. Twain's blunt verdict stood in sharp contrast to the dramatic and varied landscapes I saw and the kindness I encountered along the way; spectacular steep hills and deep wadis; the deserts and green plains; the ancient springs and glistening olive groves; countless places of antiquity and spirituality; and people that were welcoming without exception. Monotonous? No. Uninviting? Quite the opposite. Unlovely? Not in the least. Desolate? Yes, in the desert and on high hilltops, but to me that only enhanced its dramatic appeal. In 1867, it seems, Twain managed to accomplish on his own what thousands of news reports about Palestine and Israel achieve today: an impression of a region that is shrouded in misery and is unattractive for visitors.

So what explains Twain's insistence that Palestine was not worthwhile visiting? Was it an impulse to write something radical; to deal once and for all with all the worn clichés about the "sacred beauty" of the Holy Land? Twain's harsh judgment seems to stem in part from the travel books he carried along. A strong theme throughout *Innocents* was to shred to pieces the travel writing by his American contemporaries who were praising the beauty of the biblical landscape only through their hearts as devout Christians but with their eyes blind to the real world in front of them. He rejected the norm of his time in which travel books described places, especially biblical places, in jubilee style only, creating high expectations that were never met by actual travelers. Perhaps because there was so much religious zeal in the work of his fellow travel writers Twain deliberately adopted the opposite approach, embracing and emphasizing all that was unappealing to him.

But there was something else. Looking back now at Twain's five month journey across Europe and the Holy Land, it is striking how unfortunate his timing was. For starters, Twain hardly had any time to begin with. *This book is a record of a pleasure trip* the author writes in the preface of *Innocents*. But there was no time for any pleasure once the party reached the shores of the Holy Land. After some three months of traveling through a dozen countries in Europe, their steamship delivered Mark Twain and a group of American pilgrims to Beirut on September 10, 1867. The party left the Holy Land from Jaffa on the first of October. All in all, Twain visited Beirut, Baalbek, Damascus, Nazareth, Capernaum and the Sea of Galilee, Sebastia, Nablus, Jerusalem, Jericho, the Dead Sea, the Judean desert, Bethlehem, Jaffa and nearly all places of biblical significance on this route in just 20 days. He covered the entire distance on horseback and foot in one of the hottest seasons in the year. The intensity of the trip would be unheard of even today. The journey would also be impossible to complete today as myriad boundaries have long since carved up Twain's Palestine and the wider Holy Land that he traveled.

Throughout his journey, it seems that Twain was determined to endure rather than enjoy traveling in the Holy Land. No doubt it helped produce some of his most ironic and humorous writing but there was no time for the slightest diversion off the pilgrim's beaten track, for some quiet days of rest and recovery, or for any local encounter; there was always another site to visit; so much so that Twain lamented a travel weariness typical to the Holy Land:

> How it wears a man out to have to read up a hundred pages of history every two or three miles—for verily the celebrated localities of Palestine occur that close together. How wearily, how bewilderingly they swarm about your path!

And then there is the timing for the journey itself. Twain unfortunately was in all the right places at exactly the wrong time. Climate and seasons matter for any place but this is especially valid for Palestine's appeal to first-time visitors. Twain and his party arrived just near the end of Palestine's hot summer and left just before the first rains started to green the country. He traveled when the hills were monotone brown and barren, the valleys yellow and dry; a land furthest removed from the many scents and colors that is Palestine in winter and springtime. You have to walk in September to know what that feels like: the country seems so arid that you cannot imagine it will be lush and green in the next one hundred years; yet six months later you cannot conceive that it will turn dry and barren ever again. Mark Twain missed the spectacle of the mild Palestinian winter and spring, the radiance of almond blossoms, the sight of a thousand red anemones underneath the olive trees.

Twain's timing was in many ways also historically unfortunate. The Palestine that Twain visited was politically a rural backwater, located at the fringe of the Ottoman empire whose rule was still firmly in place after more than three hundred years. The Ottomans were ready, or so it seemed at the time, to continue that rule for another three hundred years. Twain thus focused on sightseeing and devoted little attention to any of the local or regional politics. Had Twain lived one hundred years later, he would have traveled a region that had just been through numerous revolts, revolutions, wars and world wars; for better or worse, it had asserted itself at the center of world attention for decades to come. But Twain traveled the historically quiet waters of 1867, and not the dramatic ones of 1967.

The emphasis in *Innocents* is on Palestine's religious sites and Twain gives serious advance warning to future pilgrims: high expectations will cater to deep disappointments. Twain laments the lack of true excitement for a traveler who moves by traditional travel guides only: a pre-determined itinerary to see pre-described places that are pre-valued as being very special. Any sense of real discovery is drained

from the experience. The disjunction between the emotions stirred up by romantic images of biblical scenes and the reality of Palestine in 1867 became apparent throughout his journey. Twain could not resist its irony:

> When I was a boy I somehow got the impression that the River Jordan was 4,000 miles long and 35 miles wide. It is only ninety miles long, and so crooked that a man does not know which side of it he is on half the time. In going ninety miles it does not get over more than fifty miles of ground. It is not any wider than Broadway in New York. There is the Sea of Galilee and this Dead Sea—neither of them twenty miles long or thirteen wide. And yet when I was in Sunday school I thought they were sixty thousand miles in diameter.

When leaving from Jaffa at the end of his journey, Twain sums up his experience with one brief phrase: "It is a dream-land." As if, perhaps, he recommended others to continue dreaming about it, but not to actually visit. A visit, after all, could only shatter pretty images of biblical serenity and sacred places. By safely imagining the dreamland from home this picture would remain untouched by reality.

Had Mark Twain made his trip once more today, he would no doubt make a different kind of journey. He would probably tick off less holy sites and divert much of his attention to more contemporary issues, not least the political geography of Jerusalem, West Bank, Israel and Gaza, and the myriad other divisions that are layered over the Palestine of 1867. Rather than ridiculing the behavior of his fellow American pilgrims, he probably would have mocked the circus of foreign diplomats running in and out of Jerusalem, Ramallah and Tel Aviv. Perhaps, he would even have written another *Adventures of Tom Sawyer* in a Palestinian-Israeli setting. And with time on his side, he would plan his journey better, stay a while longer, and walk through Palestine in the right season.

In contrast to the Palestine of *The Innocents Abroad*, where biblical pictures dominated people's expectations, the view on present day Palestine is largely fixed in people's minds through constant images of conflict and the belief that, as long as the conflict remains unresolved, today's Palestine is undesirable as a travel destination. Many travelers still opt to stay home because of this. But as in Twain's journey, pre-conceived images give a partial and twisted reflection of a diverse and complex reality. Simply put, there is another Palestine from the one filling our television screens. Mark Twain made clear that travel books cannot erase the fixed images in our minds; they tend to make it worse. Only a personal journey, a visit, an encounter, a walk, can start breaking them down.

Triple Palestine: The Story of this Book

If you relish a good fight online, type in Palestine in Wikipedia and start scrolling down the discussion page. Few names are as recognizable and controversial. When and where the word originated is only a minor part of the dispute. The Greek historian Herodotus was the first to mention it in the 5th century BC. Or was it Egyptian sources many centuries earlier? Perhaps the Assyrians? In any case, the Romans formalized the name Palestine in their administration and under the Eastern Roman Empire, three of them were declared at one point in time, dividing up the region—in a typical Byzantine way—into Palaestina Prima, Palaestina Secunda, and Palaestina Tertia. Indeed, history does repeat itself.

In today's world, predominantly two images spring to mind when the word Palestine is mentioned. One image is that of historic Palestine, the land lying roughly in between the Jordan River and the Mediterranean, a region populated by Christians, Muslims and Jews, which has been referred to as Palestine throughout many historical periods. The second image is that of the State of Palestine, to be created as a modern and sovereign country, free of Israeli occupation, and the fulfillment of the much repeated mantra of international resolutions and American Presidential declarations on "two states, Israel and Palestine, living side by side in peace and security." Over a hundred countries in the world have already recognized this State of Palestine and at the time this book went to press the Palestinians were taking their case for statehood to the United Nations. It is unclear what this will mean on the ground in terms of actual sovereignty, neither is it obvious what it holds for the part on "side by side in peace and security."

Amidst all the debate on its past and future, however, there is of course a third one: Palestine today. It is the most elusive of the three but the Palestine of the present exists: undefined at its edges, yet so alive at its core. It is the Palestine of the Palestinian people, their culture, their hospitality, their hopes and grievances, their turbulent mix of cosmopolitanism and traditionalism, their lives and minds under occupation and in freedom, their family ties across space and time, their connection to their land, their pride and steadfastness. They all make up Palestine today; not as an abstract idea but as reality. And like in the old days of Abraham and Jesus, of Mark Twain and T. E. Lawrence, this Palestine can still be explored on foot.

I first started walking out of curiosity. What was Palestine like beyond the confined view of a diplomatic car? As one of the thousands of foreign residents of Jerusalem working as diplomats, humanitarian workers, volunteers, or journalists, I had been traveling through the West Bank but never really spent time there. Ramallah and Jerusalem are the central hubs for international diplomacy on the Israeli-Palestinian conflict; an occasional visit to Nablus or Hebron is already considered quite exotic. But most diplomats hardly see anything of Palestine's rural culture and its long stretches of wilderness; they see Palestinians, but they miss Palestine.

My curiosity was split between the urge to get to know this more rural and more scenic Palestine, and a more practical question I had: could it be done? None of my guidebooks mentioned anything about places to walk; there were no maps to speak of and no information on what there was to see in and around the hundreds of small Palestinian villages that dot the West Bank hills. More generally, among Jerusalem's expatriate community, the West Bank was hardly spoken of as a place to get your mind off work and relax. Never wanting for good cars, easy border procedures and some cash to spare, diplomats generally tend to favor Tel Aviv or Jordan's Dead Sea shore as their prime leisure escape.

And so I started to explore the West Bank on foot. What I found amazed me. The question of whether it was generally possible to walk across the West Bank was easily answered. A hybrid of small rural roads, agricultural tracks, smaller paths and tiny herder's trails crisscrossed the area and were waiting to be explored. Perhaps the real surprise was that the walks were also fascinating, inspiring, beautiful, and relaxing. With every walk, the one-dimensional view of Palestine as merely a jumble of small enclaves dominated by concrete and dusty streets, its inhabitants battered by occupation, internal conflict and poverty, started to be challenged by different images: green rolling hills and spectacular gorges; mysterious caves and ruins going back centuries. And no minor detail: I also found little known, charming villages, good restaurants and very hospitable people.

One walk led to another and by 2008 going out to different parts of the West Bank became a fixed weekend routine. If I was taken over by some kind of rare West Bank walking addiction, it certainly was contagious. Over the seasons, more and more people—Palestinians and foreigners—joined the walks, eventually forming into a walking community with over two hundred members, many of them vital in testing the trail descriptions for this book. Not all of them were driven by sheer curiosity and the excitement of exploration; many just wanted to escape for the weekend, get some fresh air and enjoy the outdoors. Like in other scenic parts of the world, a hike in the West Bank gradually became the most normal and natural thing to do.

This book is the result of these past four years of walking and exploring the West Bank. It contains a selection of walks I enjoyed most, and some of the places that I found wondrous, surprising, intriguing or simply very beautiful. The list is not comprehensive. Nor is it final. On many walks I found myself somewhere in between the three Palestines that I describe above. One moment I passed the ruins of long collapsed empires; the other my mind wandered to what the future holds and whether the long overdue peace between Palestinians and Israelis can be achieved.

But as I got lost at times, literally in between future and past, I also walked the Palestine of today. On the road, I met many Palestinians who shared fascinating stories; but just as often I came across people who were busy with building and rebuilding; restoring places of antiquity to splendor, renovating old village centers and public parks, opening new guesthouses and restaurants, working centuries' old olive terraces, supporting communities through social enterprise, and bringing today's Palestine to the world. Strikingly, these people, full of energy, ideas and dreams for the future, were often the same people that told me they had given up hope in their political leaders, in the prospect for a peace agreement, and in much of the outside world. And yet they are building their country. For all the disagreements on the other Palestines, and on where it starts and ends, their Palestine is alive.

Aboud
in spring

Into the Wild West Bank

Shammet hawa is what Palestinians say when they go outdoors and enjoy themselves; it literally means sniffing in fresh air. With *shammet hawa*, just being outdoors and enjoying oneself is more important than any specific destination. Of course, walking in nature anywhere is healthy. It is physically and mentally stimulating; it relieves stress. But wandering off into the Palestinian countryside also proves to be one of the best ways to get to know Palestine. Nature lovers will see their share of unique flora, fauna and great vistas. Passionate hikers will find steep climbs and challenging desert gorges. Addicts of ancient history or contemporary politics can indulge in what they encounter along the trails: the empires of old and the conflicts of today. For pilgrims, of course, there is always the imprint of religion. Palestinian walks are inspiring and often lead to new and special encounters.

For many though, walking in the West Bank will come across as counter-intuitive. Attractive in theory; unfeasible in practice. A large misperception is that it is a dangerous place and that moving around is impossible. To people from elsewhere the term West Bank is easily associated with the image of the Wild West Bank, a place of disorder and peril, of conflict and misery throughout. Stepping through the Palestinian countryside, however, this perception quickly evaporates. The wildness in the West Bank is embodied in the dramatic scenery and the adventure of unexpected encounters.

In the areas less frequented by foreign visitors, the most common first response from Palestinians on the trail is a single worded question: *laysh? Laysh* means *why* as in *why would you be walking?* Why would you be walking when there are cars, taxis, buses, even donkeys! Even if the answer still puzzles, many such conversations inevitably lead to an invitation to sit down and drink some coffee. The question suggests that Palestinians themselves do not walk for leisure. This is only a half-truth. Farmers and Bedouin will not easily recognize why walking up and down the hills is necessary and pleasurable. And yet, an increasing number of Palestinians from cities and villages are out and about in the West Bank. You encounter groups of family and friends enjoying a picnic in the countryside, others venture out on more serious day hikes across the hills and valleys of the West Bank.

The Basics

Palestine is no Switzerland. So the risks of falling hundreds of meters from steep mountain ridges or getting stuck in a terrible blizzard are non-existent. But many of the ordinary risks of walking in nature remain exactly the same as for any other part of the world. In addition, it is important to be aware of the specific security context of walking inside the West Bank. As for walking elsewhere, risks are minimized and pleasure maximized by being well prepared before you set out.

Shat-ha and Hiking to Zarb: Who Said Palestinians Do Not Walk?

Whoever is stuck with the notion that Palestinians do not enjoy walking their own countryside should go on a hike with the *Shat-ha* group. *Shat-ha*—which means picnic in colloquial Arabic—is a Palestinian walking group founded by two academics from Birzeit University, Saleh Jawad and Samia Botmeh. Since 2006 *Shat-ha* has ventured on long hikes across the hills and valleys of the West Bank where few have gone before. The group is open to people of all ages, nationalities and religions, and apart from transport costs walks are free of charge. Their weekly off-road hikes (Friday and Sunday mornings with departures from Ramallah) have become so popular however, that the founders had to limit new members to their group. Current members of *Shat-ha* include people from a large variety of backgrounds including some well known Palestinian and international photographers and writers who have portrayed the Palestinian countryside in exhibitions and books.

Shat-ha can be contacted through samiabotmeh@yahoo.com and saleh.jawad@gmail.com.

Since 2011, a second group has been founded by the Hosh al-Elleeya café and gallery in Birzeit's restored old town. Their weekly Hiking to Zarb excursions cover walking tours in Birzeit and its nearby surroundings. Walkers are rewarded with traditional Palestinian food at the end of the walk, which often is made in so-called Zarb style, food cooked in a self-made oven of dried mud (this tastes much better than it sounds; in fact, it is delicious). Hiking to Zarb costs 100 -120 NIS pp including food, drink and transport: hosh.l.elleeya@gmail.com or Suhail.Hijazi@gmail.com (see Birzeit chapter).

Keeping healthy

Preparation starts from home. Especially if your walk is not accompanied by a Palestinian guide, make sure that you study the map and the description of the walk before you set out. Get familiar with its length and difficulty, the directions to the start, and any activities you want to combine with the walk. An early start is always recommended even on shorter walks. You will enjoy being on the trail well before the afternoon heat really sets in, and it will allow room for any sightseeing or relaxing you might want to do during or after the walk. For any walks longer than 6 hours, or for walks whose start is far away from your point of departure, an early start is required to ensure you can finish the walk before sundown. If you come from Europe or the US, remember that you are much closer to the equator in the Middle East so the sun sets early: between 6 and 7:30 pm in the summer months and as early as 4:30 pm in winter. If you have some doubt whether you or your group can complete a certain trail, study the alternatives for cutting the walk short.

Water is life. The first rule for any walk anywhere is to make sure you carry enough water. Water consumption will vary sharply depending on temperatures, length of the walk, difficulty, and whether a person sweats a lot or not. Walking a few trails will be instructive for how much water you consume, but even if that is much less than advised here, always plan on the safe side. Taking 1.5 liter is the advised minimum amount for the shorter walks in this book (below three hours). For trails that take longer than 4 hours take at least up to double that amount. Pay special attention to your water needs in the summer months and for desert walks in the winter (you should avoid desert walks in the summer). Do not postpone drinking until the moment you get very thirsty.

Protect yourself from the sun. Make sure you apply sunscreen with sufficient protection. Sunburn can happen throughout the year and even when skies are overcast. Wearing clothing that covers your skin is the best possible protection. On warm days, prevent heatstroke by drinking regularly and covering your head. Protect your eyes with sun glasses.

Avoid blisters. Blisters can normally be prevented by walking in good shoes and by checking your feet regularly. A bit of dirt or a grain of sand inside your sock or shoe can already cause blisters. When you feel a little bit of pain, stop and make sure your feet are clear. If a blister has started forming, clean the area around it and cover it with a plaster or bandage.

Be aware of wildlife. When you act responsibly, animals are very unlikely to pose any danger to you. A variety of snakes exist in the West Bank hills but spotting them is rare and when you encounter one it will usually slip away before you can grab your camera. Non-indigenous wild boars are considered a pestilence by farmers because they uproot small trees and destroy crops. Although both loathed and feared by Palestinians, they form no danger when unprovoked. Small packs of wild dogs roam in various parts of the West Bank although encountering them on a walk is rare. Should you come across them, they would normally fear you more than vice versa but be aware of any display of territorial behavior, especially from groups (you are in the Middle East so picking up a few stones is always a last resort in case the situation gets nasty). Dogs belonging to households, farms and Bedouin camps are there to bark at any approaching stranger but would usually not venture beyond the private territory they are supposed to guard. Crossing over to the opposite side of the street is often sufficient to quiet them down. Shepherd dogs guarding the flocks of goats and sheep in the valleys and hills are generally well trained and disciplined—seeing them move hundreds of animals from one hillside to another is an impressive sight—so unless you are a livestock thief you should be fine.

Walking in a conflict area

Walking is not a risk free activity anywhere and neither of course is walking in an area of conflict. While the walks in this book deliberately avoid areas that have served as flashpoints for tensions in the past, it is important to be aware of the overall security context. In the West Bank, where all of the trails described in this book are located, the conflict has transitioned from a surge in Israeli-Palestinian violence in the early 2000s (the so-called Second Intifada) to a conflict of low intensity.

The period 2007-2011 noticed a significant improvement in the security situation in the areas under Palestinian Authority control with the redeployment of Palestinian security forces across areas A and B (see below). The armed factions that previously controlled the streets in large Palestinian cities were disarmed and the Palestinian civil police returned to the streets. Israel in response reduced its presence in these areas and somewhat loosened the tight restrictions on movement that had crippled much of the Palestinian economy up to 2007. As a consequence of improved security and easier movement, tourism numbers in the West Bank have increased to record levels with over 2 million tourists visiting in 2010. While most foreign tourism concentrates in Bethlehem and Jericho, other cities and many of the smaller villages mentioned in this book are visited more and more. Ramallah is not on the standard itineraries for tourists; however, thousands of foreigners working as diplomats, aid workers or volunteers commute to Ramallah every day for work, and an increasing number live there as well.

In contrast to some other countries in the region, visitors have not been the

target of violence by any party in the West Bank, Israel or Jerusalem. There is
a small risk for visitors of being accidently caught up in events. When incidents
occur, they usually take place at specific flashpoints of conflict: Israeli checkpoints,
areas close to the separation barrier or areas where Israeli settlements and outposts
are located closely to Palestinian villages or in some cases near to or on Palestinian
agricultural land. The trails in this book intentionally avoid these areas and should
you plan to explore new walks in the West Bank you are advised to do the same.
Walkers new to the West Bank will be less familiar with the security situation in
specific areas. Going out with a local guide is recommended in those cases.

In contrast to the West Bank, Gaza was still an area of relatively high security
volatility when this book went to print. At that time, all foreign consulates in Jerusalem advised their citizens against travel to Gaza. With the exception of diplomats,
journalists and aid workers, Israel and Egypt have generally prevented foreigners
and West Bank/Jerusalem Palestinians from entering the Gaza Strip. Due to the
volatile situation and the difficulty to access the area, it was not possible to include
Gaza walks in this edition.

Health and travel insurance come in all shapes and forms. Check your policy
whether risks related to walking abroad are covered and whether it includes the
West Bank.

Travel advisories

The websites of most ministries of foreign affairs provide country specific travel advisories for their citizens that are updated regularly. On the Middle East, the information for Israel, West Bank, Gaza and Jerusalem is usually summarized in one advisory with sub-sections on these areas. While they are valuable sources of information on recent events and on the types of incidents occurring in the region, keep in mind that advisories are not meant to be travel guides, will often lack location specific detail, and their language naturally leans towards better safe than sorry. Some foreign missions seem to be most content when their advice can be summarized as "stay at home; watch Discovery Channel instead," even though actual risk levels may be equal or lower than at many mainstream travel destinations. The US advisory reads as if danger lurks in every corner of the Holy Land and only reckless travelers could consciously decide to visit the region. Most European versions tend to have an assessment somewhat closer in line with the actual situation on the ground. In general, however, advisories do not distinguish between levels of risk depending on different types of activity or whether visitors travel in groups or with a local guide. Note that regular travel insurance policies usually provide no coverage in case of a negative travel advisory (only applicable to Gaza at the time of writing).

France: http://www.diplomatie.gouv.fr/fr/conseils-aux-voyageurs_909/index.html
Germany: http://www.auswaertiges-amt.de/DE/Laenderinformationen
/Uebersicht_Navi.html
UK: http://www.fco.gov.uk/en/travel-and-living-abroad/travel-advice-by-country
US: http://travel.state.gov/travel/travel_1744.html
Netherlands: http://www.minbuza.nl/nl/Reizen_en_Landen

Confused by your country's travel advice? Ask around locally: the guides mentioned in this book and hotels and tour operators in East Jerusalem and the West Bank are good information sources.

Areas A, B, and C

Since the 1993 Oslo Agreements between Israel and the Palestinian Liberation Organization (PLO) the West Bank is divided in three types of areas: A, B and C. These three zones reflect a complex geographic mix of responsibilities divided between Israel and the Palestinian Authority (PA). The shortest possible explanation is that in Area A, the PA is fully autonomous in security matters and in nearly

Tramping on A, B and C near Sebastia

all civilian affairs; in Area B, civilian responsibilities are similar to A but overall security is in the hands of Israel with a limited role for the PA civil police; in Area C, security policy is exclusively Israel's domain. While the ABC division affects the landscape in a variety of ways there are no physical borders drawn across the West Bank on the ABC lines; you can cross them on foot without noticing. In some sections on the main roads between A/B and C areas there are Israeli checkpoints. The walks in this book cover all three areas but avoid large roads, settlements and the checkpoints located in Area C. Provided that you keep to the advice in this chapter, walks in each area are equally safe. Read the Ramallah and al-Bidaan chapters for more background on the ABC division.

Adapting to changes

The walks in this book have been carefully selected and described. At the same time, readers should keep in mind that new developments on the ground might literally cross their paths. These changes can be negative or positive and part of the challenge and appeal of walking in the West Bank lies in navigating these developments with fellow walkers. On the upside, trails presently not marked might be marked in the future; communities living close to the trails in this book might develop new ones. New restaurants or guesthouses may open in the villages on the trail.

On the downside, within the specific political and economic context of the region less benign developments may occur as well. Some of the beautiful old shepherd's paths described in this book might fall into disuse and become harder to find for walkers; dirt roads between local communities could be paved over and smaller paved roads could temporarily turn into main thoroughfares due to a change in access for Palestinians on the main roads. In the worst case, new Israeli or Palestinian construction or industrial development might directly affect the trails. For most walks described in this book, however, the chances of this happening are fairly small. If changes on the ground have affected the trail you are walking, consider whether you can get around them and still enjoy the remainder of the walk, or whether they are of such degree that further walking is not advised. The website www.walkingpalestine.org will provide updates on developments with respect to the walks in this book.

Dos and Don'ts for Walking in Palestine

Unfortunately, parts of the Palestinian cultural and natural landscape have for a long time been under threat of damage, destruction and even disappearance. The endurance of a conflict over land, decades of settlement expansion, unbridled Palestinian urban growth and too little priority given to protection and conservation continue to alter the face of the landscape. When done with respect for natural and cultural heritage, walking in nature can contribute to protection and preservation. This book aims to stimulate environmentally and socially responsible tourism. Where possible, the trails link walkers with the people and businesses from local communities giving both a stake in the promotion and preservation of their environment. On and off the trails in this book, *Walking Palestine* fully endorses the principles set by the global *Leave No Trace Center for Outdoor Ethics*: www.LNT.org.

Dos

Plan your walk and walk the plan: study the route before you set out

Allow plenty of time to finish your walk well before dark and keep an eye on the weather

Protect your eyes and skin from the sun; cover your head on warm days

Bring enough water and drink regularly

Level of difficulty

Other than the specific route of the trail and the weather conditions, the difficulty of a walk depends on your physical condition. Knowing your level of fitness is important as you plan a walk. Obviously, if you have never been on long walks before, do not start with one of the 6+ hour walks in this book. Build up gradually and you will enjoy it all the better. Generally speaking, walking in the Palestinian hills is not as demanding as long treks through mountainous terrain at high altitude so hikers with alpine experience will not have serious difficulties in completing the longest and most challenging trails in this book. On the other hand, for the average hiker there is no reason to underestimate walking the Palestinian countryside: elevation changes can be significant, temperatures high and with little tree cover in the West Bank you will be walking mostly without any cover of shade; tracks can be

Greet anybody you meet along the trail (see the Arabic on the Trail section of this book)

Leave what you find: respect history, heritage and nature

Control pets, such as dogs, especially when near local herds of sheep and goats

Be considerate of the local community: treat locals as your generous hosts as you walk through their towns and near their properties

If you explore walks outside this book, walk with a map of the area and monitor your progress (see walk #25 for tips)

Don'ts

Don't leave any waste behind (including organic waste): take it with you and dispose of it properly after the walk

Don't damage or remove pieces of historic structures

Don't take close-up pictures of people without their permission

Don't walk through planted fields

Don't enter a desert wadi during or right after large amounts of rain (danger of flash floods)

Don't drink water from streams and pipes

Don't walk up to or near settlements, outposts or military camps

Don't walk with any type of arms

Marking trails in Aboud

narrow and include scrambling over rocks. To ease planning this book distinguishes between three difficulty levels:

Easy: short walks, generally up to 2 hours (5km/3.1 mi.) and predominantly on dirt roads that are easily followed; only mild and gradual climbs are included; walks are suitable for anybody in good physical health.

Moderate: longer walks, between 2 and 5 hours; trails can vary between paved road, dirt road and single track; total elevation changes up to 500 meters (0.3 mi.).

Hard: walks that can go over 5 hours (14 km/8.7 mi. or more) and/or include a variety of (possibly steep) climbs and descents; tracks can be narrow and at times unclear; a walk might involve scrambling over rocks or down hillsides.

Estimating the average duration of a walk is never straightforward. Regardless of fitness levels, some walkers like to pause at every pretty olive tree; others love to march on as if there is a train to catch. The duration span mentioned for the trails in this book (e.g.: 4–6 hrs) relates to walkers keeping a stiff pace (4 hours) and those taking it easy (6 hours). It does not take into account stopping for picnics and sightseeing along the way.

What to wear

Good hiking shoes or boots are probably the single most important item for an enjoyable walk. Good shoes provide both stability and protection, help you keep your balance in water and on slippery surface, and prevent blisters from occurring on longer walks. Hiking shoes come in four categories: relatively light and flexible shoes for generally smooth terrain (A), mid-weight shoes for more off-road terrain (B), relatively stiff and heavier off-trail boots for rough and rocky terrain (C) and heavy duty mountaineering boots (D). All walks in this book can be done comfortably with type A or B shoes. Good walking sandals will often suffice as well, their main disadvantage being that the open space allows for thorns and insects to come in. Cross trainers or running shoes are often sufficient for the walks in this book but be aware that they provide much less balance and ankle support on stony surfaces and hill slopes. If you have bought new shoes, make sure to break them in before you start a serious walk (or suffer the consequences with fresh blisters).

As for walking attire, long loose pants and an easy fit long or short sleeved shirt are optimal for walking. For your upper body, three layers of clothing provide optimal comfort and flexibility in the winter season. Winter temperatures can move fairly sharply in both directions between early morning and late afternoon. Make sure you bring a sweater and/or a windproof jacket in this season. While compared to most neighbors in the region Palestinians are generally not very conservative with regard to dress code for women, female walkers are nevertheless well advised to leave anything resembling beach wear or gym attire at home and keep shoulders and legs covered. For men too, wearing shorts is ill-advised in all seasons. They provide no protection against a thicket of thorn bushes and invite sunburn. And if first impressions matter to you: they are looked upon as very silly by most people in the Arab world, including Palestinians.

What to bring

For the walks described in this book, a small backpack is sufficient to carry water, food and some accessories. Basic small items to pack include sunscreen, sun glasses and something to cover your head against the sun. Good binoculars are helpful for bird and wildlife watching and a pocket knife can come in handy for picnics. Pack a first aid kit; it seems a bore to bring along . . . until you need it. With the exception of a few walks, there are usually no eating options on the trail except for a self-organized picnic so make sure you bring along some snacks.

The Abraham Path Initiative

Two Palestinian organizations have specialized in organizing longer multiday treks across Palestine. These tours include local guides, arrangements for transportation, lodging, food and drink. If you have the time and stamina, participating in the following two treks is highly recommended.

Palestine is among the frontrunners in the region establishing and promoting the **Masar Ibrahim Al-Khalil or Abraham Path.** The path is the first regional initiative aimed at developing a multinational walking trail across the Middle East, drawing its inspiration from Abrahamic values that are reflected across the faiths of Islam, Judaism and Christianity. It was founded by Harvard scholar William Ury in 2006 and is supported by the UN Alliance of Civilizations, the World Tourism Organization, and the World Heritage Alliance. **The Siraj Centre for Holy Land Studies** is leading the organizaton of tours in the West Bank with the Palestinian Wildlife Society, the Rozana Association and Bethlehem University. Ranging from two days to a full week, walks along the trail cover historic sites and holy places in two segments: from Nablus to Jericho and from Bethlehem to Hebron (Al-Khalil). Walkers spend the night with local families in villages along the way and are introduced to various aspects of Palestinian culture and cuisine. Guided treks along different sections of the Abraham Path are organized year round for individuals as well as groups. Per person prices for mid-sized groups range from US$ 85 for a weekend trip to US$ 700 for a full week. Check out www.abrahampath.org (the regional portal) and www.masaribrahim.ps (for Palestine) for updates or contact Michel Awad at michel@sirajcenter.org. At the time of writing, the development of a direct trail connection between the Palestinian and Israeli chapters of the Abraham Path was considered.

The Nativity Trail follows Mary and Joseph's footsteps from Nazareth to Bethlehem. After the trail was successfully established in the year 2000, the outbreak of the Second Intifada and Israel's construction of the separation barrier stopped tours from being organized (the original trail ran through what is now the barrier). Fortunately, the trail was revived in 2008 with an 11 day tour organized by the Siraj Center and the Alternative Tourism Group (ATG). At the time of writing, the tour started in Nazareth and Mt Tabor in the Galilee and participants were subsequently driven to the north of the West Bank to start their nine days of walking towards Bethlehem passing Nablus, Jericho and wide variety of villages and monasteries in between. Accommodation during the trek varies between home-stays in villages, monasteries, Bedouin tents, small guest houses and campsites. Price per person is US$ 1370 (all-inclusive). For updates contact ATG or the Siraj Center (see the Walking Civil Society chapter).

Guides on the trail

While all of the trails in this book can be self-guided according to the methods explained below, hiring a local guide holds several advantages. The most obvious advantage is that walkers will have no worries about navigating the trail. If you prefer an entirely care-free walk and if you are not too eager to develop your path-finding skills, a guide is thus the obvious choice. But even if you like path finding, consider the other advantages of hiring a local guide. There are no better explanations about the area you walk in than those from the people that live there. A guide can also introduce you to people from the area, even if you don't speak Arabic, and by hiring one you will contribute directly to the local economy and the development of Palestinian ecotourism. Organized guiding in the Palestinian outdoors was still somewhat in its infancy when this book went into print, but a range of local NGOs have become active over the last years. Spurred on by the writing of this book, in 2011 new projects were started to train more local walking guides with foreign language skills. Where available, guide information is provided for across the walking chapters in this book and new references to local guides will be updated regularly on www.walkingpalestine.org.

Navigation

The trail descriptions in this book offer essential navigation support to any of the walks and they are particularly important for trails that are (still) unmarked. They are complemented by trail maps.

Jesus did not take the bus. Why should you?

Walkers that would like to combine Palestinian with Israeli trails have plenty of options. Many of Israel's trails are confined to its well managed nature reserves, mostly good for day hikes. Yet in recent years, Anna Dintaman and David Landis have started to change the face of walking in Israel by creating the 65 km contiguous **Jesus Trail** and over 220 km of additional trails that directly connect the various biblical sites, villages and cities in the Galilee. The trail is backed up by their motto Jesus did not take the bus. *Why should you?* It passes along Jewish, Christian and Muslim communities in the region, including locally run guesthouses and hostels. For a full description, check out the book *Hiking the Jesus Trail* or the website www.jesustrail.com where a new trail connecting the Galilee to Jenin has also been included.

The obvious advantage of marked trails is that they require minimal navigation: just follow the colored markings along the trail. Always keep in mind, however, that these markings can fade away or be overtaken by plants or tree branches. Reading the map and trail description in the book is therefore also recommended for marked trails; at the minimum it will give you extra confidence that you are going in the right direction. Note that a small number of trails are marked only partially. Also, various communities mentioned in this book were planning to mark further trails at the time it went into print.

Unmarked trails are naturally more challenging than marked ones, and depending on your taste for navigation and path finding, it might suit some pathfinders better than hikes that are well marked from start to finish. To compensate for the absence of markings, there are various means of navigation that you can combine: the trail description and map, compass, and GPS navigation. Trails that were unmarked at the time when this book went to print have an extra detailed trail description. Main junctures in the description correspond to the map through specific numbers. Use both map and text to verify you are going in the right direction. While not strictly necessary for walkers with an inborn sense of direction, some assistance by means of a simple compass will be very useful in verifying your direction. For those walkers who prefer a handheld GPS computer as their navigation guide, all trails in this book can be downloaded from the Walking Palestine website: www.walkingpalestine.org/abc-for-gps.

Walking on your own

While walking alone can hold some irrefutable advantages (freedom to go your own pace and direction; the ultimate peace and quiet, etc.) no guide book would recommend you walk only by yourself. The obvious risk is that if anything should happen there is no one to help you or get help to you. Remember that mobile phones do not have reception in all areas of the West Bank, especially the more isolated parts. If you do decide to go out on your own, inform other people where you are going, what trail you intend to do, and when you expect to be back.

Walking with children

The shorter walks labeled "easy" in this book are suitable to families with children. Take into account that unless they are so small you can still carry them on your back, walking with kids will inevitably slow you down and hence the duration is likely to be longer than estimated in this book.

Cell phone reception

Be aware that in some parts of Area C, mobile reception is patchy and sometimes non-existent. This is especially the case inside deep wadis far away from villages and settlements. If you have to make a call in these areas, your best chance is to move to a higher elevation. There are presently two Palestinian mobile phone operators: Jawal and Wataniya. Their coverage in Areas A and B is generally very good and they cover at least those parts of Area C where Palestinian villages and roads are nearby. If you have an Israeli phone number (Orange, Cellcom, Pelephone) you will have coverage in many areas in the West Bank but there is minimal to no reception in large parts of Areas A and B and the parts of Area C that are far away from settlements. If you have a foreign subscription, you are likely to have the best of both worlds as roaming is normally possible on any network.

When to walk

Visiting Palestine for three hot and dry September weeks was probably Mark Twain's single biggest planning error of his 1867 journey. If you can avoid it, don't imitate the timing of the great author: the best season for walking runs from November to April-May. Temperatures are generally mild and while sunshine usually dominates the day, the landscape is greened by intermittent winter rains. Most of the flora also blossoms in this period. Be aware that temperatures in winter and early spring vary a lot more throughout the day than they do in summer: the early mornings can still be cool, but by mid-day temperatures can rise in the high

A family walk near Birzeit

twenties, whereas the same afternoon a chilly wind can suddenly set in. Having an extra layer of clothing at hand is always advisable. As for the irregular rainfall, local weather forecasts predicting clear skies are usually pretty reliable. When rain is predicted, however, the exact day let alone the hour is mostly educated guesswork. When in doubt before your walk, bring a raincoat. Do not walk inside the deep wadis (gorges) near the desert during or directly after large amounts of rainfall to avoid the dangers of flashfloods.

Out of season, walking in summer is certainly possible and can also be very enjoyable if you pick the right walks (the shorter ones). While the landscape is invariably dry, each month will have its own charms with July to September seeing a ripening of grapes, figs and other fruits, and October usually the start of the olive harvest. If you walk in the summer months, be extra conscious of weather conditions and distances, especially in the heart of summer (July and August). It cannot be said enough: bring plenty of water. With temperatures rising over 40 degrees in some areas, you are strongly advised to avoid any of the long walks and not walk in or near the desert at all.

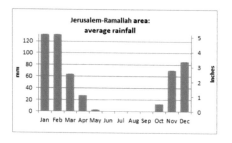

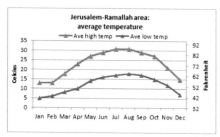

Walking and leisure

The walks in this book can often be combined with educational cultural activities: for example, the archeological heritage of Sebastia is a must-see; a walk around Ras Karkar is not complete without a visit to its castle; and the lovely trail through the rolling hills east of Jenin can be combined with a visit to Cinema Jenin. A great thing about life's most simple pleasures is that they are twice as enjoyable after a good walk: a mixed grill and *argilleh* in al-Bidaan; a fresh cold beer at the brewery in Taybeh; a splash in the pools of Jifna. On many of the trails, local leisure, food and sightseeing options are located right at the end of the trail; in some instances they are a short drive away. Another option is to combine a walk with one of Palestine's many cultural festivals (see the Festival Calendar at the end of the book). Relevant weblinks are provided in each chapter; they can also be navigated easily from www.walkingpalestine.org.

Getting there and back again

Unless you are in an organized tour group, the basic means of transportation in the West Bank are private cars, taxis or public transportation. Each chapter briefly summarizes how to get to the start of a walk by car and public transportation.

Private transportation

If you rent a car, check whether it has a yellow (Israeli) or white-green plate (Palestinian). Palestinian cars are not allowed to drive into Israel, and on some so-called settler-only roads Palestinian cars are forbidden from driving and forced to make detours through smaller roads. When renting a car, make sure you have insurance covering you both in Israel as well as in the West Bank. Some Israeli companies do not offer insurance for the West Bank but all companies in East Jerusalem and Ramallah include insurance to both sides.

The quality of roads inside the West Bank varies. The main road arteries that are used by both Israelis and Palestinians are usually of good quality. Nonetheless, special care is advised on busy roads, such as Road 60, with many Palestinians and Israelis speeding over fairly small stretches of road that meander through a very hilly landscape. The main roads connecting Palestinian villages used to be in bad shape but since 2008 major improvements have been made. A USAID funded US $300 million infrastructure program targeted larger roads connecting the main Palestinian cities, especially in the north of the West Bank. The PA also refurbished large sections of rural roads throughout the West Bank.

In addition to the maps in this book, having a detailed road atlas at hand is advised. The Applied Research Institute of Jerusalem (ARIJ) has produced the *Palestine Road Map* but it is hard to come by. *The Roadmap of Israel* (including the English version) includes all major and most minor roads in the West Bank as well, and is available at most Israeli gas stations. The UN Office for the Coordination of Humanitarian Affairs (OCHA) produces very detailed maps for each area of the West Bank, available free of charge online at www.ochaopt.org or you can pick-up the complete atlas for free at their offices (MAC House, 7 St. George Street, Jerusalem).

Taxi

You can easily find private taxis in the larger Palestinian cities, recognizable by their yellow color. Finding one in smaller villages is much harder though. In the

West Bank, taxis do not use meters so make sure you agree the price before hand, especially for longer distances. A short drive inside the city should cost you around 10 NIS. Jerusalem taxis—white color with a yellow taxi light on top—do have meters and according to Israeli rules they should be used. Ask for the meter unless you agree a price beforehand. As for trips outside Jerusalem, make sure you check the destination with your driver. While they drive similar taxis, Israeli drivers will not bring you to Palestinian cities on the West Bank (area A) whereas Palestinian taxi drivers from East Jerusalem will. If you don't find one yourself, hotels in East Jerusalem routinely arrange taxis to the West Bank.

Public transportation

Public transportation in the West Bank is not as difficult as you might think. Travelers eager for both the ride and the experience will manage their way around. See the chapter on Palestinian Public Transportation at the back of this book for more details.

Arriving from abroad

Arrival from abroad to a place that has no agreed borders can seem a complex affair. The large majority of tourists wanting to visit the West Bank should have no problems however. With Israel controlling all of its airspace, the West Bank has no airport of its own. Most visitors travel via Ben Gurion Airport, Israel's international gateway; some opt for Amman's Queen Alia Airport in Jordan and travel onwards from there. A journey over land takes place through one of the Israeli controlled border crossings. There are four land crossings: three crossings with Jordan (Sheikh Hussein, King Hussein (Allenby Bridge) and Yitzak Rabin (Eilat-Aqaba) and one with Egypt (Taba). Of these, only the King Hussein Crossing will get you into the West Bank straight away after passing through Israeli immigration and security. All other border crossings are entry points into Israel and you will have to move on to one of the various crossing points into the West Bank. For all borders, note that the entry of visitors that indicate they will solely stay inside the West Bank has become more cumbersome recently as some of them have received a so-called PA-only stamp, forbidding further travel inside Jerusalem and Israel. Tourists indicating they will visit both Israel and the West Bank should have no problems in receiving the ordinary three month tourist visa (valid across Israel, Jerusalem and the West Bank). Travelers who hold both Palestinian citizenship and a foreign citizenship can usually not enter through other crossings than the King Hussein Bridge with Jordan. If you fall into this category, check the latest information on the travel advisory page of your foreign ministry. Israeli citizens are officially forbidden

Walking amidst the yellow hues of Wadi Limoon (Aboud)

to enter areas A inside the West Bank although in practice the Israeli military order stating so is not being fully enforced.

Accommodation

A number of locations in this book provide accommodation. Hence, a long week-end of walking or a combination of walking and sightseeing is possible to combine with an overnight stay. From luxury travelers to backpackers, there are various options. Every large city has a number of hotels in various price ranges. The four and five star Palestinian hotels, however, are confined to Ramallah, Bethlehem, East Jerusalem and Jericho. A good point of reference is the Arab Hotel Association: www.palestinehotels.com which lists most hotels by city. Where these are located in close proximity to the trails, specific information about local guest houses, small hotels and Bedouin camps open to visitors is referenced in the walking chapters. So-called homestays, whereby visitors stay with Palestinian families in their houses, are another option for accommodation. On walking trails where this is available, it is mentioned in the relevant chapters.

Syrian hyrax

Further reading

Not a travel guide and yet the best reading to accompany walking in Palestine is Raja Shehadeh's *Palestinian Walks* which describes the fragility and changing character of a Palestinian landscape under occupation and the author's decades long struggle against settlement expansion in the West Bank. The book won the Orwell Prize in 2008 and has been translated in half a dozen languages. Di Taylor and Tony Howard's *Walks in Palestine and the Nativity Trail* was the first walking guide on Palestine produced by the Bethlehem 2000 project. The book has gone out of print, however, and unfortunately some of the trails described have become impossible to walk due to changes on the ground.

A few general travel books on Palestine have been produced in the last few years. *Palestine: A Guide* (Interlink Books) by Mariam Shaheen and George Azar is a richly decorated book exploring the lives of Palestinians today and their relationship to their homeland. *Palestine and the Palestinians* is a travel guide produced by the Alternative Tourism Group (ATG) containing both practical facts for travel and background information on places of interest. While most international travel guide brands include Palestine and Israel together in a single guide, a new travel guide dedicated solely to Palestine written by Sarah Irving for Bradt Guides, was published recently. An excellent locally run web portal on travel in Palestine is www.visitpalestine.ps.

Bird Paradise: Palestinian Flora and Fauna

Dust, rocks and endless dry desert plains with barely any vegetation, let alone any wildlife: this is the image often conjured when people think about the Middle East. The Palestinian landscape is a world apart from this. Located in the so-called Fertile Crescent at the crossing point of three continents, the small area boasts a high density of different flora and fauna and a dramatic variety in scenery. An estimated 115 mammal species live in Israel and Palestine, over 90 different reptiles and amphibians, some 540 different types of birds and approximately 3000 plant species.

Birdlife

Togethwer with diplomats, birds are the only species that move effortlessly between Israel, Palestine and the rest of the Middle East. Situated at the center of a route connecting Europe, Asia and Africa, every autumn and spring an estimated 500 million birds use the region as their preferred rest and recovery destination. That is not a blessing for all: due to the heavy aerial traffic the Israeli Air Force has lost more

Little green bee-eater

aircraft through so-called bird strikes than through enemy action. But it is a major magnet for ornithologists and amateur bird watchers. The Jordan Valley is one of the areas which attracts a lot of bird life. The valley is part of the spectacular geological phenomenon of the so-called Great Rift Valley which extends 7000 kilometers all the way from Mozambique to Turkey and reaches its lowest land level at the shores of the Dead Sea (more than 400 meters below sea level). The Jordan Valley is in effect one large highway, or flyway rather, for birds migrating between the continents.

A giant among birds of the Holy Land is the griffon vulture. It has a wingspan of almost three meters and can still be found in the Golan Heights, in various parts of Israel and in the Judean desert in the West Bank where it mainly feeds on carcasses of ibex, goats and sheep. Other large birds such as short-toed eagles, cranes, herons, and black and white storks can be spotted in the Jordan Valley but also elsewhere. As much as 85 percent of the world's stork population is estimated to migrate through the area. Smaller birds residing in or migrating through Palestine include kingfishers, little egrets, bee-eaters, Tristram's starlings, jays, various wheatears, blackstarts and redstarts, and a whole lot more. With their elegantly curved beak, the small Palestine sunbird can be found all across the region. It usually has a gray-brown color though breeding males gloss blue and green through shiny black feathers. The chukar is a bird you will encounter often on walks as it makes its getaway from underneath the bushes (mostly through running, not flying). If you don't see it you will hear its quirky loud song that somewhat resembles its name.

In the few areas in the West Bank that are still forested, the Syrian woodpecker can be heard hammering the bark of trees.

The spring and fall are the best seasons to go bird watching. For a more in-depth introduction into birding, or for tailor made bird watching tours across the West Bank, contact the Palestinian Wildlife Society: www.wildlife-pal.org. If you like to get started by yourself, a set of binoculars and a pocket bird guide will get you on your way. Dr. Walid Basha recently developed one for the Jenin area, but applicable to most of the West Bank. He can be contacted at bscjenin@yahoo.com.

Other wildlife

Lions are mentioned more than a hundred times in the bible and bears and croco-diles also roamed the Holy Land in ancient times. Not anymore: they were hunted into extinction very long ago or disappeared due to climatic changes. So while Palestine is abundant with wildlife, there are no ferocious creatures posing a real danger to humans. The last very large predator that still roams the Judean desert is the desert leopard, up to 1.8 meter (6 feet) in length but almost extinct. Spotting them is very unlikely as only a handful, if any, remain and they keep far away from humans. Jackals are still around across the West Bank but walkers are unlikely to see or hear them during daytime.

The mountain gazelle and dorcas gazelle are spread around different areas of the West Bank. They can survive in very arid regions and go without direct water intake by sampling moisture through the plants in their diet. Encountering gazelles on a walk is not uncommon but make sure you hold them in your gaze while you can: wary of humans they tend to leap out of sight very quickly. Larger and heavier than the gazelle, and with very impressive curved horns, the Nubian ibex can grow up to a meter long and 40 kilograms in weight. They can be found in the mountainous and arid areas of the Judean desert. More easy to spot in that area is the Syrian hyrax (or rock hyrax), a funny looking animal with the appear-ance of a rodent but, believe it or not, actually sharing common ancestry with elephants and manatees. Up to half a meter long, it is an extremely able and fast rock climber thanks to the rubbery pads under its feet. Different breeds of fox and wild cats—one size larger than their domestic cousins—can be spotted across more remote areas of the West Bank.

Frequently, yet very slowly, crossing one's path in the rural areas of the West Bank is the Mediterranean spur-thighed tortoise. While more difficult to spot during a walk, the Indian crested porcupine also roams the West Bank and hikers will often come across their black and white spines lying along the trail.

On any walk, you will spot geckos and lizards sunbathing on rocks or making their getaway between them.

Trees and flowers

The olive tree takes center stage in Palestinian culture. Its defining influence on the landscape is well illustrated in many of the walks where large swaths of land in between villages, including the terraced hill slopes, are dominated by olive groves. Other common Palestinian trees, often interspersed with olive trees, are the fig tree with its bright light green leaves that somewhat resemble a pair of human hands, and the almond, the first tree to blossom in January and February with its radiant white and pink flowers. The oak tree was once a very common sight but with the wood used for building railways and other infrastructure in the past it has become scarce. The thorny acacia tree can be found in semi-arid and desert areas providing shelter to birds and wildlife such as ibex and hyraxes. The *sabr* cactus (or in English: prickly pear) can grow up to a few meters tall. With its green pads covered with treacherous thorns, it is often found in or near Palestinian villages and sometimes still indicates a demarcation of land ownership. Its yellow red fruit ripens in summer and is a real treat; that is, if you can manage to get rid of all the thorns first (rubbing the fruit over a patch of earth before cutting it open usually does the trick). Herbs growing wild in the West Bank include sage (*maramiya*), mint (*na'na'*), and thyme and oregano (*za'tar*).

Flowers can be spotted throughout the year but they cover the hills and valleys in the winter and early spring: from December to April. As of January, beds of bright red anemones, white daisies and yellow corn marigold turn the soil of olive groves and orchards into a carpet of colors. Various irises with exotic colors, tulips, lupins, hyacinths, wild hollyhocks, rockroses and wild cyclamen can be found in abundance in spring. The plumed thistle is encountered frequently in unattended groves or to the side of roads and paths. Its large bright pink or blue flowers bloom from March to June but its thorns can be a painful reminder why wearing shorts is never a bright idea for walkers in the West Bank.

Comprehensive full color guides on Palestinian flora and fauna were not yet available in English at the time of writing. The closest thing to such a guide, and a delight for the eye because of its exquisite photography, is Jarir Maani's *Field Guide to Jordan*, covering many of the species you find in the West Bank as well, and available as a book and an app at www.fieldguidetojordan.com. Noam Kirschenbaum's *Nature in Israel* fold-out pocket guides cover the most common species in a lightweight format. These are available at most Israeli gas stations.

The Walks

LOCATION	KM/MILES	HRS	LEVEL	MARKED*
Burqin—Farming Family				
1. Canaan to Jabal Al-Baared	10.0 Km / 6.2 Miles	2.5–3.5	Moderate	No
Jenin—Ferris Wheel				
2. Jenin to Jalqamus	12.1/7.5	3–4.5	Moderate	Yes
Zebabde –Mosaic Memories				
3. Zebabde to Raba	14.9 / 9.2	4–5.5	Moderate/hard	Planned
Sebastia—Stone Empires				
4. Sebastia to Maqam Bayzeed	11.8 / 7.3	4–5.5	Moderate	Planned
5. Sebastia to Ramin over Hijaz Railway	15.5 / 9.6	4.5–6	Moderate/hard	Planned
6. Sebastia to Maqam Sheikh Sha'leh	7.6 / 4.7	2–2.5	Moderate	Yes
7. Sebastia around the City Walls	3.6 / 2.2	1–1.5	Easy	Yes
Al-Bidaan—Cool Springs				
8. Al-Bidaan around Taluza	16.9 / 10.5	5–6.5	Hard	No
9. Al-Bidaan to al-Far'a	11.8 / 7.3	3–4	Moderate	No
Aboud—City of Flowers				
10. Wadi Limoon to Wadi Sukhon	7.0 / 4.3	2–2.5	Moderate	Planned
11. Wadi Limoon Eastwards	7.6 / 4.7	2–2.5	Moderate	Planned
12. Around Aboud	8.9 / 5.5	2.5–3	Moderate	Yes
Turmus'ayya—Amreeka Amreeka				
13. Turmus'ayya to Jilijliya	13.4 / 8.3	4–5	Moderate	No
Wadi Auja—Between Springs				
14. Ain Samia to Ain Auja	10.2 / 6.3	5–7	Hard	Partial
Birzeit—Olive Branch				
15. Birzeit to Jifna to Birzeit	9.6 / 5.9	2.5–3.5	Moderate	No
Taybeh—Draft Delicious				
16. Taybeh to Wadi Habees	8.4 / 5.2	2–3	Moderate	Yes
Ras Karkar—Noble Grounds				
17. Ras Karkar to Jabal Nabi Anir	5.4 / 3.3	1.5–2	Moderate	Planned
Ramallah—City Escape				
18. Ramallah to Jifna	15.4 / 9.5	4–6	Hard	No
Wadi Qelt—Metamorphosis				
19. Hizma to Ain Fawwar	11.5 / 7.1	4–6	Hard	Partial
20. Ain Fawwar to Jericho	13.5 / 8.3	4–6	Hard	Yes
Artas—Enclosed Garden				
21. Solomon Pools to Artas	5.6 / 3.4	1.5–2	Easy	No
Mar Saba—Desert Monastries				
22. Mar Saba to Hyrcania	13.8 / 8.5	4–5.5	Moderate/hard	Partial
Battir—Hugging the Green Line				
23. Battir to Wadi Maghrour	11.0 / 6.8	3–4	Moderate	Planned
24. Battir to Wadi Jama	8.5 / 5.2	2.5–3.5	Moderate	Planned
My favorite walk				
25. From Palestine to Palestine				

*Follow trail updates on-line: www.walkingpalestine.org.

برقين Burqin: Land of Soap and Honey

The village of Burqin opens up to wide expanses of traditional Palestinian agriculture. In the hills nearby, walkers climb up to beautiful panoramas.

Boutique olive oil

Just outside the city of Jenin, the small village of Burqin looks across the so-called Araba plains where Palestinian agriculture dominates the land. Large stretches of flat land are rare in the West Bank and farmers make intense use of it throughout the plains. Agriculture remains the backbone for many Palestinian families and their wider village communities. While droughts and access to water pose serious problems, Palestinian farming here has the potential to turn from a means of survival into a mainstay for social and economic development. Burqin is also home to the **Church of St. George**, allegedly the third oldest in the world (the first two being the Nativity in Bethlehem and the Holy Sepulcher in Jerusalem). With its quiet location far off the beaten track of pilgrims and tourists, the church's small size well preserves its spiritual atmosphere and is worth a visit.

With such variety of crops around, there is probably no place more suitable to start a walk than **Canaan Fair Trade**. Their staff will be happy to give you a tour of the olive oil production line and talk about their fair trade and organic products on sale. They can also arrange a guide for the walk. This is highly recommended if you like to know more about the surroundings of Burqin and the farming in the area.

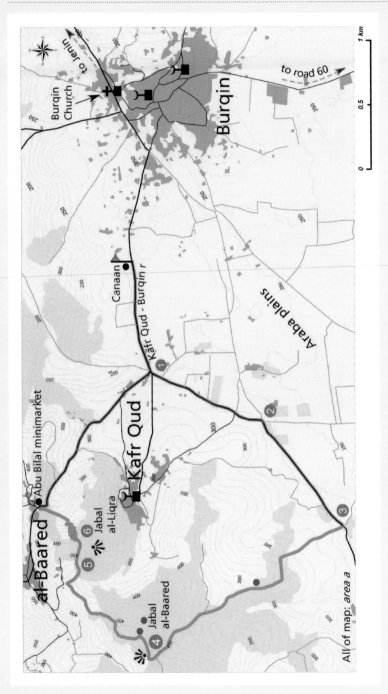

This lovely circular walk will take you from Canaan's factory and shop, W into the Araba plains and then N onto the hilltops of Jabal al-Baared and Jabal al-Liqra before looping back E to Burqin. Along the way, you will pass through the plains with its large variety of Palestinian fruit and vegetables production, past old springs and cisterns, and you will take in the expansive views over both the northern West Bank and the Galilee in Israel.

1. Farming Palestine:
Canaan to Jabal al-Baared

[0-1.8km/0-1.1 mi.] From Canaan take a R onto the Burqin-Kafr Qud road. After 800m (0.5 mi.) you reach a 4-way junction (❶); turn L and continue to follow this paved but quiet road for another 1 km (0.62 mi.). The road gives an excellent overview of the agricultural variety of the Araba plains ("*Sahel Araba*"): figs, lemons, olives, beans, cucumbers, wheat, barley, tomatoes, squash, almonds, anis and chick peas (the base for humus) among other crops grow in the fields and greenhouses along the road.

Trail: Canaan > Jabal al-Baared > Canaan

Grade: Moderate

Surface: Predominantly dirt road and paved road; minor section off-track

Marked: No

Distance and duration: 10 km/6.2 miles; 2.5–3.5 hrs

Elevation change: 275 m/902 feet ascent and descent

Start coordinates: N32 27.439; E35 14.655

[1.8-2.9km/1.1-1.8 mi.] 1 km (0.62 mi.) from the last junction you will come to a 4-way junction (❷) just underneath electricity lines: follow the main road here as it veers off to the R (W). !! After another 1 km (0.62 mi.) the trail leaves the main road and continues on a dirt road to the R (❸). The turnoff is just before the main road also bends R. The dirt road starts climbing Jabal al-Baared ("the cold mountain") between olive fields and almond trees. Canaanite dwellings made in the rock surface can be found around here and you pass a spring with water year round along the way.

[2.9-5.3km/1.8-3.3 mi.] As you walk up the dirt road, the hill progressively becomes more barren. At 5.3 km (3.3 mi.) from the start of the hike the dirt road reaches a plateau some 40m (43 yards) below the peak of Jabal al-Baared (480m/1,575 ft.) with great views over the immediate villages to the North ('aniin, Araqa, Yamun). This is an excellent spot for some rest and possibly a picnic. On a reasonably clear day Haifa's hills can be seen from here, as well as the Mediterranean to the North of Tel Aviv. Nazareth can be clearly made out to the northeast.

[5.3-7.2km/3.3-4.4 mi.] !! To continue the hike, walk up to the peak of Jabal al-Baared to the R (E). There is no path. To get there leave the dirt road (❹) (which from the plateau descends down the hill in W direction) and walk up through *za'tar* and other wild vegetation to the peak. On the peak of Jabal al-Baared there are two large water cisterns on the R (S) side. On the L (N) side you see the wall of another cistern. It is behind this cistern that you find another dirt road which leads in W direction and descends towards the next hill: Jabal al-Liqra ("the bold mountain"). Follow this dirt road until you pass a large water tank at the edge of al-Baared village. At the first house you come across, turn R and follow a path descending aside a stone wall for about 100 m (109 yards). Then continue to follow the wall as it veers L (❺) and starts climbing to the peak of Jabal al-Liqra whose edge is lined with large rocks. At the peak (464m/1,522 ft.) you have another set of panoramic views, especially of Jenin and its surrounding villages to the East. Burqin and opposite the numerous greenhouses Canaan Fair Trade can be clearly made out from here. The ruin of an ancient tomb and four aged olive trees mark the peak; each of the trees is distinctively shaped by the powerful prevailing winds that pound this hilltop throughout the year.

[7.2-10.0km/4.4-6.2 mi.] To the E side of the peak, and just below the two olive trees closest to the tomb, you will find restored terraces all the way to the bottom of the hill. Zigzag down these terraces (❻). As you walk down, you can clearly see the main road between al-Baared village and Kafr Qud. At 7.7 km (4.7 mi.) from the start, the dirt road at the bottom of the hill connects to this main road: turn R here. A mini-market,

"Abu Bilal," is located at this junction and is a good stop for refreshments. From here you follow the road towards Kafr Qud for the next 1.5 km (0.9 mi.); take a L on the next 4-way junction and after 800m (0.5 mi.) you find Canaan.

PEOPLE & PLACES

"Situated in olive country, surrounded by olive orchards Burqin has always had a special tender spot in my heart. It is a community that loves to live and laugh. Working the surrounding lands with so much natural abundance and beauty in terrains and habitat, I find Burqin's agriculture offers the essence of Palestinian culture in its natural landscape."

—Nasser Abu Farha,
Anthropologist and Social Entrepreneur, Burqin

Olive tree shaped by the winds

Logistics and Guides

Canaan can arrange a guide for the walk; costs are 200 NIS for a group: 04-2431991. **The Hakoura Center** in Jenin is another good reference for guides. Call 04-2504773 or Mohammed Atari: hike-jenin@hotmail.com or 0597-437949.

How to Get There

Car: From Jerusalem/Ramallah, it is a 1hr45/1hr30 drive to Burqin. Drive N on Rd 60 in the direction of Nablus. After having passed through the village of Huwara, do not continue towards Huwara CP and Nablus city but turn L in W direction where the continuation of Rd 60 is indicated. After 11km (6.8 mi.) you come to a junction where Rd 60 meets Rd 55; turn L here and immediately R (signs to Shave Shomron). Continue on Rd 60 for 6km (3.7 mi.) and make sure to turn R as Rd 60 turns off the main road. !! Almost immediately after the turn-off you reach a large sign indicating solely Rd 60 and Shave Shomron to the L: ignore this sign (this road leads to the settlement itself) and continue straight towards Beit Iba village. Take the first junction to the L following signs to Jenin.

You pass the villages of Sebastia, Silat e-Dahr and Jaba. !! A few km before Jenin you reach the 4-way "Qabatiya" junction (a R turn leads to Qabatiya village): turn L here onto a small road that leads straight to Burqin village. The junction is easy to miss but can be recognized by a garage for minivans and trucks on the R (and you know you went too far

Dr. Bronner's Magic Soap . . . from Palestine

Washing your hands is probably not the first activity associated with supporting Palestinian farmers. Yet when you buy olive oil soap from Dr. Bronner's Magic Soap collection, you do exactly that. In 2004, Nasser Abu Farha returned from the US to Jenin to help farming communities set up the Palestine Fair Trade Association. He then founded Canaan Fair Trade, a private company fully dedicated to sampling the best of Palestine's local produce and selling it abroad. The difference with other export initiatives in Palestine is that Canaan's marketing abroad is not reliant on expressions of solidarity with Palestine alone. Canaan's success lies primarily in product quality, elegant packaging and the philosophy and practice of fair trade. This formula helps to export over US$ 4 million annually to renowned companies such as UK's Sainsbury's and the US chain Whole Foods. In 2006, Canaan became the first company worldwide to be fair trade certified for olive oil production. The company does not own one hectare of farmland. Instead, it works with over 1700 farmers organized in small village cooperatives to produce top quality certified organic and fair trade products such as olive oil, soap, sundried tomatoes, couscous, almonds, tahini, olives, honey, oregano and other spices. This ensures that farmers earn more than twice the amount as they did previously. The factory store is reminiscent of the better whiskey shops in Scotland holding a chic display of the various kinds of Palestinian olive oil. So indulge and enjoy.

Blossoming almonds
marking a spring to come

if you pass a range of stone workshops on the L side).

Once you reach Burqin village, follow the main road until you reach the central square of the village (a few shops are located here). Turn L here and after 100m (109 yards) turn R with the main road. From here, continue straight as you drive out of the village center, passing a gas station on the road towards the village of Kafr Qud. 1km (0.62 mi.) out of the Burqin village centre, Canaan Fair Trade is located to the R on this road.

Public transportation: via Jenin; continue on ford to Burqin and Kafr Qud.

Coming from Israel, you can pass through the Jalameh crossing to reach Burqin via Jenin. If you cross in and out of Jalameh crossing as a foreigner you need to bring your passport.

Where to Park

You can park at Canaan Fair Trade, the starting point of the hike.

Eat, Drink, Relax

Restaurants nearby can be found in Jenin (15 minutes by car).

Overnight: **Haddad Tourism Resort** near Jenin is a fun place with simple but clean rooms catering mostly to local visitors: single/double room 260/340 NIS including breakfast; 04-2417010, haddadbooking@ymail.com. **Cinema Jenin Guesthouse** is the first Palestinian backpackers right in the heart of Jenin: dorm bed/double room 75/125 NIS pppn; 04-2502455, guesthouse@cinemajenin.org. **Hakoura Center Jenin** organizes homestays in Jenin city or the Jenin refugee camp for both individuals and groups: 100NIS pppn including breakfast and dinner; 04-2504773, center@hakoura-jenin.ps. At the time of writing, plans to build an eco lodge in the vicinity of Burqin were considered by Canaan. During the annual olive harvest Canaan organizes homestays with farmers for visitors; participation in the harvest and other activities are included in the program.

Places to Go, People to Meet

Canaan Fair Trade factory and shop is worth a visit. The small **St. George Church** in Burqin is also called Church of the Lepers as it was built into the cave where Jesus reportedly cured 10 lepers as he passed through Burqin on his way from Nazareth to Jerusalem. It is still used by the Greek orthodox community and they welcome visitors (A visit can be arranged through Canaan or the Hakoura Center). Belame, south of Jenin, is the site of an ancient Canaanite city and includes Bronze Age, Roman-Byzantine, Crusader and Ottoman remains, including the Belame Tunnel. **Jenin's old city** and **souk** (market) are worth exploring, as are the **Ottoman palaces in Arraba**, just south of the city. Films, theatre and other events take place in **Cinema Jenin** in the city center and the **Freedom Theatre** in the Jenin Refugee Camp. The annual Olive Harvest Festival Jenin is organized on the first Friday of November. The Hakoura Center organizes historical/archeological tours of Jenin and environs (250 NIS for half day tours; 400 NIS for a full day).

On the Web

www.canaanfairtrade.com
www.cinemajenin.org
www.haddadtourismvillage.com
www.hakoura-jenin.ps/newhak/?lang=en
www.palestinefairtrade.org

Burqin's Church of the Lepers

جنين   Jenin: Ferris Wheel

Palestine keeps surprising: a fun fair park and a university in the middle of the countryside. The gently rolling hills outside Jenin are still a hidden gem for outdoor activity.

Located in its northern periphery, Jenin is a long drive away from most places in the West Bank. Yet a visit is more than worth your while: the Jenin area is both less populated and less hilly than other parts of the West Bank, leaving ample room for agriculture, a few small forests and places where nature still has its way.

After years of isolation due to access difficulties, developments in recent years have put Jenin back on the map for local and foreign visitors. In 2008, it was the first Palestinian city where Palestinian security forces were redeployed after years of absence. Business started to return to Jenin, social and cultural venues were reopened and visitors came back to a city much scarred by the Second Intifada. Besides easier access from the rest of the West Bank, Jenin can now also be entered directly from Israel through the nearby Jalameh crossing.

The Souk in Jenin

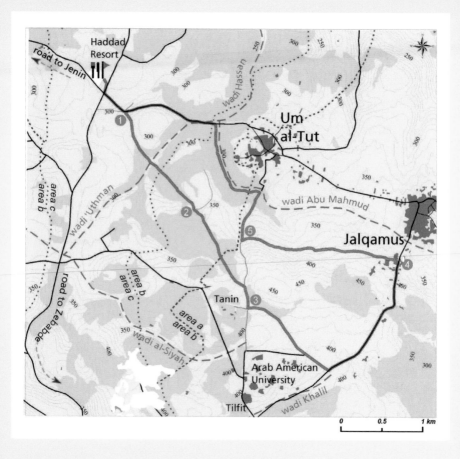

A lovely circular hike just ten minutes from Jenin. Starting at the Haddad resort, the walk will take you SE of Jenin, through the gentle hills towards Tilfit where the Arab American University is based, past the villages of Jalqamus and Um al-Tut and through their orchards of almond and olive trees. While good nearly any time of year, this hike is at its best in February and March with blossoming almond trees, radiant green fields filled with red anemones and a large variety of birds. A picnic halfway is highly recommended, and so is a meal at the Haddad resort.

2. Almonds on the Hill: Haddad to Jalqamus

[0m –500m/0-0.3 mi.] From the main entry gate of the Haddad Resort, turn R towards the 4-way junction. Take a L on this junction onto the paved road towards the village of Um al-Tut. 300m (0.2 mi.) onto this paved road, it curves to the L and at this point two dirt roads veer off on the R side (❶): take the second dirt road (located only 20m [21 yards] from the first dirt road). The dirt road descends into the fields.

Trail: Haddad Tourism Village › Jalqamus › Haddad Tourism Village

Grade: Moderate

Surface: Predominantly dirt road; minor sections paved road

Marked: Yes (red)

Distance and duration: 12.1 km/7.5 miles; 3–4.5 hrs

Elevation change: 275m ascent / 275 m descent

Start coordinates: N32 26.362 E35 19.394

[500m-2km/0.3-1.2 mi.] Follow the dirt road as it leads in SE direction going up and down the gentle hills and passing fields of wheat, olive groves and almond trees. 500m (0.3 mi.) on the dirt road, you pass a short strip of pine trees and a small Bedouin camp; continue straight up the hill after the trail crosses another dirt road near the camp. After 2 km (1.2 mi.) into the walk, you need to take a smaller dirt road that splits away from the main dirt road you are on (❷). !! This occurs just after you passed a set of cacti (*sabr*) which demarcate the border of an olive field on the R. At this point, the main dirt road will make a turn to the L whereas the trail carries on straight onto a much smaller path (should you mistakenly follow the main dirt road, it will make a U-turn and then run towards a dead end).

[2–3.6km/1.2-2.2 mi.] As you continue to follow the trail up the hill you can see villages of Jalqamus and al-Mughayer on the hills to the E. If you look back, on a clear day you can see Nazareth 30 km (18.6 mi.) to the N. Haddad's ferris wheel also stands out in the landscape. Continue to follow the trail as it meanders over the hills. 3 km (1.8 mi.) into the hike you see wheat

Dense-flowered fumitory

fields ahead with a stretch of land behind it demarcated by stone walls and a variety of different trees. While the trail gets smaller and smaller at this stage, continue to follow it in the same direction until it joins a larger dirt road connecting Um al-Tut to the **Arab American University (AAU).** Take a R onto this dirt road. 280m (0.2 mi.) from this point you reach a 4-way junction of dirt roads (❸). Instead of going straight down to the AAU campus, take a L here onto an ancient road whose

Blacksmith Tourism

With the arabic word for blacksmith as his last name, and born into a family line with that same profession, businessman Ibrahim Haddad was not exactly destined to take the business of tourism to heart. And when, in the middle of an economic crisis and with the worst of the Second Intifada just over, Haddad decided to build a new tourism village at the edge of Jenin, most Palestinian businessmen probably thought he had gone mad. In 2006, Palestinians could hardly move around within the West Bank and in Jenin the situation was especially

dire. But Haddad set his mind on creating something new and started to build regardless the gloomy prospects; first three villas for himself and his sons, then an amusement park with a ferris wheel, a restaurant and a swimming pool. And while business prospects were still dim in 2008, he started to build a hotel, conference facilities, an amphitheater and a children's museum on Palestinian heritage. The image of St. George slaying the dragon takes center stage on the facade of Haddad's villa at the center of his park and perhaps the saint was watching over

his actions. By the time the hotel was finished in 2009, internal movement inside the West Bank had started to improve, the Jalameh crossing was reopened and Arab Israelis came back into Jenin again after 9 years of closure. The positive impact on the Jenin area was immediate and busloads of school children and Nazareth families started visiting the resort. Haddad then added another wing to his hotel in 2010, leaving visitors with one remarkable novelty in blacksmith tourism: while the rooms all have a door towards a balcony, try to find a window.

old stone paving can still be traced between patches of soil and grass. The ancient road circles N of the AAU campus. The AAU is Palestine's first private university working according to the American education system. Affiliated with universities in California and Utah, it enrolls some 7000 students and its faculties include administration and finance, art and science, law, engineering and IT, dentistry and allied medical science.

[3.6-8.7km/2.2-5.4 mi.] After 1.3 km (0.8 mi.) from the last 4-way junction, you reach a T junction with a paved road connecting the AAU and the village of Jalqamus. Turn L and follow this road for the next 1.7km (1 mi.) when you reach the first houses of Jalqamus. While

Walkers exploring Jenin's rolling hills

Spiny broom near Tilfit

there is little traffic on this road, be aware that some of it drives rather fast. Soon after entering Jalqamus village and before you reach the village center, you come across a school on your L hand (**❹**). The name of the school (Jalqamus Secondary Girls School) is only indicated in Arabic but the building can be easily recognized as the first building with three floors that you come across near the village. Turn L at the school and onto a small paved road that quickly turns into a dirt road in between olive groves and almond trees. Follow this road for the next 2 km (1.2 mi.); it provides an excellent view to the N and the plains of Jenin below.

[8.7-12.1km/5.4-7.5 mi.] At 2 km (1.2 mi.) from Jalqamus you reach a 3-way junction (**❺**). Take a R here and continue your way down to Um al-Tut. Once you are at the foot of Um al-Tut, do not continue up into the village but follow the dirt road as it veers L into the wadi below the village. After 1.1 km (0.6 mi.) from this junction you will reach the main paved road between Um al-Tut and the Haddad resort; take a L here to go back to Haddad (1.5 km; 0.9 mi.).

Back to the Cinema

Marcus Vetter's film *Heart of Jenin* received a range of awards at festivals around the world. The documentary follows Jenin's Ismail Khatib whose 11 year old son Ahmed was killed by the Israeli army in 2005 when they mistook his toy gun for the real thing. Amazingly, Ismail decided to donate the organs of Ahmed to children in Israel. The film portrays his journey across Israel as he meets the parents of the children saved by Ahmed's organs. Having finished the film Vetter lamented that there was no cinema in Jenin to show it to its people. Until he was told there actually was one, in the center of Jenin but closed since 23 years and its interior buried under thick layers of dust and garbage. The idea for the **Cinema Jenin Project** originated there and then. Marcus and Ismail, together with project director Fakhri Hamad, moved heaven and earth to reopen the cinema. Starting from scratch they had a hard time gathering enough funds for an unconventional grass roots initiative driven largely by the enthusiasm of local staff and international volunteers. Fortunately, Pink Floyd's founder Roger Waters, a number of German companies, and the German government stepped in to assist and Cinema Jenin was reopened in August 2010 featuring several screenings a day in its indoor and outdoor theaters. The protagonists' ideas have meanwhile moved into other areas and include a café, a film library, and the Cinema Jenin Guesthouse, Palestine's first real refuge for backpackers. The guesthouse has dormitories as well as double rooms and a kitchen that can be used by its guests. In tribute to the many German volunteers who helped to reopen Cinema Jenin, the guesthouse also harbors Palestine's one and only beer vending machine.

Almond trees between
Jalqamus and Um al-Tut

Logistics and Guides

To arrange a guide for the walk, contact the Hakoura
Center in Jenin (04-2504773) or Mohammed Atari:
hike-jenin@hotmail.com or 0597-437949. Group
walks up to around 3 hours cost 250 NIS; longer
walks (a full day) around 400 NIS.

How to Get There

Car: From Jerusalem/Ramallah, it is a 1hr45/1hr30
drive to Haddad. Drive N on Rd 60 towards Nablus.
Pass the Huwara CP into Nablus and take a R at the
first Y junction. Continue to follow this road which
is a short cut as it circles the center of Nablus to its E
and then joins the main road from Nablus just to its

N. Continue to follow the main road N for the next 26 km (16 mi.). The first village after Nablus is al-Bidaan: make sure that after the road makes a U-turn, you turn L and immediately R to continue on the main road towards al-Far'a. After al-Far'a, you pass through the city of Tubas, and the villages of 'Aqqaba, Kufeir and Zebabde. After passing Zebabde, take the first junction to your R (the main road continues to Qabatiya) and continue to follow this road. Signs to Haddad appear a few km before you reach the park, which is located at a 4-way junction between Zebabde, Jenin and Um al-Tut.

You can also follow the directions towards Burqin on Rd 60 (described in the chapter on Burqin) and turn R towards Qabatiya, passing through the village and then head N towards Jenin and Haddad.

Public transportation: via Nablus to Zebabde or via Jenin; change to a private taxi or ford going in the direction of Um al-Tut.

Coming from Israel, you can pass through the Jalameh crossing to reach Jenin. If you cross in and out of Jalameh crossing as a foreigner you need to bring your passport.

Where to Park

You can park inside the Haddad Tourism Village

Eat, Drink, Relax

The Haddad resort offers a fairly broad menu of mezze, various grilled meats, pizza and sandwiches. The Denise (fish) is excellent as are the fresh juices. A variety of *argilleh* (water pipe) is served. You can also use the pool for a fee of 40 NIS (free if staying over in the hotel). Other restaurants nearby can be found in Jenin city and Zebabde (both 10 minutes by car)

Overnight

Haddad Tourism Resort near Jenin is a fun place

Flowering asphodels

with simple but clean rooms catering mostly to local visitors: single/double room 260/340 NIS including breakfast; 04-2417010, haddadbooking@ymail.com. **Cinema Jenin Guesthouse** is the first Palestinian lodging for backpackers right in the heart of Jenin: dorm bed/double room 75/125 NIS pppn; 04-2502455, guesthouse@cinemajenin.org. **Hakoura Center Jenin** organizes homestays in Jenin city or the Jenin refugee camp for both individuals and groups: 100NIS pppn including breakfast and dinner; 04-2504773, center@hakoura-jenin.ps.

Places to Go, People to Meet

The Jenin Governorate has developed plans for a 1.2km (0.7 mi.) environmental pathway N of the Haddad resort at the site of the former settlement

Sunset over Jenin

PEOPLE & PLACES

"We walk through the plains where fields of wheat embrace the flowers of chrysanthemums. Across the hills we go, where, on the edges, oak trees have grown old. We explore routes where the breeze carries the scent of almonds and anemones, and everything around you tells you that 'the road is from here.'"

—Mohammed Atari, Guide, Jenin

of Kadim. Dr. Walid Basha (bscjenin@yahoo.com; 0599-590284) can be contacted for more information, including on bird watching options in the Jenin area. **Jenin's old city and souk** (market) are worth exploring for visitors, as are the **Ottoman palaces in Arraba**, south of the city. Films, theatre and other events take place in **Cinema Jenin** in the city center and the **Freedom Theatre** in the Jenin Refugee Camp. Belame, south of Jenin, is the site of an ancient Canaanite city

Rambling over Jenin's rolling hills towards Jalqamus

and includes Bronze Age, Roman-Byzantine, Crusader and Ottoman remains, including the **Belame Tunnel**. **Canaan Fair Trade** factory and shop, in Burqin just east of Jenin, is worth visiting. The **St. George Church**, also Burqin, is still used by the Greek orthodox community and they welcome visitors (A visit can be arranged through Canaan or the Hakoura Center). The annual **Olive Harvest Festival** Jenin is organized on the first Friday of November. Hakoura Center organizes historical/archeological tours of Jenin and environs (250 NIS for half day tours; 400 NIS for a full day).

On the Web

www.haddadtourismvillage.com
www.hakoura-jenin.ps/newhak/?lang=en
www.cinemajenin.org
www.pace.ps

الزبابدة Zebabde: Mosaic Memories

The quiet plains of the northern West Bank give way to rounded hills in the east. From Zebabde to Raba through the pretty Wadi al-Balad.

Zebabde is one of about two dozen Palestinian villages in the West Bank that are a mixture of Muslim and Christian families living amidst a patchwork of churches and mosques. While the numbers of Palestinian Christians have been dwindling all over Palestine for decades due to emigration, relations between the two communities inside these villages are generally good.

Of Zebabde's 3500 residents about two-thirds are Christian and the town's churches represent no less than four different denominations: Latin (Roman Catholic), Greek Orthodox, Anglican, and Melkite (Greek Catholic). Zebabde's old town has a small old mosque whilst a newly built larger mosque (with the second tallest minaret in the West Bank) is located along its main road. The largest school in town is run by the Latin Patriarchate and enrolls both Christian and Muslim students.

Byzantine mosaics in
Zebabde's Latin Convent

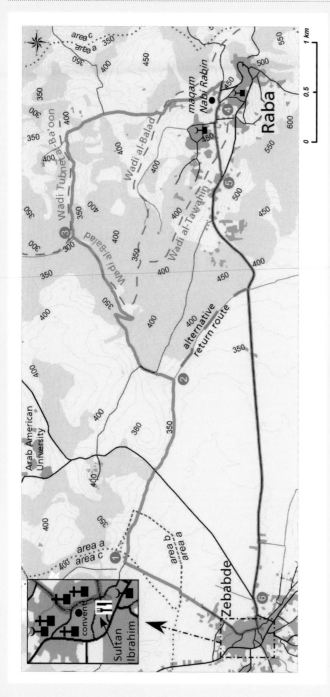

This trail from Zebabde is a long but varied circular walk. It starts from the old town of Zebabde, crosses its expansive plains and then descends into the spectacular Wadi al-Balad. It returns through the hills of Raba village and the agricultural outskirts of Zebabde. An early start on this walk is highly recommended and so is bringing along a picnic. At the start or end of the walk the old village center with its mosque and four churches is worth exploring. A walk from Zebabde is not complete without a meal at the famous Sultan Ibrahim restaurant (you can make your order before you set out on the walk).

3. The Plains and Beyond: Zebabde to Raba

Trail:
Zebabde–Raba–Zebabde

Grade:
Moderate/hard

Surface:
Mostly dirt roads;
some paved road

Marked: Yes (green)

Distance and Duration:
14.9 km/9.2 miles;
4–5.5 hrs

Elevation Change:
300m ascent / 300m
descent

Start Coordinates:
N32 23.123 E35 19.479

[0-280m/0-0.2 mi.] Start at the Sultan Ibrahim Restaurant. Standing with your back to the entrance of the restaurant, go L and immidiately take another L walking into Zebabde's old town. Continue straight as you pass the Anglican Church of St. Matthew (R) and quickly thereafter the **Latin Convent (L)** where you can see mosaics from Byzantine times in the courtyard (remains of another mosaic floor can be seen inside the convent—ask for entry at the Church of Visitation opposite the Convent). The exact date of the geometric mosaic floor is unknown but it is thought to be from the 6th century AD. A decoration above the convent's entrance honors Sister Marie-Alphonsine Danil Ghattas who spent two years in Zebabde around 1892 and co-founded the Congregation of the Rosary Sisters, the only Arab religious order in Palestine. 50m (54 yards) from the convent you pass Zebabde's largest church, the (Latin) **Church of Visitation**, named after a supposed visit of the Virgin Mary on her way to Jerusalem. Turn R at the 4-way junction in front of the church.

[280m-1.8km/0.2-1.1 mi.] Follow the paved road out of town passing the Latin Patriarchate School and the houses standing in between the old city and the outstretched plains of Zebabde. Straight ahead you can make out the campus of the Arab American Univesity, located in the hills a few km NE of Zebabde. The road turns into a dirt road that crosses the plains. Tomatoes, okra, onions, cucumber, potatoes, peppers, eggplant, zuchini, water melon and wheat are some of the crops that are grown here.

[1.8-3.8km/1.1-2.3 mi.] At the end of the fields you come across a T-junction (**❶**). Turn R here and follow the dirt road which gives beautiful views over Zebabde village. You pass a water spring in a cave to your R and olive groves to your L. Tobacco is among the variety of crops at this side of the field (visible in the fall). At 2.8km (1.7 mi.) you cross the main road between Zebabde and the Arab American University. Continue straight on the dirt road towards the large pine forest that tops the hills of Raba. Just as you have passed an olive grove to your L and some 200m (0.1 mi.) before you reach the bottom of the pine forest you come across a 3-way junction (**❷**). Turn L here onto a wide rocky dirt road.

A shepherd from Raba leading his herd

Byzantium on the Floor

It was Christians from Taybeh —a village near Ramallah— who moved to the Zebabde area early in the 19th century. The village's first parish (Greek Orthodox) of its current three was established in the 1870s. Hence Zebabde seems a relatively young town, at least when compared to many other places in Palestine. It depends how you look at it. Zebabde's origins actually go back more than one and a half millennia and its ancient origins are testified by the Byzantine mosaics in its Latin Convent.

Mosaic art dates back as far as the 3rd millennium BC but it was in Byzantine times (4th-7th century) that the use of mosaics really took a flight across the region. The most famous work is the 6th century mosaic floor depicting a map of the Holy Land in Madaba's St. George Church (Jordan). But spectacular works of mosaic art can be seen across much of Palestine as well and their

use in Christian, Muslim and Jewish places of worship demonstrates how much the three religions influenced one another artistically. Similarly, in the 8th century the three religions jointly experienced a destructive wave of so-called iconoclasm, a movement in which images of men and animals were systematically destroyed or defaced. The damage was not done by your random bunch of vandals or enemy troops, but by the religious authorities themselves, in some cases carefully removing just the individual faces from mosaics, in other cases destroying larger segments whose existence was suddenly considered to flaunt god's laws.

Fortunately, many mosaics survive to this day, and some with all living creatures still in tact. The Umayyad Palace of Hisham in Jericho, for example, contains such images in its bathhouse. In addition, it contains one of the largest continuous classical mosaic

floors in the world (850 m2), still in an amazing condition of startling colors and geometrical patterns (presently, most of the floor is covered by a protective layer of sand but there are plans to uncover it entirely). Just a few hundred meters north of the palace are the remains of the 6th century Shalom al-Israel Synagogue, beautifully decorated with floral and geometrical patterns, and Aramic inscriptions. A mosaic floor from the same century can be found inside the Coptic St. Andrew Church near Jericho's center. In Zebabde, a carpet of Byzantine mosaics can be admired inside the Latin Convent, as well as outside in its courtyard. Apart from Zebabde, walks in this book going past or nearby classical mosaics are Aboud, Jifna and Taybeh, Mar Saba, and the sites of Hisham's Palace, synagogue floors and Byzantine churches in Jericho.

The crescent and the cross cheek to cheek in Zebabde

[3.8-6.0km/2.3-3.7 mi.] Follow the road gradually up the hill. You cross onto another road coming from Raba village; continue straight and 160m (0.1 mi.) further up the road make sure you continue straight on a dirt road and do not follow the main road (which veers sharply L). You pass a large collapsed cave (to your R) after which the dirt road start to skirt Wadi al-Balad. Follow the road as it descends and zigzags down into the wadi, which is filled with a large variety of flowers in the spring. When it is at the very bottom of the wadi bed the path becomes smaller and passes under a set of newly made terraces with olive trees, and, later on, almond trees. Continue to follow the path along the wadi bed (in spring time, this trail might become less visible; when in doubt, simply continue to follow the wadi bed).

[6.0-9.0km/3.7-5.6 mi.] At 6 km (3.7 mi.) into the walk you come across a 3-way junction where a second wadi joins Wadi al-Balad from the R (**3**). This is Wadi Tubnet al-Ba'oon . A dirt road crosses the wadi bed here in between a set of stone terraces and starts climbing up Wadi Tubnet al-Ba'oon. Go R here and follow this dirt road. You continue to follow the road as it meanders in between the fields for one km (0.6 mi.) and climbs over 100m (109 yards) before reaching a T-junction on a saddle point between two hills. A few families of farmers live on either hill and their cattle is held in pretty traditional stone-built animal pens some of which can be seen from the trail. From here you have an excellent view of the surounding landscape: nearby the villages of Jalqamus (on your L) and Mughayyer (straight ahead) with some of the houses standing out because of their stark colors such as red, purple and pink; further away and just beyond the snake path of the seperation barrier you can see the Gilboa hills in Israel. At the T junction, take a R and continue your climb towards the village of Raba lying just beneath the pine forest. As you follow the trail you see the landscape on your L roll down towards the Jordan Valley and the Jordanian Rift mountains. After a slight descent the road climbs up to Raba passing a stone factory just before you reach the village.

[9.0-10.1km/5.6-6.2 mi.] At a T junction with a small paved road you have reached Raba village, its name referring to its geographical position "risen high on a hill." Turn R here. You pass a small Muslim cemetery on your R. Just above the cemetery a small path veers off to the R towards an old *maqam* named after Nabi Rabin (the site is also called Khirbet Abu Farhan). The shrine is located some 80m (87 yards) off the road and can be entered. Continuing on the paved road, at the next T junction (**4**) turn R again (if you are eager to buy drinks or snack, turn L and Abu Ahmad's minimarket

Church of the Visitation

is just 120m [131 yards] up the road) and follow the newly paved road (with sidewalks) through Raba. Continue straight through Raba for 800m (0.5 mi.) until you come across another junction with the larger main road connecting Raba to Zebabde.

[10.1-14.9km/6.2-9.2 mi.] Turn R onto the main road (❺). While there is little traffic on this road, be wary of cars and minibuses speeding along: keeping to the L side of the road is best. The road meanders down passing a pine forest. You see the villages of 'Aqqaba and Kufeir from here. Once you reach the flat agricultural plains again, you see Zebabde straight ahead: the long and somewhat dull final stretch is 3km (1.8 mi.), walking in between Zebabde's varied agriculture and the occassional stone factory along the paved road. The shortest (and fastest) route back to Zebabde is over this road, and it is the official trail. However, if you prefer a more scenic (but longer) way back to Zebabde, turn R onto the dirt road that runs directly beneath Raba's pine trees: follow this path and you pick up the first part of the trail further on, retracing your footsteps from thereon. If you walk the 3km (1.8 mi.) paved road, just before you get to the village, you reach a T junction. Turn L here and after 200m (0.1 mi.) turn R into the old city (❻). Take the first L to get back to the Sultan Ibrahim restaurant for a well-deserved meal.

Towards wadi al-Balad

Logistics and Guides

To arrange a guide for the walk, contact the Hakoura Center in Jenin (04-2504773) or Mohammed Atari: hike-jenin@hotmail.com or 0597-437949. Group walks up to around 3 hours cost 250 NIS; longer walks (a full day) around 400 NIS. An excellent local contact inside Zebabde is Rami Duaibes who handles public relations of the village: 0599-708255. Should you decide to throw in the towel for the last part of the walk between Raba and Zebabde, call Zebabde's taxi service: al-Sarah (04-2520666) or al-Ajniha (04-2520222).

How to Get There

Car: From Jerusalem/Ramallah, it is a 1hr45/1hr30 drive to Zebabde. Drive N on Rd 60 towards Nablus. Pass the Huwara CP into Nablus and take a R at the first Y junction. Continue to follow this road which is a short cut as it circles the center of Nablus to its E and then joins the main road from Nablus just to its N. Continue to follow the main road N for the next 26 km (16 mi.). The first village after Nablus is al-Bidaan: make sure that after the road makes a U-turn, you turn L and immediately R to continue on the main road towards al-Far'a. After al-Far'a, you pass through the city of Tubas, and then the villages of 'Aqqaba and Kufeir, afterwhich you reach Zebabde. As you enter the town, continue straight for about 1 km (0.6 mi.) until you reach the town center clearly visible by its yellow taxis and buses opposite Zebabde's new Abdallah ibn Rawaha Mosque. Restaurant Fountain and a small minimarket are located at this corner. Take a R here to go into the old town of Zebabde where you find the Sultan Ibrahim restaurant to the L after 40m (43 yards). Alternatively, you can follow the directions towards Burqin on Rd 60 (see Burqin chapter) and from Rd 60 turn R towards Qabatiya, passing through this village and then R (S) towards Zebabde. Public transportation: via Nablus or directly from Ramallah.

Where to Park

You can park your car either on the smaller road going into the old town close to the Sultan Ibrahim restaurant, or in front of the Fountain restaurant opposite the mosque.

Eat, Drink, Relax

Located in a traditional Ottoman house, the **Sultan Ibrahim Restaurant** (059-9763026; 056-8112240) is highly recommended. Ibrahim prepares grills, traditional Palestinian dishes such as *musakhan* and *maqloobe*, as well as steaks, sandwiches, pizzas and vegetarian dishes, including for takeout. The **Fountain Restaurant**, located at Zebabde's taxi stand, prepares burgers, shoarma and falafel sandwiches.

Flowering tobacco at the edge of Zebabde

Overnight

The only overnight option in Zebabde is the **Naim Khader Center**. Run by the Palestinian Agricultural Relief Committees (PARC), it only accomodates large groups. The center is located north of the village: 04-2510461.

Places to Go, People to Meet

Zebabde's old town is interesting to visit, including

A colorful decent into
wadi al-Balad

its four churches: Anglican, Latin (Roman Cathlic),
Greek Orthodox and Melkite (Greek Catholic). **The
Latin Convent** contains **Byzantine mosaics**, estimated
to come from the 6th century AD. **The Latin Visitation
Church** is built on the site where it is believed Jesus'
mother Mary and Elisabeth (mother of John the Baptist) met one another. The Hakoura Center in Jenin
can provide archeological, historical and walking tours
in the Jenin area, including Zebabde (250 NIS for half
day tours; 400 NIS for a full day).

On the Web
www.zababdeh.ps
www.hakoura-jenin.ps/newhak/?lang=en

سبسطية Sebastia: Stone Empires

In the small village of Sebastia the empires of old are stacked one layer on another like a historical lasagna. Amidst olive groves and fruit trees walkers stumble across millenia of conquest and pilgrimage.

Small as it may be now, Sebastia has always been an important place, both in antiquity and in more recent centuries. In the 1870s, the Palestine Exploration Fund noted *a large and flourishing village, of stone and mud houses, on the hill of ancient Samaria.* It also reported that the inhabitants are *somewhat turbulent in character, and appear to be rich, possessing very good lands.*

Turbulence and wealth have largely passed by the village in more recent times, but Sebastia remains incredibly rich in its heritage, and its people generous in their welcome. It is a unique place mistakenly ignored by most tourists. The upside is that visitors can enjoy Sebastia in peace and quiet: its impressive ruins include a Roman theater, basilica and forum, a Byzantine church, a Herodian temple, Hellenistic defence towers, a cathedral-turned-mosque and buildings from Ottoman and Crusader times, among others. A walk from the village is incomplete without a visit to its archeological site and historic town center so make sure you start walking early enough to leave time for this once you return.

Resting on an empire: young walker in Sebastia

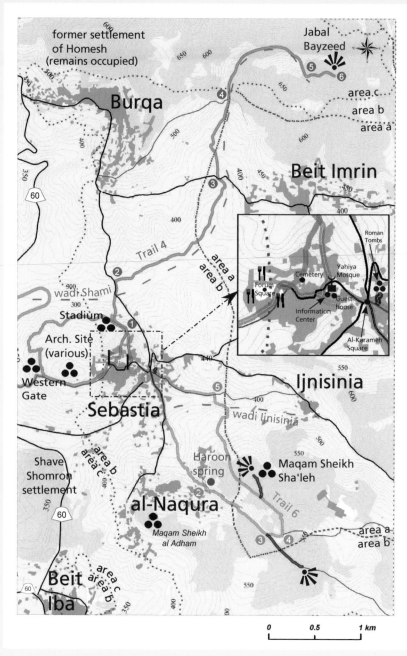

See page 93 for Trail 6 directions.

4. A Slow Rise: Sebastia to Maqam Bayzeed

While this is a so-called out and back hike, the trail leading from Sebastia village to the top of Jabal Bayzeed is so lovely and varied that you will not be bored for a moment retracing your steps in the second half of the walk. From the Forum Square put your gaze NE and you will easily make out the hilltop of Jabal Bayzeed which at 722m (2,368 ft.) is the highest point in the area. If you look closely you can discern a small structure on the E side of this hilltop; these are the ruins of **Maqam Bayzeed**. From where you are standing, it might look a day hiking away but the easy dirt roads and footpath that lead down into the valley of olive fields and then up Jabal Bayzeed will only take you around two hours to cross. Allow yourself at least another half hour to picnic and take in the impressive views at Maqam Bayzeed before heading back.

Trail: Sebastia—Maqam Bayzeed—Sebastia

Grade: Moderate

Surface: Dirt road and single track; minor paved

Marked: Planned (blue)

Distance and Duration: 11.8 km/7.3 miles; 4—5.5 hrs

Elevation Change: 550m ascent / 550m descent

Start Coordinates: N32 16.622 E35 11.617

[0-500m/0-0.3 mi.] At the Forum Square, and with the archeological site to your L and the town of Sebastia to your R (hence facing N), start the hike walking towards the village center at the NE side of the square. Take the first road L going downhill. The road passes a small cemetery where you meet a T junction: go R and follow the road as it descends between the houses at the edge of town. After 500m (0.3 mi.) you reach an intersection (❶): turn L and continue to descend towards the valley.

[500-3.3km/0.3-2 mi.] Out of town, you continue downhill until the road levels off crossing the wadi bed. Some 70m (76 yards) after the lowest point of the road, a dirt road to your R leads into the olive

Sebastia's Western Gate

fields (❷); take this road and follow it as it gently runs E across the wide valley of olive trees. While other footpaths and dirt roads will intersect with your path, continue your path straight ahead, elevating slightly above the olive trees in the valley.

[3.3-4.1km/2-2.5 mi.] After 3.3 km (2 mi.) from the start, you meet the main paved road that connects the villages of Beit Umreen and Burqa. Some 30m (32 yards) to the L of this junction a slightly overgrown dirt road continues on the other side of the paved road, also running through an olive field (❸). Continue on this dirt road (should this road be completely overgrown, an alternative is a larger dirt road 220m [0.13 mi.] further up). The dirt road eventually turns into a smaller single track gradually sloping upwards through the olive groves. Continue to follow this path which eventually runs close to the wadi bed. Should you lose track of it in between the olive trees, simply direct yourself towards the wadi bed on your R and keep close to it as you climb up the slope. The wadi bed at one stage is filled with large fig and almond trees; a pretty sight, especially when the latter blossoms in February.

[4.1-5.5km/2.5-3.4 mi.] After 4.1 km (2.5 mi.), the path meets another dirt road also connecting the villages of Beit Umrin and Burqa (❹). Cross this road as well and continue the trail upwards passing a modern water cistern. From here, you continue to walk close to the wadi bed (the path runs on both sides). Gradually leaving the olive fields, the path starts climbing up small terraces, eventually also leaving the last almond trees behind. The trail then continues to follow the wadi bed, bending R (E) and ultimately reaching a saddlepoint just below the summit of Jabal Bayzeed (❺). Especially in winter time this is a place of quiet beauty without any building or road in view. In the midst of grassy fields and in the center of the saddlepoint, 12 almond trees give shade to herders and their flocks that frequently graze around this site.

[5.5-5.9km/3.4-3.6 mi.] The footpath stops here and you can climb to the top of Jabal Bayzeed from either its L or R flank, the latter being slightly easier. Once at the top (5.9km/3.6 mi.) you will find the ruins of Maqam Bayzeed on the R (E) side (**⑥**). The history of the *maqam* is unknown; yet its location gives you a full view of the region at 722m (2,368 ft.) above sea level. On a clear day the views are among the most spectacular in Palestine: to the immediate SE you see large parts of Nablus city, to the SW Sebastia and its surrounding villages; to the W Israel's coastal plain and the Mediterannean and to the E the Jordanian hills above the Rift Valley. On a very clear day in winter, the most spectacular view to the N is Jabal al-Sheikh (Mt. Hermon) with its snow packed peak at 2200m (7,217 ft.).

[Return] On the way back, simply retrace your steps into the wadi or choose the best path on either side. Make sure you keep close to the lowest point of the wadi and ignore the occasional tracks that follow the hill higher up. After crossing the dirt road, keep the wadi bed on your L. You then cross the main Beit Umrin-Burqa road (paved) into the olive valley which leads you back to Sebastia. If you return to the Beit Umrin–Burqa road at an unfamiliar point you have probably strayed slightly to the R (W); just take a L towards the lower (wadi) point of this road and you will meet the entry to the valley of olive trees (R) that connects to Sebastia. Upon leaving the valley, take a L onto the paved road and climb straight back up to Sebastia; once you have passed the first houses of the village make sure to take a R turn at the first intersection.

Naples garlic

See page 97 for Trail 7 directions.

5. The Hijaz Railway: Sebastia to Ramin

This walk follows the old Hijaz railway line that passes below Sebastia village and snails through the landscape towards the village of Ramin. This trail is also suitable for mountain bikes and there were plans at Sebastia's Information Center to rent these out to visitors in the future. The trail passes Sebastia's old railway station, one of the last to be built by the Ottomans before the collapse of the empire. From Ramin village you will leave the railway to follow footpaths over the hills back to Sebastia. Ardent walkers or bikers can also continue to follow the railway northwards to the village of al-'Attara where the impressive 250m (0.15 mi.) long Ramin railway tunnel is still in surprisingly good condition.

Trail:
Sebastia—Ramin—Sebastia

Grade: Moderate

Surface: Predominantly dirt road; minor sections paved

Marked: planned (green)

Distance and Duration: 15.5 kms/9.6 miles; 4.5 - 6 hrs

Elevation Change: 375m ascent/ 375m descent

Start Coordinates:
N32 16.597 E35 11.588

[0-1.4km/0-0.8 mi.] Start from the Holy Land Sun Restaurant which is located just to the S of the Forum Square and at the top of the Sebastia's Columned Street. Descend W down the Columned Street where numerous Roman columns—once forming one of the city's main arteries—now stand quietly between the olive trees. Underneath the hill slope to your R lie the ruins of Sebastia's old city wall. After 1 km (0.6 mi.), a large section of the once heavily fortified wall can still be seen just as the road starts twisting and turning further downhill. Near the bottom of the road and some 200m (0.12 mi.) from Rd 60 (which is clearly visible from this point), the old railway path crosses the road (❶). The railway, which is partially overgrown here, cuts across your road just before the olive trees on the R side make way for open fields. The iron and wood have been removed from the track long ago and the iron can still be found as supporting material in Palestinian houses across the West Bank.

Damascus by Rail

From Haifa to Medina or from Nablus to Damascus by train and without showing your passport once: a dream for today's traveler, but reality nearly a hundred years back. In 1914 you could step on a train in Sebastia and make your way to Damascus in about 12 hours. Presently, a trip to Damascus is hardly undertaken by anybody. Too many borders lie in between. Too many authorities make passing them difficult.

The construction of the 1600 kilometer long Hijaz railway was the last achievement of imperial magnitude for the Ottomans. The grand finale as it were before this empire too collapsed. But when Sultan Abdulhamid II issued his order to build the railway in 1900, he had a somewhat different scenario in mind. The megaproject was aimed to restore the grandeur of the Ottoman Empire. Its public objective was to massively ease a pilgrims' Haj to Mecca, cutting the journey

from over 40 days of heat, disease and exhaustion on the road to under 3 days on the railway. Though the real purpose was to get a better millitary grip on Arabia, the Sultan's emphasis on the Haj was a smart move in public diplomacy: almost bankrupt, he managed to galvanize massive financial support for the railway from Muslims around the world, as well as technical assistance from his ally Germany.

Yet building it in the extremely harsh environment of the Hijaz proved to be an imperial headache: with extremes of heat and cold, water scarcity and local Bedouin tribes sabotaging the project, it took the Ottoman army 8 years to finish the main line to Medina; the last stretch to Mecca was never built. Laying out the various branches in Palestine, however, went much more smoothly and the connection from Haifa to Damascus was ready long before the main

line was finished. Sebastia's Masoudiya station was part of a late extension of the Hijaz line running south from Afula (now in Israel) via Jenin to Sebastia where the railway split towards Nablus and Tulkarem.

Yet the trains never got any further as the first World War and Lawrence of Arabia literally blew the Hijaz Railway off its tracks across the region. With his spectacular sabotage actions, Lawrence made sure the railway became more famous for its own demise —and that of the Ottoman empire—than for its achievement of linking people across the Middle East. The war of 1948 finally sealed the fate of the railway and the Jenin-Tulkarem-Nablus stretch became one of the many loose limbs spread across a fractured region.

Ruins of temple of Augustus

[1.4-3.8km/0.8-2.3 mi.] Take a R (N) onto the old railway: you are now walking the section between Nablus and Masoudiya stations. Continue along the path as it curls slowly around the bottom of the Sebastia hill. While walking here you can see another old Hijaz branch coming from the direction of Tulkarem to your L below (the two tracks eventually merge at the station). Keep following the railway track you are on and which passes through a gentle U turn at the N side of Sebastia. The trail then curves back in W direction towards Rd 60. Cross Rd 60 (take care as traffic is fast along this road) after which the railway disappears underneath a smaller paved road. Follow this road and after almost 4 km (2.4 mi.) into the hike you pass the long abandoned Sebastia railway station on your R (❷); despite being slowly overtaken by nature it retains a glimmer of its original elegance. The original framed marble commemorating its opening in Arabic caligraphy (depicting the station's official name and year of opening: Masoudiya, 1914) still hangs from the outer wall of the first floor. A large fig tree grows out of one of the station's former entrances.

[3.8-8.3km/2.3-5.1 mi.] From the railway station, the trail continues to follow the old railway route (now again unpaved) as it winds very gradually around the hills W of Rd 60. At times the rail's historic presence is unmistakenly evident as the trail cuts through rocks in the hillside in order to continue its gradual ascent without any deviation. As it snails around the hills and away from Rd 60, the railway provides some of the most quiet views of rural Palestine. After almost 8 km (4.9 mi.) into the trail you reach the outskirts of Ramin

Sebastia's Masoudiya station

PEOPLE & PLACES

"Sabastia is very important to me because it is a historic city inhabited since ancient times. It is considered one of the most important sites in Palestine. I have been impressed since my childhood, and I decided to study archeology to contribute to its development."

—Suheib Huwari, Guide, Sebastia

village and as you pass the first houses, the railway route becomes paved road again. Continue for about 500m (0.31 mi.) on this paved road until you reach a 4-way junction: L goes towards Ramin village; straight continues on the railway cutting through the rocks; and a sharp R turn climbs up the hill on an unpaved dirt road (**❸**). Take the latter turn to the R and start climbing on the dirt road in E direction on the hill.

A family day in the field

[8.3-10.2km/5.1-6.3 mi.] The short climb provides a clear view over Ramin village. Once over the hill, and some 700m (0.43 mi.) from the last junction, the road forks in two; keep straight (R leg) here after which the road will descend into a quiet valley. At the bottom of the valley, you come across a 3-way junction (**❹**): turn R here and continue to hike in between the fields. !! After some 700m (0.43 mi.) you come across another 4-way junction (**❺**). In spring, it can be difficult to spot but note that the slightly elevated railway where you walked before is clearly visible a few hundred meters ahead. Turn L at this 4-way junction and continue on this path as it ascends the hill to the SE.

[10.2-11.8km/6.3-7.3 mi.] Continue to follow the path as it climbs onto the ridge of the hill from where you have an excellent view over Nablus in the distance. You will pass several junctions: keep L until you are nearly above the old train station and the Mhattet Zamaan resort. At that moment you will reach a junction of various dirt roads: turn R here, then immidiately L and descend towards the station. You pass the small Mhattet Zamaan resort; if you care for a drink or a swim (boys only though!) you can stop here.

[11.8-15.5km/7.3-9.6 mi.] To turn back to Sebastia, continue past the railway station, cross Rd 60 again and retrace your footsteps all the way back to the village. An alternative return can be made by leaving the railway near the small overpass over Wadi Shami and walking through the wadi and then climb up at the N side of the village. At the time of writing, this passage through the wadi was not ready for walkers yet.

6. Nablus Vista: Sebastia to Maqam Sheikh Sha'leh

See page 82 for Trail 6 map.

If you do not want to spend most of your time around Sebastia by walking its beautiful hills and valleys, this walk from the al-Yahia Mosque to Maqam Sheikh Sha'leh is the ideal compromise. While you will get some good exercise and spectacular views you will have plenty of time left to explore Sebastia's ruins and its old city.

The trail will take you from the heart of Sebastia's old city to the Haroon spring in al-Naquura and via an old Roman road up to Jabal Sheikh Sha'leh. From the upper balconies of the Guesthouse you can get an excellent view of the aim of the walk, the *maqam* of Sheikh Sha'leh, which is located to the SE of Sebastia, resting slightly below the highest point of the hill. The trail is a circular walk.

[0m-300m/0-0.18 mi.] The start is from the central Baab al-Jaame (Mosque Gate) square in Sebastia's old town, and directly opposite the Sebastia Information Center. Walk past the Information Center on its R side. Almost immediately you pass the entry to the Sebastia Guesthouse on your L . You can walk in for a peak at the beautifully renovated Crusader's complex that now houses the guesthouse. From the higher balconies of the guesthouse you have an excellent view of Maqam Sheikh Sha'leh (to the SE). Continue past the guesthouse and walk down the small alleyway where further renovations of historic buildings have been taking place. You reach the Sebastia main road located 200m (0.12 mi.) from the start. Turn R here and walk

Trail: Sebastia > Maqam Sheikh Sha'leh > Sebastia

Grade: Moderate

Surface: Predominantly dirt road and some paved road; minor off-road

Marked: Yes (red and black)

Distance and Duration: 7.6 km/4.7 miles; 2–2.5 hrs

Elevation Change: 325m ascent/ 325m descent

Start Coordinates: N32 16.591 E35 11.754

down the main road towards the al-Karma square (**❶**). Five roads come together on this square.

[300m-1.8km/0.18-1.1 mi.)] Take the third road on your L (*Madraset al-Banaat* Street) which runs down into the direction of al-Naqura village. You pass the local girls school after which the street is named. Ignore any side roads and continue straight; the road eventually turns into a dirt road, running upwards alongside the water stream coming from the Haroon spring and passing orchards of lemon and pomegranate trees on both sides. After 1.8km (1.1 mi.) into the walk you reach a T-junction where you meet the Haroon spring (**❷**) which shares its water between Sebastia and al-Naqura villages.

[1.8-3.2km/1.1-1.9 mi.] Turn R at the Haroon spring and take a L at the next 3-way junction, just 60m (65 yards) further. From here, you start to ascend on

al-Khali road, which used to serve as the main road to and from Nablus in Roman times. You pass a few houses on the outskirts of al-Naqura and after some 500m (0.31 mi.) al-Khali road turns into a dirt road. At 2.7km (1.6 mi.) into the walk you reach a split in the road (❸): while red markers continue to the L, a black trail runs up the R leg towards a viewpoint over Nablus. The viewpoint (500m [0.31 mi.] further up the road, marked by a black circle) is certainly worthwhile the climb; from the very rural outskirts of al-Naqura it provides a fascinating glimpse into the densely urban center of Nablus and the high-rises on its two legendary mountains, Ebal and Gerizim.

[3.2-4.7km/1.9-2.9 mi.] While the dirt road you are on continues all the way to Nablus, turn-around at the viewpoint to walk back to the split and take a R to continue on the red trail. !! 200m (0.12 mi.) after

Al-Naqura village with Nablus city in the background

Spiny broom in early spring

rejoining the red markers, the trail sharply veers to the L (**4**) and leaves the dirt road for an off-road section. The trail follows an old stone wall bordering an orchard and climbs up the hill. Continue to walk up until you come across a footpath: turn L here and almost immediately you will see the ruins of Maqam Sheikh Sha'leh ahead of you. The footpath turns into a dirt road: keep following it until another split occurs with a black marked trail skirting up the hill towards the *maqam*. After scrambling over a few minor rocks, you will reach the *maqam* at 4.7km (2.9 mi.) into the walk. As you approach and walk around the ruins be careful not to step into one of the Roman caves that surround the site. You can climb on top of the ruins which provide an excellent spot for a picnic with pretty views over Sebastia and its surroundings.

[4.7-7.6km/2.9-4.7 mi.] To continue, walk back to the red marked trail below the *maqam* and continue to follow it as it descends towards Wadi Ijnisinia below. On the way down, you pass a 3-way junction (keep straight), afterwhich two more 3-way junction follow one another very closely (just 50m [54 yards] in between): keep going straight at the first one, but take a R at the second one. Take a L at the T-junction that follows. After crossing the wadi bed of Wadi Ijnisinia you reach the dirt road (**5**) connecting Ijnisinia village to Sebastia (6.4km [3.9 mi.] into the walk). Take a L here. The trail passes a range of ancient tombs on its R side. Just as you reach the first houses of Sebastia, a 50m (54 yards) short black trail splits to the R: it leads to two old Roman Tombs hidden beneath a modern house. They are worth seeing. The red trail continues straight onto Karma square. Follow the main road up to the R and turn L to walk back to Sebastia's Information Center.

7. Rounding the Romans: Sebastia around the City Walls

See page 86 for Trail 7 map.

This pretty but short walk trails Sebastia's old walls in a circle around the city. The trail runs mostly over dirt roads and single track paths in between orchards and past ancient ruins.

[0-500m/0-0.31 mi.] The start is from the central Baab al-Jaame (Mosque Gate) square in Sebastia's old town and just opposite the Information Center. Facing the impressive Yahia Mosque, walk L towards the lower side of the square. Turn R leaving the square and immediately turn L onto al-Barre street. The road descends and passes a few nice houses, one decorated with ornamental stones composing the image of a large palm tree. After 450m (0.27 mi.) the trail mixes for 60m (65 yards) with the blue trail towards *maqam* Bayzeed. Make sure you do not follow this trail but, as the paved road makes a L turn downhill, turn L onto a dirt road that leaves the paved road and runs into the fields (❶).

[500m-1.6km/0.31-0.99 mi.] On the dirt road, you quickly pass some of the remains of the ancient Roman Stadium (on your L). Some columns are still standing, scattered between a field of young olive trees. Some two millennia ago this arena (195m [213 yards] long and 58m [63 yards] wide) was used for foot-racing, boxing and wrestling. From here, continue to follow the trail as it runs in W direction through olive groves, also passing apricot trees and various shrubs. You keep to the right side of the terraces you are walking on. To your R below lies Wadi Shami and

Trail: Sebastia > Sebastia

Grade: Easy

Surface: Mostly single track and dirt road; some paved

Marked: Yes (orange)

Distance and Duration: 3.6 km/2.2 miles; 1–1.5 hrs

Elevation Change: 125m ascent / 125m descent

Start Coordinates: N32 16.591 E35 11.754

The twelve almond trees below Jabal Bayzeed

on the other side of the wadi you see the village of Burqa. After 1.2km (0.74 mi.) into the walk, you pass a Byzantine tomb: the dirt road descends before it starts to climb again and turns into a single track path that runs over the old Roman walls (the walls are still covered here). The trail turns into a single track path here. On your R side, far below in Wadi Shami, you can discern the old path of the Hijaz Railway where the green trail runs.

[1.6-2.5km/0.99-1.5 mi.] At 1.6km (0.99 mi.) into the walk, the trail runs from the top of the old city wall to a path just besides it on its R (❷). 100m (109 yards) further, you pass an exposed section of the foundations of the old wall with its huge stones clearly visible between the shrubs and trees. The trail continues for a few hundred m on an ancient stone path that has been recovered by Sebastia's municipality and restored

Maqam Mystery

A *maqam* is an ancient shrine for saints and holy men. In some *maqams* worshipping still takes place and in some parts of the West Bank it is not unusual that the same shrine is venerated by Muslims and Christians alike. The origins of the now abandoned Maqam Sheikh Sha'leh are however unknown. Sha'leh means both light and fire and one theory is that the spiritual leader residing in the *maqam* was granted the power to illuminate his surroundings because of his sanctity. Another theory assigns the original purpose of the *maqam* structure to be military. Muslim rulers in post-Crusader times would have used the ignition of fires across various hills as means of rapid communication in the case of enemies approaching the area.

A range of other *maqams* dot the other hills in the surroundings of Sheikh Sha'leh, one above al-Naqura village and the Bayzeed maqam on the region's highest hilltop to the north.

for walkers and farmers. The trail then turns sharply L and starts to climb in between the olive and apricot trees. On a 3-way junction just after a sharp uphill section you meet a colossal olive tree (perhaps itself hailing back to the Roman period). The trail takes a sharp R turn here up the hill. At 2.5km (1.5 mi.) into the walk you reach the impressive tall remains of the tower that used to contain Sebastia's western gate in Roman times.

Along the ancient columned street

[2.5-3.6km/1.5-2.2 mi.] At the tower ruins, you've reached Sebastia's columned street (❸). While some columns lay spread out besides the road, a few dozen still stand tall, lining up the ancient way into the village as an old guard honoring past glory days. Turn L here and continue to walk up the road, passing the Holy Land Sun restaurant and turning R on the Forum square to complete the circle and end at the Information Center at Baab al-Jaame.

Baby donkey in Wadi Shami

Logistics and Guides

The **Sebastia Information Center** is ready to assist with information, guides and reservations for the guesthouse: 09-2532545 and cultural_centre2006@ yahoo.com. You can also contact Suheib Huwari (0599-490856). Group fees for guided walks are very reasonable and independent of group size: around 250 NIS for the shorter walks (#6 and #7); and 375 NIS for the longer ones (#4 and #5).

How to Get There

Car: From Jerusalem/Ramallah, it is a 60/45 minute drive to Sebastia. Drive N on Rd 60 in the direction of Nablus. After having passed through the village of Huwara, do not continue towards Huwara CP and Nablus city but turn L in W direction where the continuation of Rd 60 is indicated. After 11 km (6.8 mi.) you come to a junction where Rd 60 meets Rd 55; turn L here and immediately R (signs to Shave Shomron). Continue on Rd 60 for 6 further km (3.7 mi.) and make sure to turn R as Rd 60 turns off the main road. !! Almost immediately after the turn-off you reach a large sign indicating solely Rd 60 and Shave Shomron to the L: ignore this sign (this road leads to the settlement itself) and continue straight towards Beit Iba village. Take the first junction to the L following signs to Jenin. After passing the CP (also called Shave Shomron), you take the second turn-off on your R (clearly signposted to Sebastia). Once you enter the village keep L, following the road upwards until you arrive at the central town square of the village.

Should the Shave Shomron CP be closed, alternative routes are through Nablus and via the villages of al-Sira Ashamaliya and Ijnisinya (15 minutes extra). Public transportation: via Nablus.

Panorama from Sebastia's guesthouse

Where to Park

You can park at the central square in Sebastia (Baab al-Jaame) where the starting point of two trails is located, as well as the Sebastia Information Center and the Yahia Mosque. The other trails start from the Forum Square, easy to reach by foot a few hundred meters to the W—you can also park there.

Eat, Drink, Relax

Two restaurants have long served Sebastia's guests: **Samaria Restaurant** (0599071552) and the **Holy Land Sun Restaurant** (0599212252); they are located on and just below the Forum Square; both have souvenir shops as well. At the time of writing, a small coffee shop was planned opposite the guesthouse and crusader complex and a third restaurant had opened just above the Forum Square.

Enjoying the view from
Jabal Bayzeed

Overnight

The Sebastia Guesthouse is a charming and comfortable place to stay. It has four rooms (2 doubles, 1 triple, 1 quartet); pppn 120 NIS incl. breakfast; contact the guesthouse through the Sebastia Information Center above or through the Jericho Mosaic Center at 02-2326342. For larger groups homestay accommodation with Palestinian families elsewhere in the village can be arranged.

Places to Go, People to Meet

Enough to see in and around Sebastia. **Sebastia's Archeological Site** is its prime attraction, but its small old city is definitely worth a visit, in particular the **Yahia Mosque** which contains the tomb of St. John the Baptist, the **Crusader Complex** and the **Ottoman al-Qayed Palace**. The Sebastia Information Center (opened Sat-Thu) contains a mosaic workshop and sells local crafts as well. The **Sebastia Festival** takes place in July or August every year. The city of Nablus is nearby and very much worth a visit (see the al-Bidaan chapter).

On the Web

The Jericho Mosaic Center runs many activities in Sebastia: www.mosaiccentre-jericho.com

البيذان   Al-Bidaan: Cool Springs

In a small corner below the tall hills of Nablus the cool waters of al-Bidaan are hidden to most foreign visitors. Palestinians have known better for decades; yet the pretty hills and valleys above the springs remain largely unexplored.

Three different landscapes converge on the small village of al-Bidaan. The tall steep hills of Nablus and Jabal al-Kabir tower above the village to its south and west; to its north much smoother hills roll towards the agriculture flatlands surrounding al-Far'a and its ancient ruins; and to the east Wadi al-Bidaan and Wadi al-Far'a merge towards the fertile plains of the Jordan Valley. Any walk from al-Bidaan is best concluded in one of the resorts straddling the springs of the village. Take off your hiking boots and reward your feet in the cool waters while sipping a fresh lemon juice, enjoying a mixed grill and perhaps smoking an *argilleh*.

No water shortage in al-Bidaan's *muntazahat*

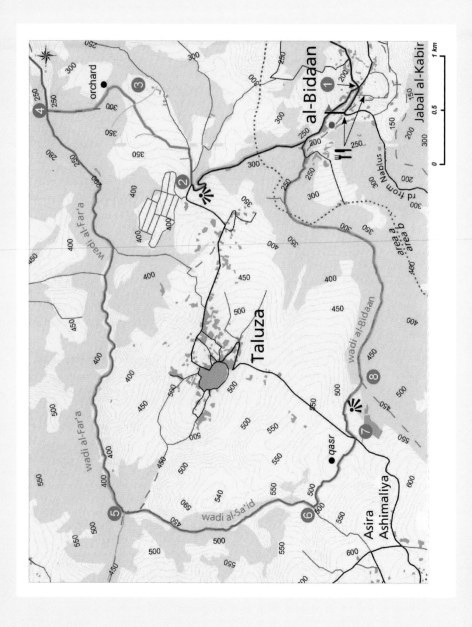

8. The Long Haul: al-Bidaan around Taluza

This long circular walk will take you up to the hills near Taluza, down into the lovely Wadi al-Far'a that circles Taluza and back down to al-Bidaan through Taluza's olive groves and the wild Wadi al-Bidaan. As this is a long walk, make sure that you bring food for a picnic alongside plenty of water (there are no refreshment options on the trail).

[0m-2.5km/0-1.5 mi.] The hike starts in front of the two restaurants (Shalalaat and Batra) located at the hairpin turn on the main road coming from Nablus. Start walking upwards on the main road in the direction of Tubas. After some 300m (0.18 mi.) you reach a 4-way junction (❶): take a sharp U-turn to your L and walk up the paved road between al-Bidaan and Taluza for about 2 km (1.2 mi.). This is quite a stretch of climbing (some 200m [0.12 mi.] over 2km [1.2 mi.]) but the incline is steady and the road has been refurbished and widened, which eases the effort. Having risen above the springs of al-Bidaan, the road is flanked by a small pine tree forest on both sides and then by almond trees. Wild boars are reported to stray in these pine forests (walking in or near the forest after dark is therefore not recommended). Just before the road reaches Taluza it goes through an S-shaped curve.

[2.5-2.8km/1.5-1.7 mi.] At the top of the S-shaped curve at an elevation of 370m (0.22 mi.) there are excellent views on Jabal al-Kabir (the big mountain) to the R (SE) standing tall between Nablus and the Jordan Valley. Further away you can see the Rift mountains on the Jordanian side of the valley. !! Coming out of the

Trail: al-Bidaan around Taluza

Grade: Hard

Surface: Paved roads, dirt roads and single track paths; some off-road walking in wadi bed towards the end of the trail.

Marked: No

Distance and Duration: 16.9 km/10.5 miles; 5–7 hrs

Elevation Change: 600 m ascent/ 600m descent

Start Coordinates: N32 15.604 E35 19.186

curve do not continue towards Taluza village but turn R for a smaller paved road going E (❷). After 100m (109 yards), keep L at a subsequent fork in this road as the paved road becomes a dirt road. After 230m (0.14 mi.) on the dirt road, take the second L onto a smaller dirt road (the first L turn is immediately after a standalone house and runs into a dead end). From here, Tubas can be easily spotted between the hills to the NE, as well as the plains of al-Far'a packed with greenhouses to the N and the village of Aqaba further away (N).

[2.8-4.6km/1.7-2.8 mi.] !! Continue down the smaller dirt road until it forks; go R at the fork and continue downhill for another 300m (0.18 mi.). You will reach a 4-way junction (❸). Continue straight at this point.

A Splash in the *Muntazah*

After a long walk there is nothing more gratifying than cooling your feet in one of the many fresh cold water pools of al-Bidaan. The abundant springs of the village run through no less than 8 so-called *muntazah*, which means resort in Arabic. If your mind associates the term resort with a 5-star pampering of tourists inside a walled enclave, adapt your expectations for al-Bidaan's *muntazahat*. The resorts here cater "exclusively" to local tourism. The oldest *muntazah*, established in 1936 and located in the hairpin turn on the main road, is appropriately named Shalalaat, or water-falls, and includes three swimming pools. In some of the larger *muntazahat* located downstream towards the village of al-Agrabaniya the flow of water culminates in entire water parks including ponds for miniature boats before streaming further downstream to irrigate farm land in the valley. The term overcrowding can get a whole new meaning when busloads of Palestinian schoolchildren fill up any *muntazah*; going next door is then advisable. Note that some places cater only for bring-your-own-barbeque, in which case an entry fee (usually 10 NIS) is charged. When in doubt, ask when entering.

The dirt road starts to climb up gradually and 300m (0.18 mi.) after the junction it meets an orchard which is closed off by a fence. !! Turn L here to continue off-road for some 250m (0.15 mi.): walk down the hill slope keeping a course parallel to the orchard's fence. Continue until you meet the bottom of a wadi bed covered by wild flowers and (in late spring) by hundreds of thorny plumed thistles, a reminder on why wearing shorts is never a smart idea in the West Bank. Once in the wadi bed turn R to follow a small single track that descends further down into Wadi al-Far'a in between the hill you came from and another hill. The single trail descends fairly steeply.

Taluza's panorama on the valley below al-Bidaan

[4.6-8.9km/2.8-5.5 mi.] Once you reach the bottom of the wadi bed (❹), turn L to continue the trail in W direction by following the dirt road running through the bed of Wadi al-Far'a. You will encounter giant rock formations on the N slopes of the wadi within 500m (0.31 mi.). Follow this wadi bed for a total stretch of

Flowering Acacia tree

4.3km (2.6 mi.); you will come across dirt and gravel roads (wide and small) and, towards the very end of this stretch, a short section of single track trail. Ignore any side roads (big or small) that skirt up either to the L (towards Taluza village) or to the R side Wadi al-Far'a. After the full 4.3km (2.6 mi.) you meet a 3-way junction in the wadi bed (❺); this is where you turn L into another wadi which is filled with olive trees (Their shade provides an excellent picnic spot as you are just over the halfway point of the trail). The 3-way junction is easy to recognize as it is the first point in Wadi al-Far'a where you can turn L without any immediate steep incline.

[8.9-12.0km/5.5-7.4 mi.] After 400m (0.24 mi.) of single track, the wadi splits into two. Continue to follow its R leg where a dirt road runs S for the next 2 km (1.2 mi.) moving through and past olive groves. At 11.2 km (6.9 mi.) into the hike, and just 100m (109 yards) after the dirt road has started to incline significantly, a second dirt road veers off to the L and into an olive grove bordered by a stone wall (❻). Take this road as it meanders through the olive grove, starts climbing the hill and passes a beautiful two story *qasr* at the highest point in the walk (529m/1,735 ft.). The *qasr* is clearly visible from the turnoff into the olive grove. (Should you accidently miss the turn into the olive grove you will reach a 4-way (paved) junction leading to the village of Asira Ashimaliya at which point you have passed the turnoff by 800m [0.5 mi.]). Just after passing the peak of the hill the panorama of hills between the Jordan Valley and Nablus opens up again. You come across a paved road that runs from Taluza to Asira Ashimaliya.

[12.0-16.9km/7.4-10.5 mi.] At the paved road (❼) turn L and immediately (after 30m/32 yards) turn R where the dirt road continues along a beautiful path following the stone orchard walls as it descends into Wadi

al-Bidaan. While the trail runs downhill and turns
from a dirt road into a single track trail, a spectacular
view opens up on the agricultural plains of the al-
Bidaan valley and the village of al-Aqrabaniya towards
the Jordan Valley. Continue to follow the small single
track trail downwards until you reach the wadi bed of
Wadi al-Bidaan (**8**). Turn L here and follow the wadi
bed in E direction. The last 2.5 km (1.5 mi.) back to
al-Bidaan village are not the easiest of the hike; while
the wadi descends only very gradually towards the
village, the wadi bed is covered with smaller and larger
rocks which reduce the pace and occasionally require
some scrambling. After 1km (0.62 mi.) in the wadi,
the path disappears from view altogether. However,
the direction is straightforward: continue to follow the
wadi. As this section comes at the end of a long hike,
walk it at a pace you feel comfortable with. At 15km
(9.3 mi.) into the trail you reach the pine forest and
the first houses located on al-Bidaan's picturesque outskirts; continue on the dirt road that runs from here.
Once you reach the paved road at the upper section of
the village, turn L; after 200m (0.12 mi.) turn R and
continue your descent towards the starting point at the
al-Bidaan restaurants and resorts.

Reward your feet in
al-Bidaan's cool springs

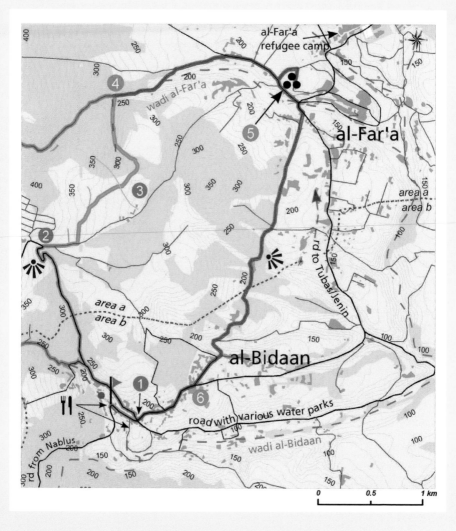

This shorter and less challenging trail starts similar to the one above, but from Wadi al-Far'a veers NW towards al-Far'a village, passing by the ruins of Tirza and returning to al-Bidaan over a gentle hill with good views over Wadi al-Bidaan and Wadi al-Far'a.

9. Tirza's Way: Al-Bidaan to al-Far'a

[0-4.6km/0-2.8 mi.] Follow the first part of the al-Bidaan around Taluza trail as described earlier in this chapter (❶-❸).

[4.6-6.8km/2.8-4.2 mi.] Once you reach the bottom of the wadi bed (❹), go R onto a dirt road following Wadi al-Far'a in the direction of al-Far'a village. Continue to follow this road when after 300m (0.18 mi.) it climbs out of the wadi and joins a wider dirt road towards the village. When reaching the paved road at the edge of the village, turn R and walk between the quiet houses and fields of lemon trees. Just after this road starts descending towards the al-Far'a main road you will notice a slight elevation to your L; this is the archeological site of Tel al-Far'a, also called Tirza. !! To reach it, take the dirt road to the L and after 250m (0.15 mi.) turn R onto another dirt road; after another 100m (109 yards) and just before reaching a house turn R onto the site (❺). In winter/spring, thick fields of grass and flowers will obscure large fractions of the site whose excavations have been partially or fully overgrown over the last decades. If you visit in February or March you understand why locals have set bee hives close to the site as it covered by thick coverage of yellow and white daisies. The site is perfect for a break in the hike, a picnic in between the ruins, or spotting the variety of birds around. It also gives excellent views over al-Far'a village, the refugee camp, and the extended agricultural activity in the area.

[6.8-11.8km/4.2-7.3 mi.] To continue the hike, walk back to where you left the paved road and turn L

Trail: al-Bidaan to al-Far'a

Grade: Moderate

Surface:
Paved road and dirt roads

Marked: No

Distance and Duration:
11.8 km/7.3 miles; 3–4 hrs

Elevation Change:
350m ascent/ 350m descent

Start Coordinates:
N32 15.604 E35 19.186

Olive harvest in al-Far'a

towards the al-Far'a main road. !! Turn R onto the main road and after 120m (131 yards) turn R again onto a small side road. Follow this small road (which eventually becomes unpaved) as it crawls up and down in S direction through the hills between al-Far'a and al-Bidaan for the next 3 km (1.8 yards). To your L (E) you will have pretty vistas over a landscape shaped by the two main wadis of the area (Wadi al-Far'a and Wadi al-Bidaan) as they run towards the Jordan Valley. Once you reach the al-Bidaan main road (**⑥**) turn R and follow this road for another 1 km (0.62 mi.) to get back to the starting point.

Logistics and Guides

Suheib Huwari (0599-490856) can be contacted for guided tours; for updates on other local guiding options, check www.walkingpalestine.org.

How to Get There

Car: From Jerusalem/Ramallah, it is a 1hr15/1hr drive to al-Bidaan. Drive N on road 60 towards Nablus. Pass the Huwara CP into Nablus and take a R at the first Y junction immediately following the CP. Continue to follow this road which circles the center of Nablus to its E and joins the main road from Nablus just to its N. Continue to follow the road as it leaves Nablus and starts its large descent towards al-Bidaan. Before entering the actual village the road will pass through a hairpin turn crossing over the wadi. This is the starting point of the walks. The location is easily recognized as it is straddled with small shops and the two best known resorts and restaurants (Shalalaat and Batra).

Public transportation: via Nablus; continue by ford in the direction of Tubas.

Where to Park

You can park on the side of the road just before or just after the hairpin turn.

Eat, Drink, Relax

Al-Bidaan's *muntazahat* are located along the springs of Wadi al-Bidaan. **Shalalaat** (0599-316555) and **Batra al-Bidaan** (0597-032132) are centrally located on the main road between Nablus and Tubas an include small craft shops at the front. Smaller places located close-by are **al-Tawaheen** (0598-036955) and **al-Rafadeen** (0598180345). The larger resorts which include water and fun fair parks are **Falasteen** (0599-888185), **Wahet al-Bidaan** (0599-585565), **al-Jazeera** (0599-646562) and the **al-Bidaan Tourism Castle** (0599-557170).

Wild flowers near Wadi al-Bidaan

Wadi al-Far'a

Each of them is located along the road from al-Bidaan towards al-Agrabaniya, running parralel to the wadi.

Overnight

There were no overnight options in al-Bidaan at the time of writing. Nearby accomodation can be found in Nablus.

Places to Go, People to Meet

Exploring **Nablus' old city** is a great way to get familiar with the largest Palestinian city in the north of the West Bank; in particular its large **traditional souk** where locals still shop for bargains in its small charming alleyways and tourists are a rare sight. Inside the old city you can also visit the **Ottoman hamam** (bath house), an olive soap factory and a range of historical buildings which incude dozens of large and small mosques, the restored **Khan al-Wikala** (traditional lodging and trading point for passing caravans) and, surprisingly, Nablus' own clock tower built by the Ottoman sultan in 1906. **Jacob's Well** is Nablus' most famous church. It has been beautifully restored by the serving Greek Orthodox priest, Justinus, who painted the spectacular frescoes by his own hands. The nearby archeological ruins of **Tel al-Balata** show the remains of biblical Shechem. Towering high above the city, Mt Gerazim is the home of Palestine's Samaritan community. Whatever you do, you can't leave Nablus without eating its celebrated **kanafa**, the city's most famous sweet and the craving of all Palestine.

On the Web

www.wahet-albadan.com
www.nablusguide.com
www.pushproject.org

A PUSH for Shared Heritage

In al-Far'a, history is covered by a million flowers. On a small mound behind the village you find the ruins of ancient Tirza whose earliest habitation according to archeologists dates back to 7000 BC and which is mentioned in the Bible as the second capital of Israel's Northern Kingdom (931 BC). All the ingredients, one would think, for an excavated and signposted site. But when you walk up the mound in early spring you stand in a sea of bright yellow crown daisies waving in the wind. If you look carefully, you can still make out the antique walls of Tirza as they rise and fall beneath the thick bed of flowers.

Tirza's historical successor as the capital was Sebastia (then called Samaria), a mere 15km to the west and a fabulous base for walks through the imprints of a history of invasions, empire building and religious mythology. King Omri moved here from Tirza to rule over Israel's Northern Kingdom; Assyrian and Persian invasions followed; then Alexander the Great took charge; later the Romans destroyed and then rebuilt the city before handing it over to the Jewish King Herod the Great. According to Greek Orthodox tradition Herod's son Antipas then gave another spin to the wheel of history when he drunkenly agreed to behead John the Baptist in Sebastia. The effect was another millennium of pilgrims visiting the city. The Crusaders built one of their largest cathedrals in Sebastia, which Saladin's forces then turned into a mosque, but also devoted to St. John.

The Holy Land is filled with countless Sebastias where human heritage is both very dense and very mixed and where the strong currents of history have made any single categorization as Arab, Jewish, Palestinian, Christian, Muslim or any other label futile. Yet the Palestinian-Israeli conflict provides fertile ground to promote a single narrative. And to make matters just a bit more complicated, the carving up of the West Bank into Areas A, B and C (see the Ramallah chapter for more background) has turned the management and protection of these historical sites into a complex affair wrought with practical, financial and political difficulties. The Oslo Agreements stipulated that all sites of historic value should be protected regardless of their origin and location. Sites were supposed to remain accessible to both sides, committees of specialists would coordinate conservation and Oslo further set out the gradual transfer of responsibility for most sites in area C to the PA.

More than 15 years later, the record on the status of West Bank sites is mixed. In some locations in A and B conservation measures have been taken but elsewhere sites such as Tirza remain abandoned and neglected due to lack of interest or funds. In area C, the situation is worse and overall political deadlock has had detrimental effects on conservation efforts. Authority over C sites has not been transferred for over a decade and sites are now either exclusively controlled, managed and excavated by Israel, or they have fallen into some kind of vacuum of authority. Sebastia's archeological site is essentially neglected. The PA is not allowed to carry out excavations or enforce protection measures and apart from sporadic visits with the army, Israeli authorities are not present either. The result of this logjam is that sites of Potential Outstanding Universal Value (according to UNESCO) remain at risk of looting, vandalism or even unchecked construction works.

Beneath the squabble over the details of Oslo, a more profound issue is that of the controversial role of archeology itself in the conflict. Palestinian archeology has been largely devoid of resources, and leans mostly on work done prior to 1967. Israeli archeology is globally respected for its high professional standards but a major critique, including inside Israel, has been the growing politicization of archeology to advance claims to more territory. Since Oslo, mutual trust was not exactly enhanced by Israel's removal of valuable artifacts, such as statues, from places like Sebastia (to Jerusalem's Rockefeller Museum) and vice-versa by the desecration of Jewish sites in Palestinian controlled areas.

Not everybody in the field of cultural and archeological conservation has given up hope however. A remarkable project bringing together academics, professionals and community members on heritage has been the Promoting the Understanding of Shared Heritage (PUSH) initiative. The project was undertaken by independent scholars outside the perilous hands of governments and politicians. Leaving the political questions of geographical ownership at the door, the project created a platform where an inclusive view of history and heritage could be discussed. One of the achievements was a first of its kind list of sites in Israel, Palestine and Jordan which describes the region's unique shared heritage (www.pushproject.org). Experts also managed to agree on a common text describing the great ancient cities of Sebastia, Pella and Beit She'an. Unfortunately, the signs depicting the text in Sebastia were removed by the Israeli military under the pretext that they were put in area C "without due permission." Another PUSH is required to defy the narrow-mindedness on heritage.

عبود Aboud: City of Flowers

Small Aboud has a great many charms. From the village's famous lemon trees, walkers explore pretty trails with ancient tombs and classical mosaics, caves, springs, intriguing murals, and one of Palestine's richest sceneries for spring flowers.

Aboud means worshipping in Arabic, a name perhaps derived from the presence of so many mosques, churches and church ruins in one place. At the end of the 19th century it was described by the Palestine Exploration Fund as large and flourishing with 200 Muslims and 400 Christians whose houses were nearly all marked with a cross in red paint. According to historians, an important Roman road passed Aboud and the village used to be called City of Flowers. This remains a very fitting name today as Aboud's springs continue to provide Wadi Limoon with a great variety of plants, trees and birds. The natural spectacle of colors is at its pinacle in spring but walkers will enjoy the walks from Aboud any time of the year.

Wadi Limoon is named after the many lemon trees that straddle the valley below the village. It is the starting point for three relatively short walks of a few hours each. Eager walkers can always opt to combine two walks to see more. The third walk combines the natural surroundings of Aboud with its many historical and spiritual sites. Many of these can also be explored seperately and a visit to Aboud's small old town is much recommended following any of these walks.

Wadi Limoon in spring

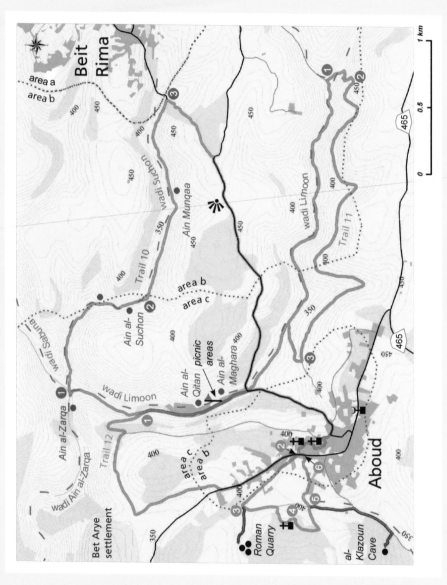

See pages 122 and 124 for Trail 11, 12 directions.

10. Sweet Lemons: Wadi Limoon to Wadi Suchon

This circular walk consists of a single track trail, following century old paths near and through the wadis between Aboud and Beit Rima, as well as some wider dirt roads. Flora adepts will love the rich diversity of flowers in spring time, in particular the variety of wild orchids across the trail. The last 2 km (1.2 mi.) are on a quiet and scenic paved road. The trail starts towards the N side of the wadi on a dirt road towards the Ain al-Zarqa spring, and then continues around and over the hills to arrive at the paved road between Aboud and Beit Rima.

Trail:
Wadi Limoon to Wadi Sukhon

Grade: Moderate

Surface: Dirt road, single track and paved road

Marked: Planned (blue)

Distance and Duration:
7.0km/4.3 miles; 2–2.5 hrs

Elevation Change: 260m ascent / 260m descent

Start Coordinates:
N32 01.398 E35 04.318

[0-1.4km/0-0.86 mi.] From the Wadi Limoon picnic area walk N (away from the paved road) over the dirt road that runs above the wadi bed. The road climbs above the wadi bed for a few hundred m before sloping downwards again. Make sure you ignore the split to the L (a dirt road which climbs back to Aboud) and continue to walk parallel to the wadi.

[1.4-2.6km/0.86-1.6 mi.] After 1.4km (0.86 mi.), the road descends towards a junction (❶) where four different wadis meet: if you follow the dirt road 50m (54 yards) to the L (W) of this point you find the largest spring in Aboud, Ain al-Zarqa, with water gushing out year round and wild mint growing beneath it. !! At the junction, various paths run in different directions: as mentioned, the dirt road to the L runs towards Ain al-Zarqa. The path to the R quickly splits in two: one clearly visible single track path turns L after 60m (65 yards) and starts climbing up another wadi to the NE; the trail, however, continues on a less visible path which crosses the wadi bed and

Pretty Maresia

continues straight onto a pretty single track which runs parallel to the R side of the wadi. Hence, you turn R at the main junction and then R again after 60m (65 yards) (crossing the wadi bed). The trail gradually climbs E. This is Wadi Sukhon (hot wadi). Continue to follow the trail which passes a great variety of flowers and shrubs as well as the occasional oak tree. The trail meanders up the wadi, gradually turns R (S) and then enters a gorge filled with various springs, some coming at the surface in the wadi bed, and others in the rocks on its R side. Depending on the time of year and the level of rainfall, you might get wet feet here.

[2.6-4.3km/1.6-2.6 mi.] At 2.6km (1.6 mi.), where the wadi bed takes a turn to the L, the trail leaves the wadi bed (❷) and starts to zigzag up the R bank of the wadi. Above the wadi, the trail turns into a wider dirt road gradually climbing up in the direction of Beit Rima (E). After you spot the first of houses of Beit Rima in the distance, you pass Ain Munqaa, a small spring forming a pool und the the rocks a few meters to your R.

[4.3-4.9km/2.6-3 mi.] Some 300m (0.18 mi.) before you would reach the first houses of Beit Rima, and just before a sharp L bend in the road towards this village, you reach an olive grove separated from the road by thick stone walls (❸). To the R of this olive grove, a small single trail runs up the hill over the natural rock surface. Follow this trail as it zigzags up the hill always keeping the olive grove to your L. The trail turns into a dirt road near the top of the hill and then meets the (paved) road between Beit Rima and Aboud.

[4.9-7.0km/3-4.3 mi.] Turn R on this road which gives excellent views to the S and W, including—on clear days—the Mediterranean coast and the Israeli city of Tel Aviv. Follow the main road as it runs over the ridge

Field of red anemones

of the hill and then descends towards Wadi Limoon. Turn R at the point where the road meets the wadi bed to reach the starting point of the hike. (Walkers keen to avoid the paved road and connect directly to the E section of Wadi Limoon, can turn L on the paved road, walk a few hundred m in E direction and take a R onto a dirt road that meanders down into the wadi, connecting midway with trail #11).

11. Olives and Hollyhocks: Wadi Limoon Eastwards

See page 118 for Trail 11 map.

This walk is a lovely circular hike through the E part of Wadi Limoon. Because of its length, overall easy paths and fairly mild incline/decline, it is very suitable as a family hike. The walk covers the E side of the wadi, first through the wadi bed, then climbing up its S hillside, and subsequently winding back to Aboud above the wadi. In spring, the terraces directly adjacent to the wadi bed are covered by a radiant yellow carpet of mustard flowers. Higher on the hill, you find a great quantity of hollyhocks and white rockrose.

Trail: Wadi Limoon to the east

Grade: Moderate

Surface: Mostly single track, some off-road and some dirt road

Marked: Planned (green)

Distance and Duration: 7.6km/4.7 miles; 2–2.5 hrs

Elevation Change: 230m ascent / 230m descent

Start Coordinates: N32 01.398 E35 04.318

[0-500m/0-0.31 mi.] From the Wadi Limoon picnic area, walk back to the intersection with the Aboud-Beit Rima paved road. Cross the road onto a dirt road that follows the wadi bed. You very quickly find yourself in the middle of nature with a large variety of birds and in spring a great variety of flowers.

[500m-2.8km/0.31-1.7 mi.] Continue on the dirt road that follows the wadi bed and eventually becomes a single trail that runs in the wadi bed itself. After 2 km (1.2 mi.), the wadi bed becomes too overgrown for easy passage. Continue on the terraces to the R side of the wadi bed but always keeping fairly close to the wadi bed (do not climb the terraces); after some 400m (0.24 mi.), a single trail continues on this side. Eventually the trail runs back in the wadi bed where it is easily traversed; the path turns into a dirt road once again.

[2.8-3.4km/1.7-2.1 mi.] At 2.8 km (1.7 mi.), both the wadi and the dirt road split in two at a clearly visible junction (❶): turn R here. !! 50m (54 yards) from this junction, a small single trail skirts away from the dirt road to the R and crosses the wadi bed to climb the hill on its S side. Follow this trail as it zigzags through natural as well as man-made rock terraces up the hill. You pass a water cistern as you move up this centuries old path and gain impressive views over the wadi below. While you follow the narrow path up to 60m (65 yards) above the wadi bed, look out for a wide dirt road starting to the R of the path (❷). Should you miss the dirt road and continue to climb upwards, the single trail will quickly disappear on the terraces. If this happens, retrace your steps down the hill and look for the dirt road.

[3.4-7.6km/2.1-4.7 mi.] From here, you follow the wide dirt road as it winds above the wadi back to Aboud village. At 6.5km (4 mi.) into the hike, and some 200m (0.12 mi) before reaching the first houses of Aboud, turn R onto a smaller dirt road (❸) that runs back into the wadi; turn L once you reach the wadi bed. You reach the starting point of the walk after 800m (0.5 mi.).

Neatly kept terraces in Aboud

12. Village Treasures: Around Aboud

See page 118 for Trail 11 map.

In comparison with the first two Aboud hikes this trail is more about the village and its direct natural surroundings. The trail provides great views over the Wadi Limoon area and then continues to explore various sites located near Aboud. If you're keen to explore the al-Kalzoun Cave, make sure you bring along a torch.

Trail: Around Aboud

Grade: Moderate

Surface:
Dirt road and paved road

Marked: Yes (red and black)

Distance and Duration:
8.9km/5.5 miles; 2.5–3 hrs

Elevation Change: 245m
ascent / 245m descent

Start Coordinates:
N32 01.398 E35 04.318

[0-2.5km/0-1.5 mi.] From the Wadi Limoon picnic area walk N over the dirt road that runs above the wadi bed. You pass the second picnic area and the road gradually climbs above the wadi bed. After 670m (0.42 mi.) a split in the road occurs (❶); take the L leg which starts climbing the hill. The road winds upward for the next 2km (1.2 mi.) and offers great views over the Wadi Limoon area. Continue to follow the road upwards and ignore any side roads coming from the L. You see the Beit Arye settlement to the W. The dirt road enters Aboud village at its N end and next to the large dirt mound which cuts Aboud's shortest connection to the neighboring villages of Rantis and al-Luban.

[2.5-4km/1.5-2.4 mi.] Turn L as you encounter Aboud's main village road (paved) and walk in the direction of the village center (S). !! After 660m (0.41 mi.) and just before a second covered cement bus stop on the R side of the road, turn R onto a smaller road that descends mildly towards Aboud's olive groves (❷) (this turn-off is just before a road on the L climbs up to Aboud's Catholic Church). The start of the road is lined with

sabr trees (cactus) and the village's one and only internet café is located just 100m (109 yards) down this road. Continue until you meet a 4-way junction (❸). To see the old Roman quarry (*al-Maqata*) continue straight following a black marked side trail for 250m (0.15 mi.) after which the site is located on your L. Sections of the ancient quarry contain tombs, ornamental decorations on the outer walls and some remaining painted decorations inside the burial chambers. Unfortunately graffiti has degraded certain parts of the site, which lies unprotected in the area C, a virtual no man's land between the Beit Arye settlement and Aboud village.

Wild cyclamen growing from a wall

[4-4.8km/2.4-2.9 mi.] To continue on the trail, walk back to the 4-way crossing you came from and take a R turn here, following the red markers again. !! 280m (0.17 mi.) after the 4-way junction a small single track path veers off on the R climbing the hill in between the rocks (this small track is a continuation of a path coming from the L but both paths are difficult to spot; if you miss it, the dirt road starts descending after 50m [54 yards]). Leave the dirt road here to follow the small single track upwards for some 200m (0.12 mi.) until you reach the tiny cave and ruins of St. Barbara Church (❹) at the highest point in the vicinity. A small church has been built around the ancient cave and just beneath the ruins of what used to be a larger church and monastery complex.

Caves of Palestine

Across Palestine, caves reflect ancient ways of life, and sometimes ancient ways of worship. Caves were used throughout history as living quarters, providing protection and shelter for their inhabitants, and a place for food storage and animal keeping. They were also used for mining and as burial grounds. In the desert, they served as the natural retreat where hermits found the seclusion necessary to get closer to god. But elsewhere too, caves were used for spiritual purposes, not least to geographically pinpoint some seminal events in Christianity, Islam and Judaism: the caves underneath the Nativity Church in Bethlehem, the Holy Sepulchre and the Dome of the Rock in Jerusalem, and the Cave of the Patriarchs in Hebron are among the best known examples.

Aboud's St. Barbera Church is located inside such a spiritual cave. Archeologists have dated monastic ruins around the cave church between the 4th and the 6th century. In the rock face near the church, an ancient wine press and a tomb were also found. According to tradition St. Barbara was a young girl persecuted for being baptized as a Christian. The cave is the location where she was imprisoned before eventually being killed. Every year on December 17 the residents of Aboud march to the site for ritual prayers and the celebration of the St. Barbara Festival. However, in the midst of the second Intifada in 2002, the small church cave was blown up by the Israeli military. The event caused outrage with Muslims and Christians residents of Aboud who both worship at the site. The Israeli Military issued an apology a day after the event stating that it had not known the religious significance of the site which it considered a hiding place for militants. The cave church has been restored in the meantime and works are carried out to also renovate the old pathways in and around the ruins of the old Monastery.

To the south of the village, Aboud's al-Klazoun Cave is large enough to stand up erect in and explore. While some daylight penetrates through the entrance and a small chimney in the ceiling, you still need a torch to properly see the base of stalactites. Unfortunately, the al-Klazoun Cave is one of many examples of a natural site in area C devoid of any protection. As in some other places around the West Bank, it has been a draw for vandals and thieves: most of the stalactites have been sawn off a few cm below the cave ceiling. When you enter the cave, be aware that bats live there. If you don't see any you will definitely notice their droppings. Do not descend too deep if you're not an experienced cave explorer.

[4.8-6km/2.9-3.7 mi.] To continue on the trail, walk to the L of the church, cross the monastery ruins and exit through a wide opening in the wall, crossing over a number of large rocks and connecting to a dirt road that runs down the hill. After 200m (0.12 mi.) you cross another dirt road. Turn L here. After 180m (196 yards) you encounter another 4-way junction (❺). To see the al-Kalzoun Cave, turn R here (follow the black markers) and, after 350m (0.21 mi.), reconnect with a paved road from Aboud. From here the cave is located at another 350m (0.21 mi.) down the paved road. To find the entry of the cave look out for a dirt road coming from the L: at this point start scrambling straight up the hill to your R. Note that the al-Kalzoun Cave is not directly visible from the road below and is located at an elevation 25m (82 ft.) above it (this is still quite a climb).

Al-Khader (St. George) slaying the dragon in Aboud

[6-8.9km/3.7-5.5 mi.)] To continue the trail walk back to the 4-way junction that came after passing the St. Barbara Church. Take a R here and walk back to Aboud village passing fields of *sabr* (cacti) strewn across large rocks. Immediately after passing the Aboud Family Park (to your R) leave the paved road for a single track on the L. The tracks runs behind some houses to reconnect with Aboud's main road (❻). Turn

Aboud amidst its olives

L at the main road and after 50m (54 yards) turn R to walk into Aboud's old village. You first pass the Latin Church and then the Greek Orthodox Church. The latter was built on a 4th century Byzantine church and the original mosaics can still be seen. Both churches are worth a visit. Continue on the small road which is decorated on either side by a large variety of mural paintings made by Bethlehem artist Taqi al-Diin: from portraits of the Savior to St. George slaying the dragon and scenes of Palestinian farmers harvesting their land. Take a L at the first 3-way junction and a R at the second one. From here continue to follow the paved road downwards and back into Wadi Limoon to the starting point of the walk.

Logistics and Guides

At the time of writing, the Palestinian Wildlife Society (PWLS) and the Aboud boyscouts were planning to train local guides from the village on the trails in this book. For inquieries contact Michel Mansour Massad at 0599-990054 or the PWLS at 02-2774373. The latter can also arrange special bird watching walks in the area. For visits to Aboud's churches, you can contact Michel Massad or the office of Father Samer Haddad (Latin Church) a few days ahead: 02-2864526 or fsamerhaddad@yahoo.com.

How to Get There

Car: From Jerusalem/Ramallah, it is a 50/30 minute
drive to Aboud. From Jerusalem, drive N/S on Rd 60
and leave it for Rd 465 towards Birzeit. From Ramallah, the closest entry to 465 is via Birzeit. Once on 465,
drive W passing the settlements of Ataret and Khalamish, and the village of Nabi Saleh. 5 km (3.1 mi.) after
passing Khalamish, the road to Aboud veers off to the
R. Once you enter the village, continue on the main
road until you pass a tall red-white telecommunica-
tions antennae; after this, take the first paved road to
your R, and an immediate turn to the L; continue a few
hundred meters and turn R onto the paved road that
descends into Wadi Limoon. At the bottom of the road
in the wadi bed, turn L onto a dirt road until you meet
the Wadi Limoon picnic area where you can park.

Public transportation: From Ramallah take a ford
to Birzeit and get out at the small bus station just before reaching Birzeit; change to a ford for Aboud.

Where to Park

You can park your car in front of one of the two picnic
areas in Wadi Limoon; they are about 400m apart
from one another.

Eat, Drink, Relax

Aboud has no restaurants but there are other options
available. Wadi Limoon has two picnic/barbeque
areas, both including small pools; you have to bring
your own food and drink and pay an entry fee to make
use of the facilities (inquire as you enter; usually 10
NIS). Since you can park the car next to these areas,
bringing along a barbeque for after the walk is easy.
The owner of the first place is called Karim Hamid
(0599-893786); the second picnic area is run by Nihad
Mustafa Abdul Majid (0599-364801). There is also a
small falafel shop behind the Greek Orthodox Church

Murals by Bethlehem artist
Taqi al-Din

"Aboud is really representing Palestine's rich biodiversity. There are hundreds of beautiful flowers in a landscape filled with history, and one of Palestine's amazing caves."

—Imad al-Atrash
Ornothologist,
Aboud

in Aboud's old village. By prior arrangement the Latin Church can also arrange meals for groups.

Overnight

Apart from homestays organized through the churches, there are no accomodation options in Aboud. Options close by can be found in the Ramallah and Birzeit chapters.

Places to Go, People to Meet

Even if you do not walk the third trail where this is included, it is interesting to visit Aboud's old village and the Latin (Um al-Awja) and Greek-Orthodox (al-Aboudiya) churches, see the ancient **Byzantine mosaics** in- and outside side the churches and look at the contemporary art murals by Bethlehem artist Taqi al-Diin. A short walk from the center you can explore the old Roman quarry, the St. Barbara Church, and the Aboud's **al-Kalzoun Cave**.

ترمسعيا Turmus'ayya: Amreeka Amreeka

Porto Alegre, Santiago and Chicago appear a world away from the tall hills of the central West Bank. But through hard-earned wealth, Palestinians from afar hold on to the villages of their ancestors.

From the quiet plains of Turmus'ayya, a walk up to the neighboring village of Mazra al-Sharqiya promises a steep climb. In return the trail offers great horizons over the central West Bank and a view up close into some of the Palestinian towns and villages that are closely tied to the Americas. Their residents once migrated there en masse in search for a better future but many of them have kept ties to their homeland and, as traders or business owners, they have started to reinvest into their mother towns.

Just enough guestrooms:
a mansion in Turmus'ayya

13. Diaspora Blues:
Turmus'ayya to Jilijliya

A great walk slinging you from past to present and back again. The trail takes you through the edges of Turmus'ayya, then up to Mazra al-Sharqiya after which it will gradually descend towards Rd 60 and climb over the hills of Sinjil towards the end point of Jilijliya's old town. Walkers ramble in between fields and olive groves of what once were rural backwaters and the villas that Palestinian migrants have built in their stead. This long walk contains two significant climbs: up to Mazra al-Sharqiya and later up to the hills of Sinjil and Jilijliya. In Mazra al-Sharqiya and Jilijliya there are small minimarkets where you can stock up on drinks and small snacks. Note that you either have to pre-arrange a pick-up or call a taxi at the end of the walk in order to return to the starting point.

Trail: Turmus'ayya >Mazra al-Sharqiya >Jilijliya (return by car or taxi)

Grade: Moderate

Surface: Dirt roads and minor sections paved road

Marked: No

Distance and Duration: 13.4 kms/8.3 miles; 4–5 hrs

Elevation Change: 475m ascent / 450m descent

Start Coordinates: N32 01.216 E35 17.475

[0-1.8km/0-1.1 mi.] From the Equestrian Club, turn R onto the road to Turmus'ayya; after about 100m (109 yards) turn L onto a dirt road that runs W between wheat fields and continues to meander through olive groves. Continue to follow this road as it winds through the olive grove until, after 1.2 km (0.74 mi.), it reaches the edge of Turmus'ayya village (❶). The trail runs through the village for 1 km (0.62 mi.). As you come across the first houses continue straight into the village. The road turns into a paved road here. !! At the first 3-way junction you come across, turn L (❷) (to your L at this corner is a furniture store).

[1.8-4.3km/1.1-2.6 mi.] After the turn to the L continue to follow the street which starts running back into the direction you came from. Continue straight at the next

133

4-way junction. As you pass the last houses of the village and the road turns into a dirt road again, the trail starts going up. On the dirt road, a long but rewarding climb awaits from about 690m (2,263 ft.) to 930m (3,051 ft.) above sea level. During the climb you will have amazing views over the area. In Turmus'ayya below, you can easily spot the ring of red-roofed houses

Beverly Hills in Palestine

Once you reach the edges of Mazra al-Sharqiya or Jilijliya you walk into something like Beverly Hills. Well, the West Bank equivalent at least. It is not as glamorous as in Los Angeles and some of the architecture is slightly bizarre—a jumble of Arab and American building styles with frivolous decorations cheering up the facades.

Exactly how many Palestinians live in the Diaspora and where is unknown. Figures suggest that about half of all Palestinians now live outside historic Palestine. Apart from the Arab world, the Americas have been the most prominent destination, for refugees as well as for economic migrants

who left early in the 20th century. With an estimated 500,000 citizens of Palestinian origin, Chile holds by far the largest Palestinian community outside the Arab world. One of its premier league football teams and two times national champion is Club Deportivo Palestino. Many of the migrants rose to become traders and shop owners across the American continent. Some became very wealthy indeed and it shows in the inter-family competition that seems to take place over who builds the most grandiose mansion.

The continuous building raises interesting prospects for Palestine. What would be the impact if families would

permanently migrate and put their skills and capital behind social enterprise and new business ventures? Israel still has a tight hold on Palestinians returning home permanently, however. Some American Palestinians deliberately outstay their visas but this gets them into trouble when they want to travel abroad again, usually making future visits impossible. Meanwhile, fellow Palestinians sometimes poke fun at the strong accent of their American brothers: the label *Falaahi Amerchani* (farmers' American) mocks their Arabic as a combination of American English and the Arabic of their forefathers in the old days.

Children learning to
ride at the Turmus'ayya
Equestrian Club

and villas that circles the old center of the village.
What used to be plains of agricultural land around the
village has largely been replaced by spacious houses
with large gardens. At the top of the hill the dirt roads
becomes a paved road that leads into the village of
Mazra al-Sharqiya (❸). Its lands once filled with vineyards have given way to an expanse of new villas.

[4.3-6.3km/2.6-3.9 mi.] Continue straight towards the
village center (S) until at 5km (3.1 mi.) into the hike,
and before reaching the center of the village, you come
across a 3-way junction: turn L here (❹). 300m (0.18
mi.) after the 3-way junction the road bends around a
large building to the R into a street lined with some
of Palestine's largest mansions. In the middle of the
street—cramped in between two large villas—you find

Abu Nawaaf's tiny Mini Market selling ice creams, soft drinks and small snacks. Orders can be made in Arabic, Portuguese, Spanish and English. Continue on this street until you reach a 4-way junction near the center of town; !! turn R here and after 150m (164 yards), turn L at the following T junction. 90m (98 yards) after the T junction you reach another 4-way junction with the small road to the R descending into the wadi below (**⑤**).

[6.3-8.3km/3.9-5.1 mi.]Take this road which quickly turns into a dirt road. Continue to follow it as it winds down into the wadi past olive trees and almond groves. At a 3-waypoint (**⑥**) halfway down the wadi make sure you keep R. After a little while you will see the West Bank's main north-south axis, Rd 60, run across the bottom of the wadi. Continue to descend up to the

Boys in Jilijliya

A Saddle for the Kids

As a child, Ashraf Rabi loved one thing above all else; riding the one horse his family owned in the village of Turmus'ayya. There was not enough money for a saddle but that was little deterrent for Ashraf who rode his stallion bareback. Growing up with little opportunities in the West Bank, he took the step that so many of his fellow villagers had taken before: emigration to the Americas. Following in the footsteps of his cousins and uncles, Ashraf started his own department store in Panama selling bargains to shoppers from Costa Rica. After 12 years, Ashraf moved on to the US setting up businesses in Brooklyn and New Jersey. Slowly but surely he acquired the wealth necessary to realize his life-long dream: a horse-riding club in his home town of Turmus'ayya.

The idea for a true Equestrian Club in Palestine was not spontaneous. It had deeply rooted in over two decades of life abroad: Ashraf made sure to travel back home once every year for 27 years in order to hang on to his so-called *hawiya*, the Palestinian ID administered by the Israeli authorities. With all these trips back home, Ashraf thus avoided the fate of so many Palestinian Americans who "lose their ID" after not being present for a certain period.

While most of them can still visit their homeland, they can only do so temporarily through three months tourist visas. In 2007, Ashraf finally made the big leap back to Palestine, buying a bare strip of land on the edge of Turmus'ayya and, from scratch, he built the Turmus'ayya Equestrian Club. The club is now home to some 25 horses and has over 150 members who visit it throughout the week and in weekends, taking lessons from Khaled, the club's full-time professional instructor. A large part of the membership are children who can learn to ride like Ashraf did 40 years ago. Yet this time on an actual saddle.

point where the dirt road gets you very close to Rd 60 but starts going up again. Leave the dirt road here to go across Rd 60. On the other side, you reconnect with another dirt road which is clearly visible to your L. !! Be very careful here as traffic can be fast and furious on the West Bank's main highway.

[8.3-11km/5.1-6.8 mi.] On the other side, follow the dirt road that goes along the wadi and gradually ascends

Almonds to be in
Turmus'ayya

the hill for the second (but more gentle) climb of this walk (from 750m [2,460 ft.] to 890m [2,919 ft.]). After a while up the dirt road you can make out the edge of the village of Sinjel (named after the famous French crusader leader Raymond of St. Gilles) straight ahead. At the first T junction (**❼**), turn L heading further up the hill, and keep L once more at a following Y junction. !! Shortly after this, you reach a junction: turn L again here for some more gradual climbing and keep R as the dirt road gently meanders up the hill and heads W(towards Jilijliya). You can clearly make out Mazra al-Sharqiya on its hilltop to the E (in the opposite direction). While other dirt roads join from either side, continue to follow your road heading W towards Jilijliya. Note that at 10.5km (6.5 mi.) into the hike, there is a side road (not part of the trail) running S to the highest point in the area (914m/2,998 ft. **❽**); this is an excellent picnic spot you could consider. However, to continue on the trail, keep following the main path, which gradually veers off to the R (W direction).

[11-13.4km/6.8-8.3 mi.] After 11 km (6.8 mi.) into the hike, you start seeing the outskirts of Jilijliya, another example of significant Diaspora investment from the Americas. 11.5km (7.1 mi.) into the hike, you take a L and join the main (paved) road at the edge of Jilijliya (**❾**). From here, it is another 2 km (1.2 mi.) past large mansions to get to the old village center with its beautiful ottoman structures and spotless mosque square. Opposite the mosque are two abandoned traditional Palestinian homes (unfortunately in a fairly bad shape at the time of writing). In these traditional homes, the single space is divided in upper and lower floors (*rawyeh*). The upper one was used for living, sleeping and food storage whereas the lower floor served as a stable for all types of livestock. [return] To get back to Turmus'ayya, arrange a taxi (see logistics section).

Logistics and Guides

The Turmus'ayya Equestrian Club can arrange local guides for the walk: 02-2803933 or call Khaled at 0598-246000. Costs are approximately 300-350 NIS depending on group size. If you do not have a guide to make arrangements, getting back to Turmus'ayya after you finish your walk is easy: arrange your own pick-up beforehand or call Taxi Abween (the next village to the E; Jilijliya does not have a taxi office) at 02-2807333 and ask for a pickup in Jilijliya. The cost for a oneway trip back to the Equestrian Club is around 40-50 NIS. While waiting for a taxi, you can get refreshments and small snacks at the mini market located on the main road 200m (0.12 mi.) E of Jilijliya's old village center.

Spring colors near the Equestrian Club

How to Get There

Car: From Jerusalem/Ramallah, it is a 40/30 minute drive to Turmus'ayya. Drive N on Rd 60 towards Nablus. After having passed the junction towards Birzeit and Atara (Rd 465), continue N for another 4km (2.4 mi.) and the turn-off to Turmus'ayya is located to your R in the midst of a flat meadow. You enter the village

A grand entrée in Mazra' al-Sharqiya

along a chic line of palm trees. The Turmus'ayya Equestrian Club is reached by driving a few km further on the village main road and just after passing the sign for the neighboring village of Khirbet Abu Fallah; in true American style, the club is signposted throughout the way. Note that the last sign indicating a R from the main road towards the club has a different color than all previous signs.

Public transportation: from Ramallah, take a direct ford to Turmus'ayya (if possible via Khirbet Abu Fallah).

Where to Park

You can park at the Turmus'ayya Equestrian Club

Eat, Drink, Relax

There are no restaurants in the villages on this route so packing a generous picnic is recommended. The club has a small cafeteria serving coffee, tea and soft drinks.

Overnight

The closest lodging options are in Ramallah, Jifna and Taybeh (see relevant chapters)

Places to Go, People to Meet

The Turmus'ayya Equestrian Club is one of three Palestinian places for horse riding (the other clubs are located in Jericho and Gaza). Lessons are available for children as well as adults. 8 lessons cost 350 NIS and horseback trips in the countryside are also possible (experienced riders only). Cherien Dabis' film *Amreeka* portrays the drama and comedy of relations between Palestinians in the American Diaspora with those who stayed behind.

On the Web

www.palhorse.com
www.amreeka.com

العوجا Wadi Auja: Wild Seclusion

Wadi Auja slowly carves its way deep into the desert hills. Descend through its quiet gorges to the wide expanse of the Jordan Valley.

Most trails in the West Bank contain a few places of perfect quietness; spots where the wind and the birds are your only companions. In Wadi Auja, you can have that solitary experience throughout. It is among the least frequented and most spectacular walks described in this book, providing seclusion in the depths of the wadi as well as on its ridges above.

At the end of the trail you meet the Auja spring, the traditional water source for Auja village which lies 7km (4.3 mi.) further east and not far from the river Jordan. Auja is Jericho's small neighbor and worth visiting as one of the few Palestinian villages in the plains of the Jordan Valley. The Center for Environmental Education and Eco-Tourism in the village has a guesthouse and offers walking and other tours in and around the valley. Its local guides are much recommended as walking companions through Wadi Auja.

After a long hard walk, a refreshing dip in Auja spring

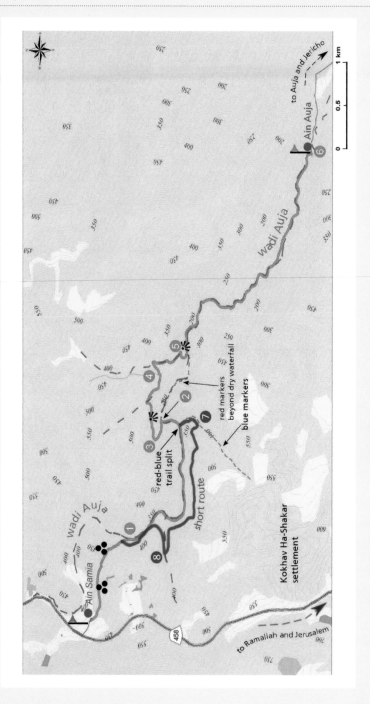

14. Between Springs: Ain Samia to Ain Auja

This trail takes you from the Samia spring at 410m (1,345 ft.) elevation to the Auja spring located at sea level at the W edge of the Jordan Valley. In contrast to Wadi Qelt you will hardly encounter other walkers on your way. The trail described below is well marked apart from a 2km (1.2 ft.) section above the wadi bed where it temporarily leaves the red markers. The full trail is challenging, requires a good level of fitness and an early start. It includes scrambling over large boulders, climbing up a steep ridge, and making your way down dry waterfalls. Winter is the best period to do this hike with an abundance of flowers and wild vegetation covering the wadi bed and the hill slopes growing lavishly green. Late fall (November) and early spring (March-April) are also good choices though. Always mind the weather as heavy rains can lead to flash floods.

If you prefer a good peek into Wadi Auja but do not want to do the whole trail, you can opt for an out-and-back walk into the wadi or take the shortcut described separately at the end (8.1 km [5 mi.] and 4 hours). Note that the short-cut can still be challenging, especially with walkers dealing with vertigo. There are no places along the route to stock up on food and drink so make sure you bring plenty, especially water (take 3-4 litres minimum for the full walk). Note that to get back to your starting point, or to continue to Auja village or Jericho, you will have to (pre-)arrange your own pick-up at the Auja spring.

[0-1.3km/0-0.8 mi.] The trail starts at the dirt road running from the Ain Samia water pumping station. Follow the red trail markers. 100m (109 yards) after the pumping station the dirt road veers sharply L.

Trail: Ain Samia to Ain Auja

Grade: Hard

Surface: Single track and wilderness (includes scrambling)

Marked: Partially

Distance and Duration: 10.2 km / 6.3 miles; 5–7 hrs

Elevation Change: 170m ascent / 600m descent

Start Coordinates: N31 59.096 E35 20.106

Butterflies enjoying the
Artichoke Cotton-thistle

You leave the dirt road here to follow the red marked trail that starts running up the hill slope to the R of the dirt road. The markers are fairly clearly indicated at 50m (54 yards) intervals. The trail passes ruins that overlook the valley below and then pass over a saddle point where another set of ruins lie, probably the remains of ancient animal pen. From here, the trail descends into Wadi Auja. At 1.3km (0.8 mi.) the trail reaches the wadi bed where two pretty Christ's Thorn trees guard the surroundings (**❶**).

[1.3-4.1km/0.8-2.5 mi.] From here, the trail follows the wadi bed for the next few km. At first the wadi is wide, more like a valley, but gradually it becomes more narrow as it cuts deeper into the rock surface. The scenery becomes greener with shrubs and flowers amidst the smooth boulders. At 3km (1.8 mi.) large trees appear in the wadi bed and the scrambling down numerous small dry waterfalls becomes more serious. !! At 3.7 km (2.2 mi.), just before the wadi bed turns sharply to the L, you come to a split in the trail with blue markers skirting off to the R and climbing up between a large boulder and the cliff wall. If you want to do a shorter trail, turn R here (see inset for continuation). If you walk the full trail continue to follow the red markers until, at 4.1km (2.5 mi.), you meet a dry waterfall with a sheer drop of about 6m (19 ft.) (**❷**).

[4.1-4.4km/2.5-2.7 mi.] You are not advised to make your way down the waterfall and continue on the red trail unless you are experienced climbers with sufficient equipment. In any case, the following loop around the waterfall is not only more safe but also more spectacular. From the dry waterfall walk back 40m (43 yards) and to the R you will see an accessible gully. It is the only place amidst the otherwise steep wadi cliffs on either side where you can scramble up. This climb is still

Rising above Wadi Auja

slightly steep at some points, however, and people with vertigo might have problems even though it is technically not very difficult and no equipment is required. As you do this, simply follow the gully upwards and continue to climb it until you are 100m (328 ft.) above the wadi bed. Unless you have an altimeter it will be very hard to estimate how high you have climbed. Therefore, the following visual aids will help: at 70m (229 ft.) above the wadi bed a single tree stands out in the middle of the gully. 30m (98 ft.) above the tree you will see three large square rocks that stand out from their environment. Climb up to these rocks (❸) and at this point you find a small herders' path that moves along the gradient of the hill.

Water without Borders

In a perfect world the spectacular walk from Ain Samia to Ain Auja would end with walkers refreshing their feet under the gushing streams of the Auja spring. Unfortunately, the flow of the spring has been greatly reduced over the last decade. Ain Auja used to feed the 7km long aquaduct running to Auja village for 7 months of the year, supplying both Bedouin and farmers in the area with a reliable source for irrigating their crops and feeding their livestock. Droughts over the last years have brought the flow down to about 3 months per year though, significantly limiting Palestinian use of the Jordan Valley's highly fertile land.

Out of the so-called "core issues" that need to be addressed in a final peace agreement (Jerusalem, security, refugees, borders, water and settlements), the issue of water is probably the one receiving least attention in the media. Reflecting the large disparity in wealth standards, the average Israeli uses about four to five times more water than the average Palestinian. While Israel is renowned for its high-tech water infrastructure, Palestinians still lack basic infrastructure, efficient water management and, most pressingly, the opportunity to do something about it. Since both sides tap from the same limited sources, fair distribution, knowledge transfer and cooperation on water issues seems the sensible answer.

Yet in the West Bank (as in Gaza) the conflict strongly conspires against both a more sustainable and more equitable division of water resources. One feature of the problem is that water constantly moves across the "yet-to-be-agreed borders": water that is replenished through rainfall in one area, seeps through the land surface, drains down the mountain aquifer and eventually emerges elsewhere. In the West Bank, a lot of the rain that falls on the hills in the west and north east (the so-called western and north-eastern aquifers) eventually emerges in springs inside Israel. Nearly all of the rain that falls on the eastern side (the eastern aquifer) flows down to the Jordan Valley.

In the mid-nineties the issue was tackled in the Oslo Agreements: for an interim period of 5 years specific quantities to either side were allocated and a Joint Water Committee (JWC) was set up to foster cooperation. The structure of the JWC is such that the drilling of new Palestinian wells (including those in areas A and B) has to be approved by the committee. This gives Israel a de facto veto over any new water resources under Palestinian control. With the potential negative impact on its own springs inside Israel in mind, Israeli water authorities have refused all Palestinian requests for drilling new wells in the western and north eastern aquifers, though some 85% of the water in these aquifers is replenished by rainfall in the West Bank, not Israel. Drilling wells in the eastern aquifer (the hills sloping down into the Jordan Valley) is allowed under certain conditions but Israel also drills its own deep wells there.

Ain Samia, the location of the start of the walk, is located above the eastern aquifer and Israel did allow the construction of an additional Palestinian well there. From 250m below Ain Samia, water is pumped up to the Ramallah municipality located some 20km away. The water crosses the highest hills of the West Bank on its way, an upward journey of some 1000m. Although Ramallah lies geographically much closer to sources in the more efficient and productive western aquifer—which is shared with Israel—drilling any wells closer by is not allowed. Hence, Ain Samia is Ramallah's only Palestinian source; it supplies about 30% of its water with the remaining 70% being bought from Israel's national water company, Mekorot.

At the end of the walk, just 200m (0.12 mi.) east of the Auja spring, the Israelis maintain their own well which supplies the agriculture of settlements in the Jordan Valley. Israeli settlements consume around 44 million cubic meters per year of water extracted from wells within the West Bank, a figure which equals roughly half of total Palestinian water consumption in the same area. One of these settlements is Yitav, very small in terms of inhabitants but large in agricultural output: a few km from the end of the trail the vast green expanse of palm trees for date production can be seen from afar. As in Israel, Israeli farmers in Yitav buy their water at subsidized low prices.

The Israeli well near Ain Auja collects water at 2000m depth, according to most hydrologists far too deep to have a negative impact on the supply of the nearby Auja spring. Even so, Israeli and Palestinian access to water

for consumption and agriculture remains inequitable, providing a basis for more conflict in times of drought. With the exception of Jericho, the water situation is especially daunting for all Palestinian towns throughout the Jordan Valley. Many have to resort to buying water for their personal use directly from Mekorot or from mobile water tanks that drive around selling water to isolated communities. This water is too expensive to be used for crop irrigation however, and water infrastructure built without Israeli permission is frequently demolished. It is one of the factors behind the steep contrasts of Palestinian poverty and Israeli green high-tech lying side by side in the Jordan Valley, causing some Palestinians to give up farming their own land and to take up work in the settlement green houses next door.

A rock climbers' challenge:
towering above Wadi Auja

[4.4-5.3km/2.7-3.2 mi.] Veer R here and move along
this single track path as it moves along the ridge. The
views over the hills and the Jordan Valley in the distance are stunning, as is the view of Wadi Auja below.
Keep following the path which stays mostly level. After
500m (0.31 mi.) you pass through the next gully. Continue on the path for another 400m (0.24 mi.) when
you meet a second gully (❹).

[5.3-6.1km/3.2-3.7 mi.] Leave the path (which runs
away from the Wadi Auja in N direction) here and

descend down the gully. The descent can be made anywhere but is more easy towards the L (N) where you need no scrambling. Once you reach the gully bed below, turn R and follow it as it slopes down towards Wadi Auja. Along the way you meet a 12m (39 ft.) steep dry waterfall. Get around it by climbing a few m to the R and going back down into the bed of the gully just underneath a set of large cliffs, 100m (109 yards) from the gully. Continue to follow the gully bed until, at 6km (3.7 mi.) into the walk, you arrive at the edge of a cliff which drops off into Wadi Auja (**❺**). The views here are spectacular and the spot on the edge of the cliff, below the pillar of natural rocks is the best spot for a picnic on this walk.

[6.1-6.4km/3.7-3.9 mi.] In case you are wondering how to get back to the wadi bed without jumping the cliff, don't worry, the way down is surprisingly easy. !! Facing the wadi, 30m (32 yards) to your R you see a large formation of rocks whose peaks are higher than the cliff you are standing on. In the middle of these rocks there is a small 2m (2 yards) wide passage. To get there safely from the cliff, simply retrace your steps for 40m (43 yards) and circle towards the passage. On the other side, you can zigzag your way down to the wadi bed over a moderate slope (use the larger rocks to avoid slipping).

[6.4-10.2km/3.9-6.3 mi.] Once in the wadi bed turn L and continue to follow the red markings again. The wadi turns into a set of smooth little gorges carved out patiently by the passing of time. Some scrambling is necessary once again. At 7.5km (4.6 mi.) into the walk the wadi widens, becomes much easier to traverse and you can see various cave dwellings dotted across the slopes above the wadi. A single track starts which follows the red markers all the way to the Auja spring. You find bamboo, palm trees and Sodom apples (with

Gorge in the wadi bed

large purple flowers in fall) along the way. At 10km (6.2 mi.) into the walk you pass beneath sea level and reach the Auja spring (**⑥**), which is dry except in winter time. Aquaducts run from the spring to the village of Auja located 7km (4.3 mi.) to the E. A paved road runs from here and 200m (0.12 mi.) beyond the spring, you pass the Israeli run water pumping station.

Mobile reception on either the Jordanian, Palestinian or Israeli networks should be fine by the time you arrive at the spring which will allow you to arrange your pick-up or a taxi if have not done so in advance. Note that if Auja village is your destination you still require a pick-up from there as it is another 7km (4.3 mi.) from the spring to the village. The paved road running from the spring towards Jericho and Auja village is a nice one and you could consider walking a bit further until you meet your transport. On the journey back to Ain Samia, as the sun starts setting in the W, you can take in another set of spectacular views on the landscape you just crossed.

Wadi Auja: the "short" way

This circular route will still take you about 4 hours and includes a lot of scrambling, including on steep sections of trail. The trail follows the red markings, then continues on blue and circles back to the starting point through an unmarked section.

[0-3.7 km/0-2.2 mi.] Follow full trail as described.

[3.7-4.1km/2.2-2.5 mi.] The blue trail splits away from the wadi behind a giant boulder. After 30m (32 yards) you encounter a serious scramble of about 2.5m (8 ft.) almost straight up the rock but with helpful cracks to provide support. Inexperienced walkers might need

Descending into the wadi

Young walker enjoying
a break

the help of more experienced climbers here: make
sure you support one another while managing this
step, and let the most experienced climber go last.
Having mastered it, the blue trail continues with a
steep but much easier scramble up the hill. While
technically not difficult, walkers with vertigo might
have a problem in the sections that follow from here:
at all times, take it easy while you scramble up the
gully. After a few minutes of climbing the views over
Wadi Auja are magnificent and the smooth gully in
which the trail runs provides an excellent location for
a picnic. Follow the blue marked trail up until, at an
elevation of 360m (1,181 ft.) (❼), you catch the first
sighting of the Kokhav Ha-Shakhar settlement located
far above you (560m/1,837 ft.); at this point you leave
the blue trail (which continues to run all the way up to
the settlement) by walking on the slope to your R.

[4.1-5.7km/2.5-3.5 mi.] Maintain approximately the
same elevation above the wadi as you walk back in the
direction of the starting point (W) with Wadi Auja on
your R. There is no clear path here. While the slope
is easy to negotiate, it remains steep for quite a while.
400m (0.24 mi.) after leaving the blue markings you

will encounter a clear herder's path (single track) which also follows the contours of the slopes of the wadi and gradually slopes down towards it. Continue along this path for 1.5km (0.9 mi.). From the path you see Wadi Auja below being joined by a second smaller wadi coming from the L (W).

[5.7-8.1km/3.5-5 mi.] The trail back to the start runs via Wadi Auja and not the smaller wadi that runs into it. To get back into Wadi Auja, however, follow the smaller wadi for around 200m (0.12 mi.) to where you can cross the wadi bed (**8**). Once you are on the other side of the smaller wadi walk back towards Wadi Auja. From here you continue to keep Wadi Auja below on your R. Around 1km (0.62 mi.) from the start you will reconnect with the red trail markers. As you meet the large Christ's Thorn trees in the center of the wadi, note that from here the red markers skirt up the hill again (to the L). Follow them as you make your way back to the starting point.

Steep cliff in wadi Auja

Logistics and Guides

In Auja village, Friends of the Earth Middle East founded the **Jordan Rift Valley Center for Environmental Education and Eco-Tourism**. Working with local guides, the Center offers a range of guided walks in the area, including for the Ain Samia to Ain Auja walk (fees for a group are around 400 NIS for an entire day). Lunch at Auja Village costs around 40 NIS pp. The Center also runs the **Auja Village Guesthouse**: 02-2310424; fadi25@foeme.org or call Fadi Jueejat at 0595-293007.

If after Ain Auja you would like to continue to Auja village, make sure you arrange a pick-up beforehand (unless you would like to walk another 7 km to the village). A pick-up by taxi (around 50 NIS) can be arranged through the Auja Village Guesthouse. To get back to Ain Samia after the walk, either arrange this through the Guesthouse or call a taxi from Jericho; e.g. Taxi Abu Ali: 02-2322525 (make sure you make clear that you want to be picked up at the Auja spring which is Ain Auja, and not Auja Village (qariyet Auja)). It is a 25-30 minute drive back to Ain Samia; costs are around 100-120 NIS for a regular taxi fitting 4 people.

How to Get There

Car: From Jerusalem/Ramallah, it is a 40/30 minute drive to Ain Samia. Jerusalem: N on Rd 60. Pass Jaba junction and look out for a signposted turn-off towards Rimonim settlement (green) and Taybeh (spelled Tayibe—white) on your R (this is Rd 457). Continue on this winding road and continue straight at the 4-way Rimonim Junction (Rd 458) afterwhich there is another 10km (6.2 mi.) of winding road. Ain Samia can be recognised by the plains of agricultural fields that are situated to the R of Road 458 as it reaches the valley below the village of Kafr Malek. 500m (0.31 mi.) after the road descends into flat arable land, look out for a small paved road to the R, leading to Ain Samia, which is a Palestinian water pumping station. Ramallah: fastest via Beitin and Rammun (road blocked at time of writing); alternative via Jaba (as above) or via Ain Yabrud, Deer Jreer and Taybeh.

Public transportation: difficult from Ramallah as walk starts far from nearest village (Kafr Malek); a private taxi or ford is advised.

Where to Park

You can park next to the small paved road where it passes the fenced-off water pumping station of Ain Samia. The red-marked trail starts here.

Avoiding the steep dry waterfall through a climb up the gully (4.1 km into the trail)

Eat, Drink, Relax

There are no eating or drinking options along the way; make sure you stock up on water and food. Nearest options from Ain Auja are Auja village and Jericho; near the start it is Taybeh.

Overnight

Staying overnight in the Jordan Valley is possible in Auja village or Jericho. **The Auja Village Guesthouse** (see above) provides bed and breakfast for 100 NIS pppn, and lunch and dinner for 40/50 NIS. For Jericho options, see the Wadi Qelt chapter.

Places to Go, People to Meet

Bike rental, bird watching and educational tours can be arranged through the Jordan Rift Valley Center in Auja village (see above). For Jericho, see the Wadi Qelt chapter.

On the Web

www.jrec.ps

www.foeme.org/www/?module=projects&record_id=174

PEOPLE & PLACES

"Wadi Auja each year is different. I've been there so many times, but the rain keeps changing the rocks in the gorge. Sometimes, I walk through and it feels as if it is my first time there again."

—Mohanad Saaideh, Guide, Auja Village

بيرزيت Birzeit: Well of Oil

The town of Birzeit cherishes both modernity and tradition. Its pleasant university campus breathes the future; its restored old city provides a stylish home to the past.

A peak at Birzeit's old city from its olive groves

Birzeit literally means well of oil, a fitting name for a village surrounded by expansive stretches of olive groves. While located close to the urban conglomerate of Ramallah, the village has retained its own distinctive charm. **Birzeit University** is Palestine's most famous academic institution with a turbulent history in the 70s and 80s when it was closed down several times by the Israeli military. Once established in historic Birzeit, the university's modern campus now enrolls its 9000 students on a hill southwest of the village.

Meanwhile, the Rehabilitation Project of the Historic Area of Birzeit (run by Rozana and Riwaq) has put new life into Birzeit's old city. Many traditional Palestinian homes are used again, including as gallery, mosaic workshop and restaurant. The **Ween a-Ramallah** restaurant (named after a classic Palestinian song) and the **Hosh al-Elleeya** are both located in these restored buildings. The Hosh is Palestine's best rural restaurant with traditional Palestinian dishes creatively reinvented, including vegetarian options. It also hosts art exhibitions, live music on Thursday and Saturday nights, weekly film nights (Tuesdays), and organized hikes on weekends. The old city is also the location of the **People's Museum** and the **Greek Orthodox Church**. Rozana can arrange guided tours of Birzeit and its surroundings.

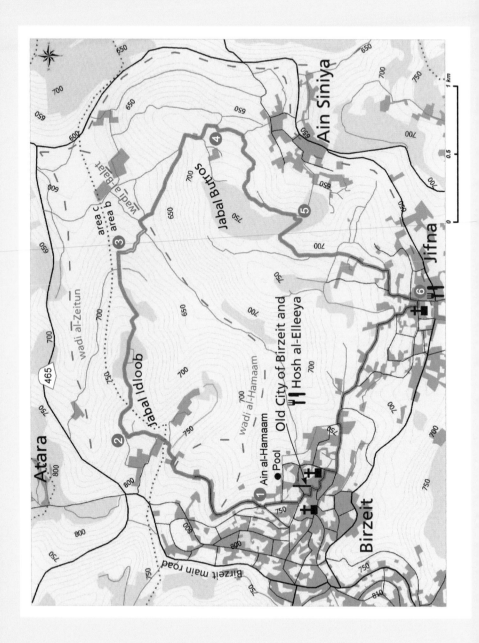

15. Circling the Olives: Birzeit to Jifna

This walk is a circle going clockwise. The trail runs from the old city of Birzeit over the outstretched hills to its N (Jabal Idloob), down into Wadi al-Balat (E) and over Jabal Butros to Jifna village before returning to Birzeit. The trail runs mostly through a terraced landscape filled with olive trees. It it is a lovely hike any time of the year, especially around the olive harvest in October or the flower dense period of early spring.

Trail: Birzeit—Jifna—Birzeit

Grade: Moderate

Surface: Predominantly dirt road; minor sections paved road; two short stretches off-road

Marked: No

Distance and Duration: 9.6 kms / 5.9 miles; 2.5–3.5 hrs

Elevation Change: 325m ascent / 325m descent

Start Coordinates: N31 58.189 E35 12.053

[0-500m/0-0.31 mi.] From the Hosh al-Elleeya cafe go L into Al-Balad street and after 40m (43 yards) take a R into Al-'Ein road. You pass the Ween a-Ramallah restaurant which is located in a restored building: continue straight and at the edge of the old city you pass the People's Museum of Birzeit (*Mathaf al-Shaab*). Turn L here and at the subsequent 3-way junction turn R and walk down the road. You see the Ain al-Hamaam swimming pool located on your R; continue straight and look out for a small side road that veers off to the R. !! Continue on this small road (❶) which is located some 300m (0.18 mi.) from the 3-way junction and appears just after the wider road has started to climb again.

[500m-2km/0.31-1.2 mi.] From here, you start walking the outskirts of Birzeit overlooking the olive groves of Wadi al-Hamaam to your R and passing a number of standalone houses and small farms. At 1.2km (0.7 mi.) into the walk the road turns into a dirt road. Continue to follow it as it passes more farms and gradually starts climbing onto Jabal Idloob. Keep following the dirt road, ignoring other dirt roads that veer off to the R.

As you continue to climb to the top of Jabal Idloob you reach a 3-way junction where a L turn will take you to a small block of houses. Keep straight however, onto the plateau of Jabal Idloob from where you can spot the village of Atara perched on the ridge ahead of you (N). From here, take the second (wide) dirt road (❷) to your R (the first will quickly run into an olive grove).

[2-3.4km/1.2-2.1 mi.] This wide dirt road runs over Jabal Idloob in E direction and slowly descends down to Wadi al-Balat. Stick to this road and ignore other (smaller) dirt roads crossing it or skirting away from it. The views on the surrounding hilltop villages from the plateau of Jabal Idloob are excellent: Atara to the N (to your L); Silwad to the E (straight ahead); Ain Yabrud to the SE and Jalazon and Ramallah to the S (R). At 3km (1.8 mi.) into the walk, another road joins from the L side: keep R and follow the dirt road as it descends. At some point you clearly see an unfinished housing estate lying at the edge of Wadi al-Balat below.

[3.4-3.9km/2.1-2.4 mi.] !! At 3.4km (2.1 mi.) into the walk, at what seems to be a T junction (the options seem only L and R), a smaller footpath actually continues straight down the hill towards Wadi Al-Balat. Follow this for about 100m (109 yards) until the path disappears along the terraces (❸), many of which are not maintained anymore. From here, you should easily spot the wide dirt road starting in the valley below you and climbing up Jabal Butros, which is the hill opposite the one you are on. Continue off-road to descend down the terraces (some scrambling might be required) for some 300m (0.18 mi.) in the direction of the dirt road. Once down in the wadi bed the wide dirt road onto Jabal Butros runs some 300m (0.18 mi.) to the R (W) of the unfinished housing estate.

[3.9-5.2km/2.4-3.2 mi.] Follow the dirt road up Jabal Butros where you pass a very large water storage tank. Continue on the road which winds down towards the small village of Ain Siniya. At a split in the road keep

The old city of Birzeit: observing Ramallah's ever growing skyline

Hosh al-Elleeya: traditional
food reinvented

R (❹). ‼ 200m (0.12 mi.) after this split, another split occurs with the L leg running down to Ain Siniya (clearly visible from here) and the R leg (dirt road) going up the hill. Take the R leg. After another 250m (0.15 mi.), a third split occurs: again you keep R and continue to climb until the dirt road takes a clear U-turn towards a house.

[5.2-6.3km/3.2-3.9 mi.] ‼ At the center of the U-turn you leave the dirt road and cross into an olive grove to your R. For the next 200m (0.12 mi.) you walk along the terrace of the grove which holds a set of very ancient olive trees in a bizarre variety of shapes. Stay in the direction of the stand-alone white house at the far end of the terrace. Walk around the house on its R side to reconnect with another road (❺).

[6.3-7.8km/3.9-4.8 mi.] On this road, go R and start walking up again. Keep following the road as it winds through the olive groves to the high outskirts of Jifna

The Olive and the Tree

If Palestine would choose its national tree there would only be one candidate. The olive tree is the single most recurring feature of the Palestinian landscape, a national symbol of steadfastness and resilience, and an important economic resource for most villages around the West Bank. It has its deep roots in literature and religion too, with the olive mentioned in the Quran, the Torah, the Bible and the Greek and Roman classics.

During spring time, the olive tree produces small creamy white flowers, almost hidden between its leaves. But its visual appeal is year round: the varying colors of olive groves—silver blue to dark green depending on the time of the day—the distinct unique shape of individual trees and of course their legendary age. Many trees can survive for up to two or three centuries and in exceptional cases a few thousand years. Several millenary trees still survive today (the most famous ones in Jerusalem's Garden of Gethsemane) though few of these trunks have been subject to any rigid science. As their age proves, olive trees are incredibly strong, fending off drought, disease, storms and even fire.

There are over 700 different olive varieties and it is probably the tree with the widest range of uses to mankind: the fruit and oil is used for food preparation, light, heating, olive soap and cosmetic products. Olive wood is superior for furniture and construction. For many Palestinian families olive oil remains a staple produced and consumed locally but the production of professionally branded high quality oil to western markets has been on the rise in the last decade. In case you wondered, the words extra virgin stand for oil with the finest quality and an acidity level of less than 1%.

In October and November walkers will notice individual farmers or whole families harvesting: trees are milked in various ways, ranging from climbing up and handpicking the fruit to hitting the branches with poles. In the harvesting season you can buy fresh oil in large jerrycans in nearly every Palestinian village. To produce the tasty olives that you eat as a snack, the fruit has to go through a rigorous process of curing in salted water that is regularly refreshed (try them straight off the tree and you will have a very bitter experience indeed). If you believe the talk of the trade and some of the science, there is no end to the health benefits of olives and their oil: it improves digestion, lowers blood pressure, prevents heart disease and counters muscle aches. According to some it is also responsible for strengthening nails, countering wrinkles, and making hair look shinier. It is said that drinking a shot of pure oil can even prevent a hangover.

village. At 7.1km (4.4 mi.) you reach the first pretty houses of Jifna; the road becomes paved again and starts going downhill. At a T-junction, keep R. Continue to follow the road as it descends into the old city of Jifna, which is worth exploring. You are at its heart when you reach Jifna's large Catholic Church (**6**). While the trail turns to the R here to climb back up to Birzeit, any hungry or thirsty walkers can relax at one of several Jifna restaurants below. The Tabash and Basha restaurants are located just 170m (0.1 mi.) past the Catholic Church at Jifna's roundabout (several others as well as the Dream Swimming Pool can be found not far from the roundabout).

[7.8-9.6km/4.8-5.9 mi.] To continue on the trail take a R at the Catholic Church (if you come back from the roundabout the direction, of course, is L), pass the Jifna Kindergarden and take a R at the next T-junction. Continue to climb up through Jifna's narrow streets and keep L at the next split in the road. On the outskirts of the village the road turns into a dirt road again. As you climb up further you pass a large cement factory on a little stretch that is no doubt the least scenic of this hike. Keep L at the next split in the road and walk on until you reach the edge of Birzeit at a roundabout. Go R here and after 90m (98 yards) take the first L as the trail leads back into the old city and to the Hosh al-Elleeya cafe.

Slow life in Birzeit

Logistics and Guides

The Hosh al-Elleeya/Suhail Hijazi organizes weekly Hiking to Zarb walking tours, which depart from the cafe/restaurant by the same name in Birzeit's old city. The hikes include a traditional Palestinian zarb meal at the end of the walk—food prepared in a self-made

oven in the ground. Hiking to Zarb walks cost 100-120 NIS pp including food and drinks. Contact the Hosh or Suhail at hosh.l.elleeya@gmail.com and Suhail. Hijazi@gmail.com (0599-963991). Rozana, a local NGO based in Birzeit, also regularly organizes tours in Birzeit and its surroundings: 02-819850.

A herd enjoying the afternoon sun

How to Get There

Car: From Jerusalem/Ramallah, it is a 40/15 minute drive to Birzeit. From Jerusalem, drive N on Rd 60 until you meet Rd 465. Drive on Rd 465 in W direction until you cross under the bridge connecting Birzeit to Atara. Take a L here, drive up the hill and turn R, followed by another R; from here, continue on Birzeit's main road until you meet the roundabout with the statue of Abd al-Qader al-Huseini (a famous Palestinian resistance leader who died in the '48 war). Make a near full turn at this roundabout and veer R onto a wide road which leads to Birzeit's old city. Drive for 1 km (0.62 mi.) passing the large Catholic Church and the Birzeit Municpality building (on your L). At the first roundabout after the municipality turn L and

PEOPLE & PLACES

"As the name implies Birzeit (olive oil well) is a hilly town decorated with endless groves of olive trees, some of which date back to Roman times. It acquired this name because inhabitants used to store the olive oil in wells dug in the ground. Birzeit today is a university town and a gateway between Ramallah and the north of Palestine. Its central location, the diversity of its cultural heritage, the hospitality of its people and the richness of its history make Birzeit a must visit place."

—Raed Saadeh, Board Member Abraham Path Initiative, Birzeit

take the first road L immediately after this where you enter the old city. From Ramallah leave the city to the N passing the villages of Surda and Abu Qash before entering Birzeit on its main road. Continue to follow the main road in N direction until you come across a roundabout with the Al-Huseini statue. Take the second (wide) road that veers R (NE) from the roundabout and follow the directions above.

Public transportation: via Ramallah to Birzeit.

Where to Park

You can park at the (small) square in the old city (opposite the Hosh al-Elleeya cafe). If there are no parking spaces there, try the municipality building nearby.

Eat, Drink, Relax

Inside the old city of Birzeit there are two nice restaurants: **Ween a-Ramallah**: 057-770776 (Kamal); and **Cafe and Gallery Hosh al-Elleeya**: 0599-868914 (Mazen), both are siuated in restored buildings. On the main road running from Birzeit to Ramallah there are a number of eateries as well. The center of Jifna boasts a handful of grill restaurants and two guest houses (see the Ramallah chapter).

Overnight

The Activity Center of the Edward Said National Conservatory of Music runs a guesthouse in Birzeit, located on walking distance from the old city. It caters for up to 70 people and has rooms with 3-5 beds each. Pppn including breakfast: 70 NIS. Contact: 02-2819155 or 0599-835434 (Amjad); and info@ncm. birzeit.edu.

Places to Go, People to Meet

The Old City of Birzeit is nice for a small walkabout (Rozana can organize a tour). You can visit the **Mosaic Workshop** and the **People's Museum** (*Mathaf al-Shaab*). Rozana organizes an annual *Maftool* (couscous) Festival but dates have been varying (check online). **Jifna's Old City** is also worth seeing. At the time of writing, apart from hiking tours, the Hosh al-Elleeya was active organizing horse riding and camping trips.

Ready to be harvested: olives in Birzeit

Birzeit's old city

On the Web

www.rozana.ps
www.birzeitsociety.org
www.riwaq.org
http://ncm.birzeit.edu/new/page.php

الطيبة Taybeh: Draft Delicious

Legend has it that when Saladin conquered Palestine and visited this Christian town, he coined the name Taybeh as he found its people *taybeen*—generous in their hospitality.

Located on the highest hills of the West Bank, Taybeh lies in between the urban sprawl of Ramallah and the dramatic desert scenery sloping down towards the Jordan Valley. With sales in Germany, Japan, the UK and the US, the village is famous for brewing Palestine's one and only beer. Beyond the brewery and Taybeh's pretty surroundings, other places worth visiting are its historic old city center and its various churches.

Walkers exploring
Wadi Habees

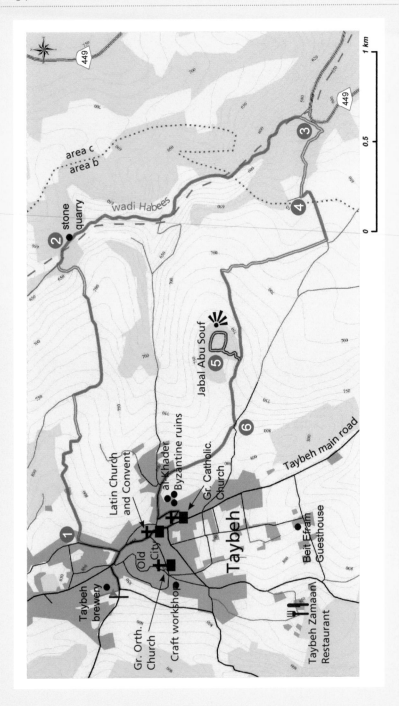

16. From the Brewery: Taybeh to Wadi Habees

This circular walk will take you from the brewery through the expansive olive groves E of Taybeh, gently descending into Wadi Habees before turning back to the village. On your way back you will pass the pine trees of Jabal Abu Souf with its great views towards the Jordan Valley: a great place for a picnic. Once back in the village the trail passes the pretty ruins of Taybeh's Byzantine al-Khader (St. George) Church, which is certainly worth a stop.

Trail: Taybeh > Wadi al-Habees > Taybeh

Grade: Moderate

Surface: Predominantly dirt road; minor single track; minor paved

Marked: Yes (blue and black)

Distance and Duration: 8.4 kms/5.2 miles; 2–3 hrs

Elevation Change: 320 m

Start Coordinates:
N31 57.337 E35 17.848

[0-500m/0-0.31 mi.] The hike starts from the brewery; walk out of its gate and turn L towards the village center; at the small roundabout go R and then take the first road L. After some 200m (0.12 mi) on this road and having past a small factory, take the small paved road to your R leaving the village and descending into the fields (❶).

[500-2.5km/0.31-1.5 mi.] After a little while this road becomes a dirt road: continue to follow it E as it winds down between the olive groves; ignore smaller paths that cross it along the way. As you leave the tranquil village behind you, expansive views of the olive groves of both Taybeh and Deer Jreer open ahead of you. At 1.5 km (0.9 mi.) into the walk, you meet a T junction with a dirt road coming from Deer Jreer: go R here. This road formally separates the olive trees belonging to Deer Jreer (to your L) from those belonging to Taybeh (to your R). As you continue your gradual descent towards the wadi, the well-tended olive fields become olive terraces and the dirt road becomes smaller, in parts overgrown. Once the wadi bed is clearly visible,

Performance at Palestine's most popular festival

the path can become more difficult to see but simply continue your descent into the wadi. Once in the wadi bed (❷), you turn R following the wadi bed in SE direction on another dirt road and passing an old stone quarry.

[2.5-4.4km/1.5-2.7 mi.] From the wadi bed, you can see Taybeh's olive and fruit trees extending upwards on terraces L and R. Large natural caves can be spotted just underneath the rock ridges above. Continue to walk in the wadi bed. At 3.3km (2 mi.) into the walk you reach a 3-way junction. The dirt road going upwards to your R provides an alternative but much less attractive route (cutting the hike by about 1 hour but also passing a stone quarry and a solid waste site along the way). For the main route, continue to follow the wadi bed.

[4.4-5.1km/2.7-3.1 mi] At 4.4km (2.7 mi.) into the hike, the wadi bed meets (and crosses underneath) a sharp U-turn in Road 449 (❸). Do not follow or cross Road 449 but leave the wadi by climbing up the slope directly to the R (W) of the U-turn in Road 449. !! There is no clear single track path here but the rocky surface is easily traversed; as you climb up keep the ridge of the hill you are climbing to your L (the ridge of the hill is covered with olive trees) and a line of farmer watchtowers (*burj*) to your R. Once you climb higher up, the pine tree covered hilltop of Jabal Abu Souf is a good marker for direction; after a few hundred meters of walking into the direction of Jabal Abu Souf, you meet another dirt road (❹); follow it to your L as it winds up in an S-curve and heads back towards Taybeh village.

Oktoberfest in Palestine

From a rural backwater once far off the beaten track of the tourism itinerary, Taybeh village is gradually transforming into a mainstay for alternative travel in Palestine. Its magnet? Beer. Pretty churches, spectacular archeological ruins, a beautifully restored old city and a handicraft workshop; they all help to attract visitors to one of the most pretty and rustic Palestinian villages. But it is the **Taybeh Brewery** that has become its distinctive feature and the annual Oktoberfest its truly unique attraction. With advertisements for alcoholic beverages being forbidden in Palestine, Oktoberfest became the vehicle to spread the word on Palestine's only beer. And with tremendous success. First staged in 2005, ten thousand visitors now attend the annual festival which showcases the odd but cheery combination of Palestinian *dabka* dancers, German brass bands, Japanese karate athletes, Ramallah rap groups and more. The festival revelers are made up of Palestinians from near and afar, a battalion of foreign diplomats, aid workers and journalists, tourists, and a handful of Israelis keen to experience a different Palestine to the one in their newspapers. Palestinian food is served and local community organizations promote their honey, handicrafts, and olive oil. But let's not kid ourselves: it is all about the beer.

Taybeh's restored old city

[5.1-6.6km/3.1-4.1 mi.] 270m (0.16 mi.) after the S-curve, and just 20m (21 yards) before meeting a clear dirt road junction to the L, a smaller dirt road veers off into the olive fields to the R (N): take this road to the R and continue to follow it as it climbs towards Jabal Abu Souf (❺). Two forks in this road follow: keep L at both of them. After 6.6km (4.1 mi.) you have reached Jabal Abu Souf: to climb to its peak underneath the pine trees take the dirt road up on your R. A black marked trail takes you in a circle around the hilltop with wonderful views all around, including Jordan's

Rift Mountains (on a clear day). On weekends you can find families from Taybeh enjoying the shade underneath the trees with a picnic or a barbeque.

[6.6-8.4km/4.1-5.2 mi.] From Jabal Abu Souf, walk down on the same road you climbed up and then continue your way back to Taybeh village by turning R at the first junction and then follow this road into the village (❻). Once in the village and just prior to reaching the main Taybeh road at the Latin Secondary School, a small side road veers up on the L: take this road which will take you to the ruins of the Byzantine al-Khader (St. George) Church. The scenery over the valley to the E of the church is wonderful and it gives you a good overview of the hike you have just been doing. Turn R after the church and R again on the main road. You pass the Latin Convent and the entrance to Taybeh's old city center (L), which is located on the village highest point and has been beautifully restored in recent years. It is well worth a small detour if you are still up for it. To get back to the brewery, simply follow the main road until you reach the roundabout where you turn L.

A curious herd near Taybeh

Logistics and Guides

The Taybeh Brewery is opened 8:00-16:00 Monday-Saturday and staff will gladly give you a tour: 02-2898868 and taybeh@palnet.com. Guided tours for the walk can be arranged by contacting (preferably a few days in advance) the brewery or George Mashriqi (0597-267086). Prices for groups are approximately 250 NIS.

How to Get There

Car: From Jerusalem/Ramallah, it is a 30/25 minute drive to Taybeh. From Jerusalem, drive N on Rd 60.

PEOPLE & PLACES

"Taybeh is my favorite place because it's a small quiet town and when walking down the street your hand is always in the air saying hello to every person you pass. Anyone visiting Taybeh just feels right at home because the town and the people give you that sense of belonging no matter who you are and where you're from in the world."

—Madees Khoury, beer brewer, Taybeh

Pass Jaba junction and take the signposted turn-off towards Rimonim settlement (green) and Taybeh (spelled Tayibe—white) on your R (this is Rd 457). Subsequently, turn L at the so-called Rimonim Junction (4-way junction). Once in the village, continue on the main road until you reach a small roundabout: turn L at this roundabout (the brewery is signposted) to reach the brewery after 150m (164 yards). From Ramallah, the fastest connection is normally via Beitin and Rammun (road blocked at time of writing); an alternative is via Ain Yabrud and Deer Jreer or via Jaba (as above).

Public transportation: via Ramallah; catch a ford to Taybeh via Deer Jreer.

Where to Park

Visitors can normally park inside the brewery grounds; however, inform the brewery staff about this upon your arrival. If you like a brewery tour after your hike, it is good to tell in advance. Parking in the village is also safe.

Eat, Drink, Relax

The brewery has no bar but you do get a complimentary beer with the tour. For a proper meal visit the **Taybeh Zamaan Restaurant** which is located at the edge of the village on the road to Rammun; call Khaldoun (0599-774092 or 02-2899411).

Overnight

Lodging options in Taybeh include the **Beit Efram Guesthouse** which is unpretentious, modern and clean and has 15 rooms with 1-4 beds and ensuite bathroom: NIS 80-120 pppn incl. breakfast; dinner can be ordered and guests can also use the kitchen. It is located on the road to Rammun. For details, contact Father Raed: Taybeh@lpj.org, 02-289 8020. **The Charles de Foucauld Pilgrim's Hostel** in the Latin Convent is another option. It has 13 small and basic rooms catering mostly to pilgrims: 80 NIS pppn incl. breakfast (the hostel is closed from Dec to Feb). Contact Sister Marie Martine, scjtaybe@palnet.com, 02-289 9364 (fax and phone). When this book went into print, the Khoury family, also owners of the brewery, was building Taybeh's first hotel.

Façade of St. George Church

Taybeh's view on Jabal
Abu Souf

Places to Go, People to Meet

Palestine's most famous festival, the **Taybeh Oktoberfest**, is held for two days in September or October every
year (check the website for updates). Apart from the
Taybeh Brewery, a site much worth visiting in town
is the 4th century ruins of the Byzantine **St. George
Church**. The three still functioning churches in the
village are Greek Orthodox (old city), Greek Catholic
(opposite St. George Church) and the Latin (Roman
Catholic) Church (part of the Latin Convent on Taybeh's
main road). In the Latin Convent, you can also visit the
Parables House, an example of a traditional Palestinian
home. Elevated just above the main road, the restored
Old City of Taybeh is great to walk through. The craft
workshop of the **Olive Branch Foundation** produces
and sells oil lamps, candles, olive oil, olive soap and
more. Daoud Nasser (054-5523549) runs an antique
floor tile workshop at the edge of town.

On the Web

www.taybehmunicipality.org
www.taybeh.info
www.taybehbeer.com

رأس كركر Ras Karkar:
A Sheik with a View

Once this quiet village commanded regional power.
What remains is its grand Ottoman castle, spectacular
views and the scenic surroundings of ancient springs
and mysterious ruins.

A short drive into the hills west of Ramallah, the
small village of Ras Karkar stands out because of its
peculiar shape. The top of the village seems to barely
hang onto the steep slopes it is built upon. At its peak
stands the **Qal'at Ibn Samhan**, the 240 year old castle
built in Ottoman times and once the hallmark of power in the area. A tour of the castle provides expansive
views from its top floor and is highly recommended in
combination with the walk.

Smiles in Ras Karkar

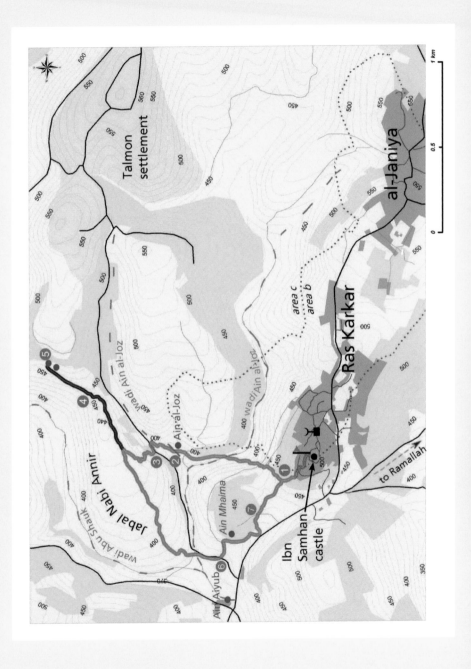

17. Noble Grounds:
Ras Karkar to Jabal Nabi Annir

The Ibn Samhan castle is located at the very top of the village with its entrance on the N side. The trail runs from here, down into wadi Ain al-Joz, climbing Jabal Nabi Annir and then circles back down to the wadi and up the steep slopes of Ras Karkar. Though the walk is short in distance, the trail does involve quite some climbing and small single track paths.

Trail: Ras Karkar > Jabal Nabi Annir > Ras Karkar

Grade: Moderate

Surface: Dirt roads and single track

Marked: Planned

Distance and Duration: 5.4 kms / 3.3 miles; 2–2.5 hrs

Elevation Change: 250m ascent / 250m descent

Start Coordinates: N31 56.630 E35 06.203

[0m-180m/0-0.1 mi.] Facing the entrance to the castle, turn L into a small alleyway; descend down the stairs until a small path veers off to the R. Take this path which continues downwards until you meet the road. Turn L here and walk for about 100m (109 yards) until another set of narrow stairs appears on the R in between a couple of houses. Take the second set of stairs. Follow the trail down here as it reaches the outer edge of Ras Karkar with a splendid view over the wadi and hills to its N. To the L side the trail continues on a single track that squeezes through a set of large rocks.

[180m-800m/0.1-0.5 mi.] From here, the trail runs sharply down the hill. The military purpose of building Qal'at Ibn Samhan (Ibn Samhan Castle) on this hill becomes clear as you negotiate your way down; its steep slopes make it very difficult to attack from any side. Faded green (Israeli) markings of a previous trail can still be seen here. !! After some 200m (0.12 mi.), you reach a plateau in between the rocks above and the olive terraces below. (❶) Here the trail splits but not very visibly however: keep R and walk down towards the lovely wadi Ain al-Joz below. You pass a large gray shoebox-shaped building: keep L and as you

The Ibn Samhan castle

reach another dirt road, keep L again and immediately take R onto an old single track path that zigzags further down the hill towards the wadi bed.

[800m-1.3km/0.5-0.8 mi.] Once you reach the wadi bed amidst the olive groves, cross over it and continue the single track trail on the other side. Coming across another dirt road turn R and almost immediately L to reach the Ain al-Joz spring (❷). The spring flows year round and is used for irrigating the orchards in the surroundings. Passing the spring, continue N along the trail which runs past the old stone walls of the spring's orchard (pears, apple, and raspberries grow here). The trail passes an abandoned building, follows the wadi bed to the NE and then starts running parallel to the paved road above, eventually climbing up to it.

[1.3-2.4km/0.8-1.5 mi.] !! Once the trail reaches the paved road (which runs towards the Talmon settlement to the R), turn L and walk along the paved road for 70m (76 yards) until you notice a path on the R climbing steeply from the road onto the hill (❸). Climb up here and follow the trail upwards as it climbs Jabal al-Nabi Annir. The small trail zigzags up the hill. After some twists and turns you reach the plateau of the hill which is crossed by a dirt road. While the trail turns L here (following the dirt road to circle back to Ras Karkar), you would not have climbed this far to miss the ruins of Jabal al-Nabi Annir and the

The Throne and the Castle

Entering the small village of Ras Karkar, it is the size of Qal'at Ibn Samhan that stands out most. The castle has three floors, numerous larger and smaller rooms and a spacious courtyard at its center. At the top of the castle, the sheik's private quarters hold phenomenal views over the surroundings and the Mediterranean is easily visible on a clear day. It was under Ottoman rule that Ras Karkar (then called Ras Ibn Samhan) gained the status of throne village, a system by which Istanbul decentralized authority to local sheikhs across its large empire. The title of throne village gave the ruling family large powers, in particular in tax collection. The thick walls and the steep slopes on which the castle is built are testimony to the rivalries that existed between the various throne villages, with the two main Arab tribes controlling them, the Qaisis and the Yemenis, in regular conflict. The castle's 18th century founder, Sheikh Ismail Ibn Samhan (Qaisi), was killed by the Yemeni family from the rivaling Abu Gosh throne village. After Ottoman times, the castle fell into disuse. In recent years, with Dutch and German sponsorship, the Palestinian NGO Riwaq helped save the castle from slowly falling into ruin. The Samhan family, who are still the owners, have since then stepped up efforts to use the castle for cultural events. Among the special occasions is the regional **Sounding Jerusalem Festival** which takes place in summer every year and brings classical musicians to perform in the castle's courtyard (www.soundingjerusalem.com).

Samhan springs. To see these, turn R on the dirt road. After some 300m (0.18 mi.), you will notice some ruins to the L. The main road continues L and a smaller dirt road veers off to the R. Take the latter road and after 100m (109 yards) you will find the main ruins amidst centuries old oak trees, including the impressive remains of a mosque (❹). The origins of the site are mixed with Hellenistic, Roman, Byzantine, Umayyad and Ottoman infleunces. Archeological surveys have been conducted here around terraces, ancient oil and wine presses, burial caves and several buildings on Jabal al-Nabi Annir. To reach the Samhan springs (❺) continue for another 400m (0.24 mi.) on the wide dirt road that runs directly behind the mosque ruins. The road quickly turns into an old single track path passing two pools before reaching the Samhan spring. Near the spring you pass grape vines and fig trees; the outskirts of the village of Deir Ammar located high up the next ridge to the N can be seen to your L.

[2.4-4.2km/1.5-2.6 mi.] To complete the walk, retrace your steps from the springs, pass the ruins and follow the dirt road you walked on earlier. The dirt road gradually runs over Jabal al-Nabi Annir amidst the olive groves in the direction of Ras Karkar (SW). Once you reach the valley, turn R onto the paved road but only for 130m (142 yards) when you turn L onto another dirt road (❻).

A crab near the Samhan springs

[4.2-5.4km/2.6-3.3 mi.] !! Follow this road for 120m (131 yards) until after a bend to the L you find a small single track veering off to the R. This track passes the Ain Mhaima spring located in an orchard underneath giant rock formations. Pass the spring and continue along the trail as it starts climbing up the rocky slopes in the direction of the main road that leads to Ras Karkar. While coming close, you don't connect with

the main road to Ras Karkar. Instead, you follow an old winding path that starts to your L and approaches the village as it climbs the hills in between impressive large stone walls. You cross over a small private road (running towards a Palestinian house) along the way (❼); keep straight and follow the old path. At 5km (3.1 mi.) onto the trail you reach the point of the first split just below the village; keep climbing up until you reconnect with the path running in between the houses at the edge of the village. The castle is located slightly above these houses to the L.

Farmer in Wadi Ain al-Joz

Logistics and Guides

To arrange a visit to the castle and a guide for the
walk, contact PACE at 02-2407611, pace@p-ol.com, or
the Samhan family in Ras Karkar: Zaghloul Samhan
(0599-264225) or Mohammed Yousef Samhan (0599-
353665). Guided tours for groups of 5 or more cost
around 180 NIS pp through PACE and include lunch.

Ruins on Jabal Nabi Annir
(*left*)

How to Get There

From Jerusalem/Ramallah, it is a 50/30 min drive to
Ras Karkar. From Jerusalem, drive on Rd 443 in the
direction of Tel Aviv. After Modiin CP turn R at the
second traffic lights. Continue straight until you pass a
small CP. 3km (1.8 mi.) after the CP you come across
a small roundabout: turn R here. The roads meanders
past Nili and Naale settlements until you reach an
odd-shaped junction: continue straight. The road will
climb a steep hill. At the top of the hill turn L into Ras
Karkar. Once in the village, follow the main road and
take the second turn-off to the L. The road circles up
to the very top of the village where Ibn Samhan castle
is located. From Ramallah, the easiest route is via
Betuniya (W of Ramallah), then through the villages
of Ain Arik and Deir Ibzi', and then following Rd 455
(which connects the settlements of Dolev and Modiin
Ilit) in W direction until a sharp turnoff on your R
leads into Ras Karkar.

Where to Park

You can park on the road which leads to the castle.

Eat, Drink, Relax

The closest restaurants are located in the nearby village of Ain Arik at the main road to Ramallah and are
opened daily: the **Falaaha Restaurant** (02-2905124 and
0599-842042) has specialized in the famous Palestinian dish *musakhan* for over 16 years; across from it,

Overlooking Wadi
Ain al-Joz

the name of the **Ain Arik Barbeque Restaurant** (02-2905205 and 0599-719481) speaks for itself. Alcohol is served in both places.

Overnight

PACE can organize homestays with Palestinian families for 140 NIS pppn including dinner. The closest regular lodging options to Ras Karkar are in Ramallah and Jifna (see the Ramallah chapter).

Places to Go, People to Meet

There is not much else to visit in Ras Karkar apart from the worthwhile **Samhan Castle**. Attending a courtyard concert of the **Sounding Jerusalem Festival** is a special experience; the festival usually takes place in June/July. At the time of writing, a small museum was planned for to be located next to the castle.

On the Web

www.pace.ps
www.soundingjerusalem.com

رام الله Ramallah: Walking through Oslo

From a sleepy mid-sized town, Ramallah has grown into the bustling heart of Palestinian culture and commerce. Venturing away from it is a journey from urban to rural, from hectic to scenic and from present to past. No Palestinian would forsake Jerusalem as their national heart and soul and future capital. Yet Ramallah (meaning Height of God) harbors its free mind and spirit. Ramallah's rapid expansion has been underway for a while. From a second-tier place for business, the Oslo Agreements first started to tip the balance in the mid-nineties and wealth once located in places such as Bethlehem, Gaza or Jerusalem was diverted towards the city. With the establishment of the Palestinian Authority and Ramallah as its administrative center, new government ministries were established.

Pretty yet thorny; thistles near Jifna

Even if the situation of internal movement has improved across the entire West Bank, Ramallah remains its central hub and a refuge for those with cash to spare. The city also hosts a battalion of local NGOs and foreign aid agencies. In recent years the boom has crept into the night-life of the city: new restaurants and cafes open frequently, new hotels are being built and as a small Beirut, Ramallah today has a number of venues catering for good music and dancing. In the coolest places across town, an art movement calling itself Ramallah Syndrome has put up white canvasses with uneasy questions aimed at a new generation of well-to-do Palestinians: one reads *Am I resisting by enjoying my life in Ramallah?*; and another *Is Ramallah the capital?*

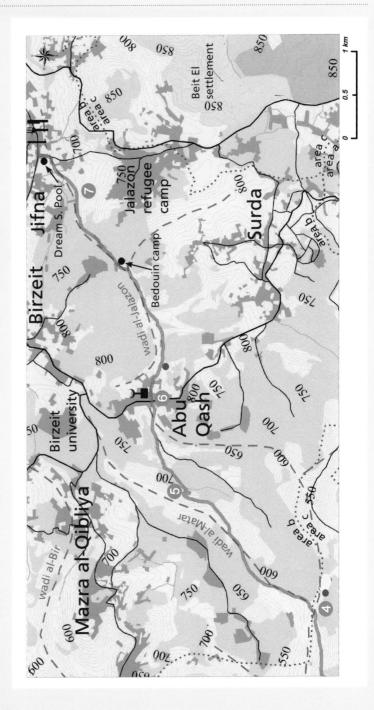

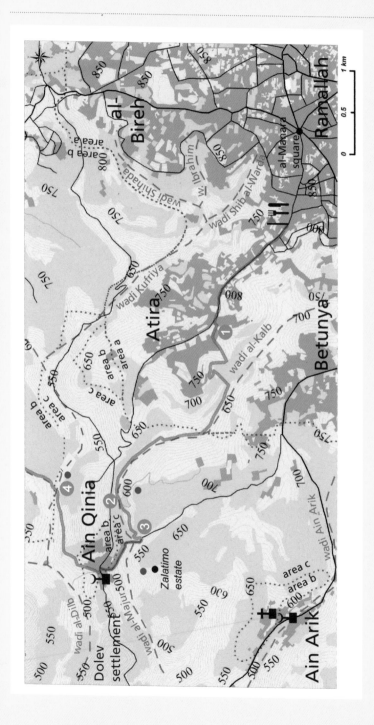

18. City Escape: Ramallah to Jifna

A walk starting in Ramallah is not too obvious as the city continues to expand in every direction possible, cramping its building frenzy against the boundaries of area C. Fortunately, some options remain to escape city life and walk through the quiet hills and valleys of its surroundings. This scenic and long walk across Ramallah's surroundings starts with a walk along the upmarket Atira area; then descends through the wadi to the tiny old village of Ain Qinia before resuming through the countryside to Abu Qash and ultimately Jifna. Before starting, walkers can prepare for the day in uptown fashion and treat themselves to an early morning espresso at Café Zamn, Arabic for time. Note that the return to Zamn is by taxi or through public transport.

Trail: Ramallah > Jifna

Grade: Hard

Surface: Single track and dirt roads; minor sections paved road

Marked: No

Distance and Duration: 15.4 kms / 9.5 miles; 4–6 hrs

Elevation Change: 375m ascent / 550m descent

Start Coordinates: N31 54.382 E35 11.540

[0m-2.9km/0-1.8 mi.] From Zamn Café start walking away from the city center (in NW direction) following the main artery of Atira, al-Teereh Street. The road has convenient sidewalks and is part of the latest trend to assign street names to Ramallah's more uptown areas (in both Arabic and English). You follow the road for 1.6km (1 mi.), first passing the youth center of the First Ramallah Group, later the Chinese Embassy, and along the road a variety of pretty side streets with upmarket apartment complexes. In between the built-up areas, you have good views over the hills of Betuniya to the L (SW) and al-Bireh to the R (NE) which have grown with equal intensity over the last decade. Having passed the al-Huda gas station, you see the al-Mustaqbal (the Future) school to your L (❶). Leave al-Teereh Street here and pass through the parallel side street of the school. Take the first street on your L after passing the school. Follow the road running down the hill until it sharply bends R. Continue to

follow the road. The street ends near an old *qasr*. At
the *qasr*, you have a good view over Wadi al-Kalb (Wadi
of the Dog) to the E and on the opposite hill the village
of Betuniya. A century ago this wadi used to be filled
with grapes until a disease destroyed all vines; now it
is a mixture of olive terraces and more wild growth on
its steeper sections as well as various *qasrs*. A few meters below the *qasr* you can spot fossils of ancient coral
reefs on the rocks that make up the terraces. !! From
this *qasr* you will descend all the way to the wadi bed.
There will be no clear path, which means you have to
gradually climb down the slope. An easy way to
descend is to follow the terrace from the *qasr* towards
the L until you reach a gully in the slope of the hill.
From here a descent is easily managed.

Ramallah's uptown: street
names are the norm

[2.9-4.8km/1.8-2.9 mi.] Once in the bottom of the
wadi bed, take a R and follow the wadi bed as it trails
towards Ain Qinia. After about 1km (0.62 mi.) in the
wadi bed, a dirt road veers off from the wadi bed to the
R and continues to run parallel to it between the olive
trees. When you get close to the paved road connecting Ramallah to Ain Qinia continue walking on the
dirt road which runs a few m below the paved road.

[4.8–5.8km/2.9-3.6 mi.] At 4.8km (2.9 mi.), the dirt
road crosses the wadi bed from the R to the L side (❷)
and starts to climb the hill gradually. !! 300m (0.18
mi.) after this point and just as the dirt road starts
climbing more steeply up the hill, a smaller and more
overgrown dirt road veers off to the R. Take this road
which descends slightly and continues to run above
the wadi (the main dirt road zigzags up the hill back
to Ramallah). The smaller dirt road eventually turns
into a single track running between the olive trees
from where Ain Qinia village becomes visible. Straight
ahead and across the hill from Ain Qinia you can

The sea in Ramallah: coral reef fossils

make out the Zalatimo estate as it lies between large pine, cypress and oak trees. Continue to walk in the same direction. Even if the single track becomes momentarily unclear, you quickly pick up a herder's path. Follow it downwards and make your way towards the small paved road connecting Betuniya and Ain Qinia. On your way down you pass a set of large rocks, olive and almond trees.

[5.8-7.9km/3.6-4.9 mi.] As you reach the small paved road (**❸**) in the wadi below, turn R towards Ain Qinia village. Passing the signposting for the village, the road veers L and climbs up towards the center of the village (6.5 km/4 mi.). Reaching the main road, you find the Salaam minimarket on your R, a good place for small refreshments. To continue the walk, turn L on the main road and after 70m (76 yards) turn R at the town's main junction and R again at the split in the road that immediately follows it (do not take the road that descends to the L steeply into the wadi). The paved road you are on leaves Ain Qinia, passing its cemetery. As the road winds E into the wadi you pass olive terraces, fruit trees and fields of vegetables. You then pass a Bedouin camp at the bottom of this wadi (**❹**).

[7.9-11.5km/4.9-7.1 mi.] At the camp, make sure you turn L at the only junction here, crossing over the wadi bed and following the single track trail that runs up the next wadi. For the next 1km (0.62 mi.) you continue to follow the single track trail in this very quiet wadi. A few *qasrs* are dotted across the slopes to your L. The trail crosses back and forth over the wadi bed until, at 9.4km (5.8 mi.) into the hike, it runs in between two lines of olive trees. Straight after the olive trees a smaller but well used single track trails starts zigzagging up the R side of the wadi (**❺**). Follow this track as it rises above the olive trees. From this point

Round *qasr* in Wadi al-Kalb

A Farmer's Castle

They are as much part of the Palestinian landscape as the olive and fruit trees that surround them: the *qasr* and the *burj*, literally translated castle and tower. In the midst of a walk they appear as sudden stone giants, elegantly erected along the elongated agricultural terraces that look over the wadis of the West Bank. They were built by Palestinian farmers generations ago, the result of hand work (no cement was used) and the laborious process of matching larger and smaller pieces of rock. The solid round structures of the *burj* were traditionally used as watch tower by farmers guarding their land; a few meters high, they are usually located at elevated places where large swaths of land can be easily overseen. The *qasr* is a more sophisticated structure, often two levels high with internal staircases all the way to the roof. *Qasrs* were used as temporary overnight shelters by farmers during periods of intensive farm work. They also provided shelter to animals such as donkeys and provided storage space for harvests. While in some places wild plants shoot from the crevices in between their ruins, some of the *qasrs* remain remarkably intact and they are worth exploring on the inside. Where they stand amidst thickets of wild growth and on long-abandoned terraces they remind of times when the surrounding land was cultivated by its owners.

you can see the large campus of Birzeit University to the N at the far edge of the wadi. After 9.8km (6 mi.) into the walk the single track reaches a dirt road: take a L here and continue to climb up. Take another L at the next junction and follow the dirt road as it becomes the paved road to Abu Qash. Before you enter the village you pass a set of ruins and ancient walls. You have a good view of Ramallah to the R (SE). Keep L following the paved road as it runs down and then up to reach Abu Qash village.

[11.5-14.5km/7.1-9 mi.] As you reach the main road running from Birzeit to Ramallah through Abu Qash (❻), the trail continues straight ahead (hence: simply cross the main road). If you would like to buy some refreshments, there are shops along the main road (to your L). As you continue on the trail you pass the old mosque of Abu Qash, a few of the village's big villas and a girls school. The road descends until it leaves the village behind and enters the valley between Abu Qash and Jifna. Grapes grow here and wheat is planted to make use of an area that is relatively even-leveled. The road turns into a dirt road. At a split in the road, keep L and continue to descend into the valley. Located at a similar elevation as the rocks in Atira, you can also find coral reef fossils here on the rocks scattered across the valley. In the center of the wadi you pass another large Bedouin camp; continue to follow the dirt road straight ahead as it reaches the edges of Jifna.

[14.5-15.4km/9-9.5 mi.] The last stretch to Jifna village is through an olive field (❼). The contrast between Jifna and the Jalazoun refugee camp perched on the hill to the R could not be larger. Jifna is spaciously laid out with one and two story houses, churches and a mosque surrounded by farm land. With a population of just below 2000 it has a total land area of 6000

Passing through Wadi al-Kalb

The ABC of Walking Palestine

ACBCB is probably the briefest summary of the long walk from Ramallah to Jifna. You could call this its Oslo Code. It inspires a cryptic invitation: We're walking "ACBCB" today: would you like to come along? Many Palestinian walks can attain a unique code in this fashion. From Hizma to Jericho: BCA; the circle around Taybeh: BCB; the walk through Aboud: CBCBC. There are also simpler grades of Oslo Code: A for Canaan to Jabal al-Baared; C for Ain Samia to Ain Auja. And the list goes on.

A, B and C is the land nomenclature inherited from the 1993 Oslo Accords and detailed in the 1995 Interim Agreements agreed between Israel and the Palestine Liberation Organization (PLO). The division of Palestinian and Israeli control across areas A, B and C is a complex affair. Initially, it was meant to cover only a transitional period of 5 years after which a final peace agreement should

have been reached. But for better and mostly worse, it is still in place in the absence of a final agreement. In area A, the Palestinian Authority (PA) is in charge of civilian matters and security; in area B, civilian issues also fall under the PA and some security, but Israel has end responsibility for the latter; in area C, Israel is fully in charge of everything except for the provision of basic services to Palestinians living there (which again falls under the PA). All large Palestinian cities are A; most Palestinian villages are in B; and in C lies a combination of Palestinian agricultural land, some Palestinian villages and all Israeli settlements, roads connecting the settlements and military bases.

Immediately after the Oslo Accords, the land division had little influence over people's freedom of movement. But this gradually changed and since the outbreak of the Second Intifada in 2000 restrictions have been raised: by Israeli military order Israeli

citizens are not allowed into area A (where many visited for shopping and leisure prior to 2000); red warning signs in Hebrew mark the entrance to A and sometimes B. Palestinians often have to pass through checkpoints moving through area C by car or public transportation. In the last few years, some of these restrictions were relaxed and some Israelis have gone back to visit area A although formally the military order is still in place.

Of all the land in the West Bank, 60% is area C. Although much of it is registered as under private ownership of Palestinians, the possibilities to use area C land are very limited. Any water, electricity or road network that passes through C requires prior agreement from Israel. Permission to build houses in C is exceptionally rare and those who build without permission risk the demolition of their new home. For Palestinians, the ABC division is among the strongest symbols of occupation. Together with the checkpoints located in between A and B areas, the restrictions in C also impact most harshly on their daily lives. The PA has long demanded that control over more land be transferred to them. Israel sees the issue as one of final status, a matter that should be resolved by a peace agreement with agreed final borders. The Interim Agreements signed between the two sides include provisions to gradually handover C land to B and B land to A, hence from Israeli to Palestinian control. Yet no such handovers have been agreed to in the past 10 years and not all those agreed prior have been fully implemented. Much of the ABC of the Israeli-Palestinian conflict is thus literally the ABC of land designation. Status changes for even small bits of land usually get mired into the larger political wrangling.

On a walk into the countryside the exact division into A, B and C land is not visible at first sight. There are no signs where B ends and C starts for example and given the archipelago style carve-up of the West Bank it would be quite impossible to put down notices in all places anyway. And yet there are various good indicators of where you are: where building activity takes place, you are almost surely walking in A or B; where land lies fallow, is used for agriculture only, or where half finished buildings or roads lie abandoned, you are most likely wandering through C. Similarly, you are in C when close to Israeli settlements or when you meet one of the larger roads passing through the West Bank.

The Ramallah-Jifna walk is a good example. Because building in C is hardly possible, building in A and B is all the more frantic. Early in the walk you pass the luxury but high rise built-up areas of Atira, clearly a part of Ramallah's area A. Not before long this walk could have started from the edge of the city center and go straight into Wadi al-Kalb. But construction here has already moved down to the lowest part of the wadi bed (also A) making it an unattractive route. The construction has damaged the ancient character of the wadi with its terraces, old qasrs, and springs; it has also been environmentally harmful as new buildings and roads block the scarce flow of water down to the rest of the wadi. One could argue that if it was not for area C taking on the role of buffer zone, harmful large-scale construction would be rampant throughout the Palestinian landscape. But that argument ignores the difficult planning environment that Palestinian local councils face due to the scarcity of land. With only a fraction of the land available to build and with land prices doubling on a yearly basis in the past years, the pressure to use the land remaining in A and B keeps mounting. With more land available, a better balance between the urban and the rural could be struck.

Further north in Atira the trail reconnects to a steep part of the wadi which is still intact. Down in the wadi bed the trail crosses into area C, a stretch filled with olive terraces and old *qasrs*, before entering Ain Qinia. The village is located next to the settlement of Dolev and is a typical example of a village whose area B borders have been drawn very tightly around the existing build-up areas. Even though the people in the village own much of the land around it they cannot expand the village boundaries. The alternatives here are to build on top of existing structures or to move residence into the conglomerate of Ramallah. Despite its high prices, Ramallah remains a magnet for Palestinians living in area B villages: it falls entirely under Palestinian control and its residents are less affected by checkpoints placed in between villages and urban areas.

Continuing further through the wadi north of Ain Qinia, the trail moves from B into C again and passes a Bedouin camp in the wadi bed. Their nomadic lifestyle of periodically changing location predates the Oslo Accords by a few thousand years, and with few other places to go, Bedouin mostly set up their camps in the remote corners of area C where their livestock can still access grazing land and water. Occasionally, these camps are demolished by Israeli authorities leading to displacements of the families. The break down of the camps is done on grounds that the Bedouin hold no permission to build in area C. Yet they have little alternative than to look for the few remote corners where they can still move: in many instances, these lie in C once again.

The trail then continues northwards into area B towards the village of Abu Qash and later Jifna. New Palestinian building projects can be seen at the top of either side of the wadi's steep slopes. Here, on the hills between Birzeit, Abu Qash and Surda, the land in B is actually an expansive stretch where there remains some space for planning urban development. The beautiful wadis around these villages have been left mostly untouched to date. For walkers, hopefully that remains so.

Ruins in area C

A herd sheep and goats near Abu Qash

dunams. Jalazon nowadays has a population of around 9000 and is built on just 253 dunams of land. Just before entering Jifna village you reconnect with the paved road. Continue straight on the first 4-way junction and turn L at the 2nd 4-way junction. You pass the Dream Restauarant and Swimming Pool before reaching Jifna's main road. This is the end of the walk. Most of Jifna's main restaurants are located to your R on the main road.

· ·

Logistics and Guides

For transport from Jifna back to Ramallah take one of the standard minibuses (4 NIS) or order a taxi from Birzeit (+- 35 NIS to Atira): Taxi Zeitoun (02-2817777); or Taxi Sahed (02-2811411). A tour of Jifna can be organized by PACE (02-2407611). For updates on other local guiding options, check www.walkingpalestine.org.

How to Get There

Car: From Jerusalem, it is a 30-40 minute drive to Atira in Ramallah. Pass the Qalandia CP and continue straight for the next 5.5km (3.4 mi.) on the main al-Bireh-Jerusalem rd. After passing the al-Bireh municipality, you come to a 4-way junction: turn L here towards al-Manarah square. At the al-Manarah roundabout take the 3rd turn-off (R) and continue straight for another 1km (0.62 mi.). Zamn Café is located on a corner on the R side of al-Teereh street and opposite the First Ramallah Group (Sarayet Ramallah).

Public transportation: via Ramallah and private taxi or ford to Atira.

Where to Park

You can park in the side street next to Zamn Café.

Eat, Drink, Relax

Ramallah's **Zamn Café** is opened daily between 7:00 am and midnight. Jifna traditionally has some of the best grill restaurants in the Ramallah area: **Tabash** (02-2810932), **al-Basha** (0599-609050), and **Laylet al-Farah** (0599-787767) are all located along Jifna's main road; they all serve alcohol. Entry to the Dream swimming pool (just off the main road, close to the restaurants) costs 35 NIS (02-2811548) and you can also eat there.

Caffeine before the walk in Ramallah's Zamn Café

Overnight

Jifna has two charming guesthouses: the **Khouriya Family Guest House**: 130 NIS pppn incl. breakfast; 02-2811485, 0599587476, rkhouriya@yahoo.com; and the **Reef House Pension**: 75-100 NIS pppn incl. breakfast; 02-2810881, 0599-266499, reefpension@gmail.com. There is a large number of hotels in Ramallah, most of them catering to business customers but with some budget options: www.palestinehotels.com.

Ramallah nightlife

Places to Go, People to Meet

Ramallah is the West Bank's bustling capital; yet without many sites developed for tourism. Hanging out is the best way to enjoy the city and breathe in its atmosphere, for example around the busy **al-Manara square**, the nearby **souq** and **the old city**. The monthly magazine *This Week in Palestine* offers a good overview of culture, cuisine and nightlife in the city. Jifna is an important historic town lying on old trade routes that go back to Roman and Byzantine times, but the village was important in the crusader period as well. The old city of Jifna and its churches are worth exploring. Famous for its tasty apricots, Jifna hosts the 2-day **Apricot Festival** in early May. Birzeit is another nearby option worth visiting (see the Birzeit chapter).

On the Web

www.thisweekinpalestine.com
www.firstramallahgroup.com
www.jifnadream.com

وادي القلط Wadi Qelt: Metamorphosis

From the dense heights of Jerusalem to the tranquility of the Jericho oasis, walkers cut through some of the most spectacular and varied scenery in the West Bank. An intense walk, rewarded with the leisure and slow pace of the world's oldest city.

Wadi Qelt is among the most varied walks one can do in Palestine. Amidst the limestone cliffs, the wadi has abundant wildlife—and especially bird life—year-round, pink oleanders and other flowers flourishing on its springs, and pools with fish, crabs, frogs and hovering dragon flies. It is not all wilderness, however: there are traces of civilization stretching back at least two millennia with ancient caves and hermit cells, archeological ruins, aquaducts and the Monastery of St. George perched on the cliffs near Jericho. You will likely come across Bedouins, either near the Qelt spring or elsewhere as their large herds of goats and sheep venture along the slopes above the wadi. These encounters continue all the way down to Jericho, some 850m (2,788 ft.) below the wadi's starting point just outside Jerusalem.

Walking any of the two trails described in this chapter requires a good level of fitness and some experience with scrambling up and down rocks. However, shorter and easier options are available as well (see the section on Wadi Qelt in three ways). In the winter season, be aware of flash floods that can occur during or after heavy rains. Year round, make sure you bring plenty of water and enough to eat along the way. If you like to visit the Chariton or St. George monasteries, make sure you wear or carry clothing that covers legs and shoulders.

Water from Ain Qelt making its way to Jericho

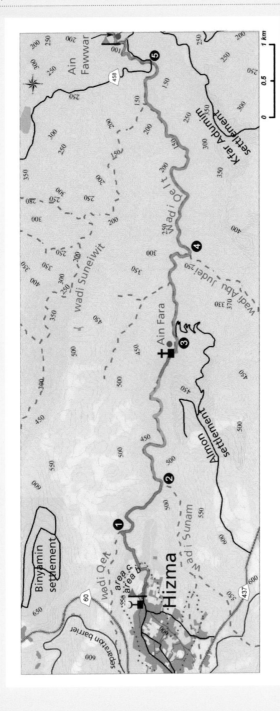

This trail is a bit shorter in distance as compared to the lower Wadi Qelt section but it is as demanding as it includes crossing water streams multiple times and scrambling over a variety of rock surfaces. The orientation for this section is straightforward as you follow the descent of Wadi Qelt in E direction. Note, however, that the first 2.5 km (1.5 mi.) of the trail are unmarked and that because of ongoing changes at the edge of Hizma some pathfinding might be required to make your initial descent into the wadi.

19. Rocky Scramble: Hizma to Ain Fawwar

Trail: Hizma to Ain Fawwar
(upper Wadi Qelt)

Grade: Hard

Surface: Single track (includes
scrambling)

Marked: Partially (fully from
Ain Fara onwards: red and
blue)

Distance and Duration: 11.5
km/7.1 miles; 4–6 hrs

Elevation Change: 200m
ascent / 700m descent

Start Coordinates:
N31 50.198 E35 16.115

[0-2.5km/0-1.5 mi.] From the square facing Hizma's mosque and cemetery, walk past the last houses of the village (E). The road quickly turns into a stony dirt road on which there are several deposits of quarried stones; follow the road downward. After 500m (0.31 mi.), the road splits: turn L and turn R at the split immidiately after: the road runs towards a set of pine trees; passing these, continue towards an olive grove beyond which you can see Wadi Qelt. !! Turn L at the olive grove and leave the dirt road (which meanders further up to the L). From here you start to walk down into the wadi: there is no path but the descent down a landscape full of large rocks is fairly easy and not steep (the direction you should maintain is that of the Adam settlement clearly visible on a ridge to the N of the wadi). Once you reach the bottom of the wadi bed (❶), turn R and continue in the wadi bed itself. The trail involves scrambling down small but steep dry waterfalls. Take care as these can be challenging (you can scramble around them as well; just make sure you stay close to the wadi bed). At 2.5km (1.5 mi.) into the walk, you reach a point where a second wadi, Wadi Sunam, joins from the R (S). !! You leave the wadi bed here (❷) by following a blue marked trail that runs from the bottom of Wadi Sunam up to the R side of Wadi Qelt. Blue markings (some fo them faded) cover the trail from here.

[2.5-5.4km/1.5-3.3 mi.] The trail gradually climbs some 50-70m (164-229 ft.) above the wadi bed. At 3.5km (2.1 mi.), below the settlement of Almon, the trail markers turn green (i.e. a green train trail coming from Almon joins your path). At 4.5 km (2.7 mi.),

An easy stretch beyond
Ain Fawwar

the green markers suddenly take a sharp R turn climbing up the hill. !! Do not follow green here, but instead continue straight past a wall and a set of ruins. From the ruins, you see the nature reserve around Fara spring. Continue to descend towards a group of olive trees and keep L untill 200m (0.12 mi.) after the ruins you come across a blue marked trail again: turn L here and zigzag your way down into the wadi passing a giant cave and the Chariton Monastery, which some believe is the first desert monastery established in the Holy Land around 330 AD. Its founder is the famous monk Chariton who also established the Mount of Temptation Monastery above Jericho. The monastery is now under the protection of the Russian Orthodox church and is sometimes open for visitors (call ahead for inquieries from Father Oleg; 052-5399075).

You have now reached Ain Fara (called En Prat by Israelis), location of the first of three main springs in Wadi Qelt, and the entry point for many visitors by car

(via the Almon settlement). Park rangers might ask
you to pay the standard entry fee applicable to visitors
(20 NIS). In Hasmonean (2nd century BC) and Roman times, an aquaduct started here and connected all
the way to Jericho, among others to King Herod's Winter Palace. The aquaduct would take in water at the
downstream Fawwar and Qelt springs along its way.
Many traces of the two millenia old aquaduct can still
be seen on the trail. If time allows it you can go for a
picnic, do some rock climbing, or buy a stiff espresso
at the small shop. You can also set up your own barbeque under the pine trees though the chance that you
brought one in your daypack will be pretty slim. Ain
Fara is one of the rare spots in the West Bank where
Palestinian and Israeli families and groups of friends
enjoy the outdoors in the same location. West Bank
Palestinians are in the minority though; it is difficult
for them to reach the reserve by car, although some
still come out. Saturdays are very busy at Ain Fara but
otherwise it is nature and not people dominating life
in the wadi.

[5.4-7.2km/3.3-4.4 mi.] To continue on the trail (still
blue), walk away from the park offices and shop (❸)
which once housed a British pumping station that
supplied Jerusalem with water from Ain Fara. Pass
the picnic area located in a eucalyptus grove next to the
wide road where cars can park. When you reach a split
where the paved road goes up and a dirt road veers L,
follow the latter. The trail markers are red from here for
the next km, following the wadi bed on its R side and
passing some natural rock pools. 1km (0.62 mi.) past
Ain Fara the trail splits in two with red following an
old water pipe onto the ridge of the wadi whereas blue
stays close to the wadi bed. Follow the blue trail which
is the more spectacular of the two. You pass through
large rock formations, crossing the wadi several times;

Directions in Jericho

while you can use stepping stones most of the time, you cannot always keep dry feet, especially in winter and spring. Apart from in the wadi bed itself, water can be seen and heard floating down the rocks to the R side of the wadi at several points. At 7.2 km (4.4 mi.) the path descends onto a plateau of smooth rock formations; you find a small, lovely waterfall here; a great spot for some rest and possibly a picnic (❹).

[7.2-11.5km/4.4-7.1 mi.] The blue trail is very well indicated in this section, with frequent markers. From the waterfall onwards you will need to scramble over rocks at various stages. At the more tricky points, iron bars firmed into the rocks will help you through. Another recurring feature are bushes of bamboo-like reeds of

Crossing the rock bridge
near Ain Qelt

up to 7m (22 ft.) tall; park authorities usually do good
upkeep on the trail, however, so you should be able to
pass underneath various tunnels of reeds. !! At 9.7km
(6 mi.), the blue trail veers up some 50m (164 ft.) above
the wadi bed on the R side. You walk over old traces
of the Roman aquaduct here. The trail then descends
again and merges with the red trail coming from the
other (L) bank. You continue on red from here. At
10.7km (6.6 mi.) you come across Rd 458 (paved) (**❺**),
which you cross. Follow the red markers for another
700m (0.43 mi.) before you reach Ain Fawwar. To
return to Hizma, you need a pick-up from Ain Fawwar. Note that cars cannot reach the actual entry to the
spring but there is a parking lot (signposted En Mabo'a)
300m (0.18 mi.) to the R from the entrance.

Wadi Qelt in Three Ways

A walk through Wadi Qelt can be the most challenging hike you ever do in Palestine or it can literally be a "walk in the park." You decide which type of walking attracts you most.

The walk in the park. If you like to enjoy some of the beauty of the wadi but want to keep the time and effort limited and under your control you can drive up to one of the two entrances that allow for cars to be parked near the wadi bed and start an out-and-back hike from there. As for the walking trail, simply follow the colored markings and retrace your steps to the starting point from a self-selected "halfway" point along the trail. The entry point of Ain Fara (indicated as En Prat on Israeli road signs), located underneath the settlement of Almon, is by far the busiest (especially on Saturdays) but also has facilities such as toilets, picnic tables, a small (coffee) shop and a number of climbing routes on nearby rock walls. There are also a

few natural pools suitable year-round for a refreshing dip. The area is particularly suited if you are bringing children. Opening hours are 8 AM-5 PM April-September and 8 AM-4PM October-March (call 02-5715859 for inquiries). The Ain Fawwar entry is located on Road 458 and is much more quiet. Both sites are administered as Israeli Nature Reserves and while park rangers are present at both sites, an entry fee (child/adult 20/9 NIS) is only charged at Ain Fara.

Walking a part of the wadi. Walkers eager to go further into the wild should opt to walk one stretch of Wadi Qelt. There are various possibilities with different levels of time and effort. This guide cuts the entire wadi length into two, more or less, equal sections of 12-14 km (7.4-8.6 mi.) covering the upper wadi below Jerusalem and the lower wadi ending at Jericho. If you keep a reasonable pace both stretches will take

you between 4-6 hours (not including breaks). If you like to do a little less than this you can also cut these sections short in the following way:

**Ain Fara to
Ain Fawwar**
Duration: 3–5.5hrs

**Hills above
Ain Qelt to Jericho**
Duration: 3–4.5 hrs

**Ain Fawwar to
St. George Monastery**
Duration: 3–4.5 hrs

**Hills above Ain Qelt to
St. George Monastery**
Duration: 2–3 hrs

**St. George Monastery
to Jericho**
Duration: 1.5–2.5 hrs

Whatever you decide you need to arrange transport at the end point of your hike. In Jericho this is fairly easy to do through a local taxi, but on the other points mentioned it is wise to arrange it before-hand. Remember that mobile phone coverage is often patchy inside the wadi.

Wadi Qelt all the way. While a long haul, fit walkers will enjoy the experience of hiking Wadi Qelt all the way. The journey is 25km (15.5 mi.) long and the difference in elevation between start and end is a staggering 850 meters. To state the obvious, you need to be in very good shape to complete the full stretch in one go. If you are inexperienced in walking in the region you are strongly advised not to "just give it a try." Remember to take very large amounts of water, plenty of food and to rise early (a 6 AM start is advised). The journey takes between 9 and 12 hours.

How to get there? Except for Palestinian public trans-port to Hizma village there is no public transport to any of the following entry points to the wadi. If you do not have your own wheels, a private taxi is your only option. In addition to Hizma and Ain

Fawwar (see section How to Get There), the following are driving directions to the other entry points from Ramallah/ Jerusalem:

Ain Fara: drive towards Jer-icho on Rd 437 passing Hizma village; take the L turn-off towards Almon settlement; drive into the settlement (there is a guard who will ask you where you are going) and take the signposted turn-off towards the Ain Fara (Ein Prat) nature reserve; you pay the entry fee at another gate before you zigzag down a steep paved road towards the parking area.

Hills above Ain Qelt: drive towards Jericho on Rd 1 and take the L turn-off towards the Mitzpe Yeriho settlement (Wadi Qelt and St George Monastery are also signposted here); don't enter the settlement but turn L onto a paved road. About 800m (0.5 mi.) from the turn-off the road meets a T-junction. Turn L here onto a small road to reach the start of the trail towards Ain Qelt at an unpaved parking

lot 70m (76 yards) further (on the R). From the parkling lot visitors can climb up to a viewpoint over Wadi Qelt and the dessert. To the L of the viewpoint a black marked trail descends into the wadi on a dirt road for about 1.5 km (0.9 mi.) (4WD vehicles can handle this road all the way close to the wadi bed). It takes about 30-40 minutes to reach the wadi bed from the black trail, which then veers L towards Ain Qelt and its small waterfall (you pass the ruins of a large bridge that used to support an aquaduct, and a large Ottoman mansion now inhabited by Bedouin). From the spring another trail (red) runs towards the Monastery in E direction.

To reach St. George Monastery by car, drive as above but turn R on the T-junction. Continue on the winding paved road for about 4km (2.4 mi.) until it ends at a parking lot where a large gate with a cross welcomes visi-tors. From here, it is another 10-15 minute walk down a small picturesque road.

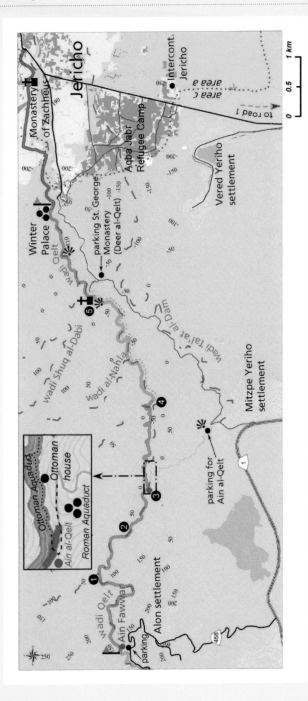

The trail starts at Ain Fawwar where there is a ranger station manned by the Israel Nature and Parks Authority. No entry fee is charged, though there were plans to upgrade the station at the time of writing. The orientation for the walk is easy: the red marked trail always follows the downward direction of the wadi (E) as it flows towards Jericho. Through various scrambles, the trail moves up and down between the wadi bed and the cliffs above. The first and final sections have clear red trail markers. The middle section trailing the aquaduct is unmarked.

20. Along the Aquaduct: Ain Fawwar to Jericho

[0-2.5km/0-1.5 mi.] The trail starts at the Fawwar spring where remnants of the ancient Roman aquaduct can still be seen. The first part of trail goes past and at times underneath tunnels of thick reeds (depending on the season, these can be wet and muddy); in the winter season you will spot gushes of water streaming down the rock surface on the R bank of the wadi (where the old aquaduct is broken). Some scrambling is necessary here and there, including over large boulders that lie across the stream. Within an hour from the start (at 2.5km [1.5 mi.] into the hike) the wadi opens itself (❶) and beds of delicious smelling mint surrounding what is now a much gentler stream with an easy path to its side; the walking gets easier from here onwards.

Trail: Ain Fawwar to Jericho (lower Wadi Qelt)

Grade: Hard

Surface: Single track (includes scrambling)

Marked: Yes (red and green)

Distance and Duration: 13.5km/8.3 miles; 4 - 6 hrs (15.8km/9.8 mi. to Jericho's center)

Elevation Change: 450m ascent and 800m descent

Start Coordinates: N31 50.402 E35 20.922

[2.5-4.6km/1.5-2.8 mi.] While the going gets easier as the wadi opens, the red trail markings gradually become less frequent. !! At 3.7km (2.2 mi.) into the hike, the red trail leaves the wadi bed through a sudden climb on the L of the wadi bed (❷). It climbs up the L bank up to about 50m (164 ft.) above the wadi bed from where it continues in E direction (should you miss the red marking at this point and instead continue in the wadi bed, you will notice that about 400-500m [0.24-0.31 mi.] further into the wadi bed huge boulders block any further walking through the wadi). The trail skirts the wadi from above and crosses a natural rock bridge (4.2 km/2.6 mi.). Pay attention here as 200m (0.12 mi.) thereafter the trail markers take a sharp turn to the R and downwards to the wadi bed. Here, the red trail intersects with a black trail.

Tulips in the wadi flower
in February

If you follow the black trail back for 50m (164 ft.) upstream you come to a small pool and waterfall (❸) beyond which is Ain Qelt, the third and last of the large springs in the wadi. There is an inscription in calligraphy above the waterfall lauding Huseini, a wealthy family from Jerusalem, for building the dam, the flour mill and the modern aquaduct that runs from here to Jericho. This is a good place for a refreshing plunge into the basin below the waterfall, especially in summer, or for a picnic alongside the pools.

[4.6-7.7km/2.8-4.7 mi.] To continue on the trail, walk back to the red trail and follow it as it runs directly adjacent to the well-maintained aquaduct. The aquaduct's path gently leads you past an oasis with a 19th century Ottoman house that used to belong to the Huseini family, from where taxes were levied for the use of Ain Qelt. The house and the nearby old flour mill is now inhabited by Bedouin. There are no red markers along the aquaduct but just continue to follow the gentle stream. The aquaduct flows across three smaller side wadis: climb down and up these wadis and keep trailing the aquaduct. Take care as the surface here can be slippery. !! At 6.8km (4.2 mi.) into the walk you come across a sign (❹) indicating a green (aquaduct) and a red trail (wadi bed), both leading to Deer al-Qelt (St. George Monastery). Follow the sign here, thus leaving the aquaduct and descending towards the wadi bed. You cross a small bridge and quickly thereafter find the red and green trail splitting with red following the wadi stony bed and green running back up to the aquaduct. The green trail is more spectacular so take a L here and follow green, which gradually runs back up the slopes. At 7.7 km (4.7 mi.), you reconnect with the aquaduct.

[7.7-10.2km/4.7-6.3 mi.] Keep following the water. At 9.2km (5.7 mi.), the aquaduct leaves the trail and skirts

Waterfall near Ain Qelt

down to your R after which it crosses the wadi over a
bridge below; continue straight on your path here on
the last km towards the Monastery. About 5 minutes
before reaching the Monastery you come across a large
cross on a rock overlooking Deer al-Qelt below; a great
spot to enjoy the vistas and to take some of your best
pictures. You reach the Monastery (**❺**), located some
70m (229 ft.) below sea level, at 10.2km (6.3 mi.).
[10.2-13.5km/6.3-8.3 mi.] From the Monastery towards

Jericho the trail follows an easy path with clear red markers. After about 30-40 minutes, you will get the first spectacular views on Jericho down at the wadi end. !! Reaching the edge of Jericho (12.5km/7.7 mi.), do not follow the red markers as they suddenly run down into the wadi bed to the R. Instead, keep straight

Jericho as the Royal Refuge

In winter, a journey from Jerusalem to Jericho exposes the opposite ends of life in Palestine. Close in physical proximity, they are far apart in almost every other sense. With modern transport, you can cover the distance in just 25 minutes. But for a more natural and physically gratifying journey, the walk through Wadi Qelt is much more satisfying and Jericho's oasis a just reward for tired hikers. As you move down different ecosystems in the wadi, the journey holds more than just a change of scenery; it is a mental change from the density of urban Jerusalem and its surroundings towards the vast spaces of Jericho, the most rural of Palestin-ian cities, and, allegedly, the oldest in the world (10,000 years). For ages, Palestinian families in Jerusalem have owned houses and land in Jericho's oasis to escape the Jerusalem winter when the city is often shrouded in a single gray wet cloud. In that season, temperature differ-ences up to 10 degrees are not uncommon. Historically, Jericho as a refuge was not much different: King Herod the Great and the Umayyad Caliph Hisham established their winter palaces there, probably as much for their personal and physical comfort as to expand their legacies as great builders of their time. In its sheer spaciousness and laid-back atmosphere, Jericho is Jerusalem's mirror image on all counts: a flat drawn out city with wide roads, side-walks and an abundance of green space. Looking down from the Mount of Tempta-tion, there is nothing really urban about the city with small dots of built-up space spread around green and fallow lands. The gardens of single story houses are filled with citrus trees and bougain-villeas. Jericho's road network covers the flattest part of Palestine and is a haven for bikers big and small. So for those who suffer from any mild form of Jerusalem psychosis—and in particular its incessantly clogged and aggressive traffic—a visit to Jericho is the antidote.

on the path and keep moving in E direction towards Herod's Winter Palace (which you can see located next to agricultural field and green houses). The path first runs to the L of the wadi and eventually runs back into it. Continue straight ahead in the wadi bed until you meet a road crossing it at a concrete washout valve. Go L here and climb up the hill to visit the ruins of the Winter Palace.

Hugging the cliffs: Deer al-Qelt and its oasis

The trail ends here. You can either order a taxi to pick you up (the Arab name for the palace is Tulul Abu al-'Alaieq) or, if you still have some stamina left, walk through Jericho's quiet rural outskirts towards its center (2.3km/1.4 mi. on flat surface). To do so, walk back down from the ruins, take a L and walk until you meet a paved road. Go R here and walk 1 km to the Monastery of Zachheus located at a T-junction. Take R again and once more at wide paved road you come across. The paved road leads to Jericho's small city center (keep straight) and its main road. Stopping a taxi is easy at this point.

Logistics and Guides

Hijazi Eid (0599-523844) and Suhail Hijazi (0599-963991) are guides with significant hiking experience in Wadi Qelt. Various Palestinian NGOs also have experience in organizing walks through the wadi, among them Siraj (02-2748590), the ATG (02-2772151), PACE (02-2407611) and the Palestinian Wildlife Society (bird watching tours: 02-2774373). If you have questions about weather and walking conditions (threat of flash floods, etc.), you can call the hiking coordinator of the Israel National Park Authority: 057-8936708. A taxi office in Jericho: Abu Ali (02-2322525).

How to Get There

Hizma: from Jerusalem/Ramallah, it is a short drive (20 min) to Hizma. From Ramallah, drive to Hizma via Jaba and turn L into the village just before reaching Hizma CP. From Jerusalem, leave Jerusalem at the Hizma CP and take a L; after 500m (0.31 mi.) take the R turn into Hizma village and turn L at the first 4-way junction. Follow this street as it curves through the village in E direction for 1.5km (0.9 mi.) until you note a mosque and a cemetery on your L. Ain Fawwar: From Jerusalem/Ramallah it is a 25/40 minute drive to Ain Fawwar. Drive down towards Jericho on Rd 1. Having passed the turn-off to Kfar Adumim settlement, you come across a L turn onto Rd 458 to Maale Mikhmas (also called 'Alon road'). The nature reserve is also signposted here. Take this junction and continue to follow Road 458 as it passes the Alon settlement and winds further down between the hills. A few hundred m after passing the settlement you find the entry to Ain Fawwar.

Where to Park

Hizma: on the small square next to the Hizma cemetery and mosque.

Ain Fawwar: just before Rd 458 crosses the wadi bed and passes the trail, there is a parking lot (signposted "Ein Maboa"). Since this is a fairly deserted stretch of road, and you are heading off for a long hike, it is advisable to leave a note on the inside of your windshield stating that you are hiking Wadi Qelt and your mobile phone number.

Eat, Drink, Relax

Apart from the small cafeteria and shop at Ain Fara early on in the upper Wadi Qelt section there are no places on the trail where you can buy refreshments. Stock up well before you set out. In the Jericho oasis you will find a few garden restaurants along Ain e-Sultan Street (including the **Green Valley Restaurant**: 02-2322349) and there are magnificent views from the **Sultan Restaurant** on top of the Mount of Temptation (reachable by cable car from Tel e-Sultan). You can also find a good mixed grill on Jericho's central square. To literally reward a long walk with a splash, you can relax at one of Jericho's resorts: the **Intercontinental Hotel** (120 NIS) and the **Jericho Resort** (85 NIS) allow day visitors to use their pools and restaurants. Note that the places mentioned here are located several km away from Herod's Winter Palace where the trail ends. A taxi is advised for those craving for food, drink and cool waters.

Jerusalem to Jericho step by step

217

Jericho's juicy oranges
on sale

Overnight

Intercontinental Jericho is Jericho's most upscale
resort: a double room costs 700 NIS and includes
breakfast; Jerusalem-Jericho Rd; 02-2311200, jericho@
interconti.com. The **Jericho Resort** is less luxurious
than the Intercontinental but still very comfortable
and fun for families with kids: a double room costs
between 450-560 NIS including breakfast; Bishan
rd near Hisham's Palace; 02-2321255, reservation@
jerichoresorts.com. The friendly **Sami Youth Hostel**
has very basic double rooms (150 NIS per room) and

very very basic triple rooms (120 NIS per room); it is located in the Aqba Jabr Refugee Camp near Jericho's main entrance: 02-2324220.

Places to Go, People to Meet

Jericho and surroundings are rich with sites to visit. The 8th century ruins of the enormous Umayyad **Palace of Hisham** are impressive by themselves; the mosaics inside its former bathhouse are truly spectacular. Only the celebrated Tree of Life figure is presently visible but there are plans afoot to uncover the entire bathhouse floor of some 850 m2 of continuous classical mosaics. Further mosaics can also be admired in the **Coptic Church of St. Andrew** and in the remains of two decorated synagogue floors, one near Hisham's Palace, the **Shalom al-Israel Synagogue**, and the other in north Jericho, the **Ain Duyuk (or Na'aran) Synagogue** (coordination with local officials is required for a visit to either). Located near the city's main entrance, the **Jericho Mosaic Center** is the city's main resource and activity center on Jericho's varied heritage of classical mosaics; it also sells a variety of mosaic products in its workshop (02-326342). **Tel al-Sultan** is a mound that showcases layer upon layer of Jericho's ancient remains starting with the neolitihic period 10,000 years ago—give or take a few years. Though the extensive excavations might not speak to your imgaination if you are not a professional archeologist, Jericho is the oldest city in the world and the tel holds its oldest remains. Much of Jericho's fortunes have been due to its oasis springs, one celebrated one which is **Elisha's Spring** (Ain al-Sultan) right next to the archeological park. From here, a modern cable car (55 NIS) takes visitors up to the Mount of Temptation where the **Monastery and Temptation Church** is a highlight for both secular and religious visitors as it barely hangs on from the cliffs overlooking the city. A stroll through

Mosaics of Hisham's Palace

PEOPLE & PLACES

"Jericho is considered one of the most ancient urban settlements in the world. A place where natural components have been subject to transformations made by humans since thousands of years. Located in an oasis surrounded by a fragile environment, the city survived thanks to human actions of watering and canalizing, based on subsistence farming that allowed the continuity of its landscape components."

—Osama Hamdan, Director, Mosaic Center, Jericho

Jericho's small town center is worthwhile and so is a visit to its latest tourism draw there, the somewhat grotesque and Kremlin-like **Russian Museum**, built on land once owned by the Tsar. Sites outside the city include the desert *maqam* of Nabi Musa, the St Gerasimus Monastery and the Dead Sea.

On the Web
www.jericho-city.org/english.php
www.jerichoresorts.com
www.interconti.com

أرطاس Artas: The Enclosed Garden

There is plenty to explore in the valley of Artas: with the ancient **Solomon Pools** under threat, the 19th century **Monastery of Hortus Conclusus** retains a scenic backdrop in a landscape full of change.

The Solomon Pools to Artas walk is one of the most scenic short walks but also among the most threatened trails in this book. Plans for construction works near the pools, the uncontrolled urban expansion of Artas and the multiple damaging effects of the separation barrier built on land belonging to the village hem in the historic Artas Valley from various directions. Ironically, while only built just over a century ago, the Monastery of Hortus Conclusus actually preserves some of the traditional cultivated landscape of the area and remains its most scenic attraction.

Artas was among the first traditional villages in Palestine that attracted outside interest in Palestinian society and culture. In the early 20th century Hilmeh Granqvist, a Finnish anthropologist, started to make detailed accounts of village life and traditions. Meanwhile, village anthropology has been taken forward by local residents through the **Folklore Center** and the annual **Artas Lettuce Festival** in spring. Apart from the Hortus Conclusus Monastery, a second spiritual place that is often overlooked is the **Monastery of al-Khader**, located 2km (1.2 mi.) to the N of the pools.

Sunflower in the Hortus Conclusus

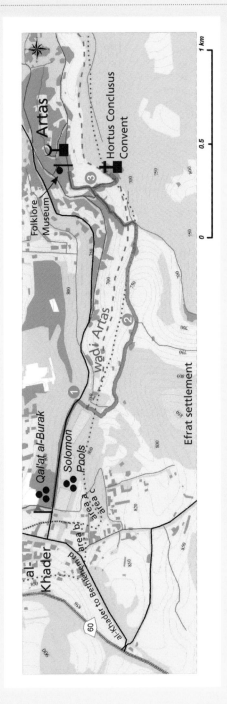

The walk from Solomon Pools runs E into the valley of Artas ending at the Hortus Conclusus Monastery and Artas Folklore Center. Visitor access to Solomon Pools was uncertain at the time this book went into print, which is why the start of the trail runs parallel to the site.

21. A Visit to the Sisters: Solomon Pools to Artas

[0-750m/0-0.46 mi.] The walk starts at the top of the road running parallel to the pools (if open to the public, an nicer alternative start is on the R side of the pools). Walk down the road passing Qal'at al-Burak (Castle of the Pools—built by the Ottoman ruler Suleiman the Magnificent in the 17th century) on your L. While the pools (on your R) are now fenced off, at certain sections you can get a good sense for their size and depth. Each pool is more than 100m (328 ft.) in length, 65m (213 ft.) wide and 10m (32 ft.) deep and together they can hold around 200 million liters. The first pool is the smallest of the three; the third the largest. After 600m (0.37 mi.) (❶) and almost directly after passing the third pool (and with the fences ending), leave the road and walk to the R onto the area immediately below the third pool. As you pass the bottom of the pool you can spot a small old path running down towards the valley.

[750m-1.4km/0.46-0.86 mi.] Here the path meets a dirt road. Follow the dirt road which runs along the slope to the R of the valley and veers up. Do not take the smaller side road which skirts down into the valley (leading to a dead end). As the road slowly climbs up the hill, you start seeing the outskirts of Artas village which have spread to the slopes of the valley. To your R the land is more barren and a few hundred meters away the separation barrier cuts through the landscape. The valley contains a large variety of crops and fruit trees: apricot, figs and pistachio grow here, as well as grapes.

Trail: Solomon Pools to Artas

Grade: Easy

Surface: Paved and dirt roads; some single track

Marked: No

Distance and Duration: 5.6 km/3.4 miles; 1.5–2 hrs (out and back)

Elevation Change: 200m ascent / 200m descent

Start Coordinates: N31 41.383 E35 10.049

The End of Solomon Pools?

Solomon Pools is one of Palestine's most impressive archeological wonders, an accomplishment of architecture and hydrology stretching back some two millennia. At first sight, the sheer scale of the pools is their most impressive feature. The first and smallest pool is 110m (360 ft.) in length and 70m (229 ft.) wide. The third and largest pool is 180 x 70m (590 x 229 ft.). Their depth varies around 10m (32 ft.) and their total water capacity is around 200 million liters. Underground springs and aquaducts in the area used to fill the pools which would supply another system of aquaducts all the way to Jerusalem and Herodion. As recently as 1946 parts of this elaborate water system were still in use. Given its strategic location, various armies, including Saladin's forces, set up camp at the site. Opposite the pools, the Qal'at al-Burak (Castle of the Pools) built by Suleiman the Magnificent

was witness to centuries of Ottoman rule here. The title of the pools is somewhat deceiving, however, as neither King Solomon nor the Ottoman Suleiman built the pools. Archeologists and historians believe they were actually built in phases, by Maccabeans, Herod the Great and then Pontius Pilate.

Naturally the best possible starting point for a walk from Solomon Pools to Artas village is the pools themselves. Since time immemorial, this has been a location for short walks, picnics and barbeques for the people from Artas, al-Khader and Bethlehem. Unfortunately, free and undisturbed access to the ancient pools has recently been put into jeopardy. A Palestinian business venture obtained not less than a 100 year lease from the Palestinian Waqf, the institution responsible for administrating religiously endowed land, which the pools are part of. The lease

was used to build the Bethlehem Convention Center just opposite the pools. However, it also included the pools and the natural area around them and for a few years plans have been afoot to build a large entertainment area right onto one of Palestine's most spectacular archeological sites. Apart from a restaurant it could include exploitation of one of the 10m (32 ft.) deep pools as a swimming pool and developing another pool into a theater of sorts. At the time of writing, preliminary works had been carried out without any specialist oversight, among others covering some of the ancient aquaducts connected to the pools from various underground springs in the area. Fortunately, awareness of the precarious situation of the pools was rising among the PA and heritage experts, with alternative plans being tabled to better match conservation needs with tourism.

[1.4-1.9km/0.86-1.1 mi.] !! Where the road takes a sharp turn to the R towards the wadi to the S (moving towards the separation barrier and a garbage dump) continue straight (❷), leaving the dirt road, and continue on a beautiful path running atop a centuries old stone wall. On the L side are small fruit orchards while on the R the remnants of cave dwellings and tombs can be seen. The stone path will take you down into the valley of Artas, turning first into a single track trail, then a dirt road, and, as you enter Artas village, a paved road.

[1.9-3.0km/1.1-1.8 mi.] Once you reach the bottom of the valley and pass the first Artas houses follow the paved road as it crosses the valley bed and starts climbing up on the other side. You see the impressive Hortus Conclusus (enclosed garden) Monastery ahead to your R. After 2.2km (1.3 mi.) into the walk you turn R to enter the grounds of the Monastery (❸) and cross the impressive bridge built over the wadi. The Monastery and church were established by a catholic order at the end of the 19th century and some of the sisters serving here come from Latin America. While the doors to the church are normally closed you can ask the sisters to open them for you: ring the bell near the door to the R of the main entrance. To reach the Folklore Center leave the Monastery grounds and continue straight down the road further into Artas village. You pass the Artas spring and then the mosque, after which the center is located to your L in one of Artas' last remaining traditional homes (climb up the stairs to reach the entrance).

Children playing at Artas spring

To return, retrace your steps. For those not keen to walk back up to Solomon Pools on the same path, regular public transportation (yellow *fordaat*) runs between Artas and al-Khader from the Artas main road below the Folklore Center (5 NIS). Indicate to the driver you want to get out at Solomon Pools (*Burak Sulayman*).

Christian Monasteries in Muslim Villages

The name Artas is derived from the Latin word hortus (garden) and a walk through the Artas Valley down to the monastery makes clear why. With plenty of water from the pools, the wadi bed just below the monastery traditionally has been considered one of the most scenic spots in Palestine, called the Hortus Conclusus, or enclosed garden. Part of the lush valley is nowadays tended by the Monastery of Hortus Conclusus, whose building, completed in 1901, was funded through donations from Catholics as far away as Argentina and Uruguay. The monastery and church were built in honor of the Virgin Mary (also called Lady of the Garden), who is symbolically seen to represent an enclosed garden (the garden representing the fullness of all virtues, and the enclosure Mary's virginity). A small community of sisters takes care of the monastery. Though the population of Artas is completely Muslim, relations between the monastery and the town have remained close. The monastery is involved in organizing various activities and many children from the village attend its kindergarten.

Nearby Artas lies another monastery in the center of a small Muslim village. Al-Khader is the name of the village but also the Muslim name for St. George, the Patron Saint of Palestine (and a long list of other places around the world; among them England and Russia, Barcelona and Beirut). Even if you are not religious you will recognize the image of St. George killing the dragon, a symbol of good conquering evil that can be found across churches worldwide. The monastery in al-Khader is built on the site where according to tradition the saint was kept prisoner and tortured. While the priest of the Greek Orthodox monastery is the only Christian resident left in the village, his church is frequently visited by both Christians and Muslims who come to pray at the church and ask for the saint's blessings. Muslims sometimes sacrifice sheep and goat, or provide other donations to the church. In Islamic tradition, al-Khader is strongly associated with providing health, making the land fertile (al-Khader literally meaning the green one), and blessing new born children.

Artas Mosque with the Monastery in the background

Logistics and Guides

The **Artas Folklore Center** can organize guided walking tours in the area. Contact Nidal Fahmy Ayesh; 0599-992509 or artasfcenter@gmail.com. Another organization active in the area is the **Palestinian Wildlife Society**; 02-2774373 or pwls@wildlife-pal.org.

The Hortus Conclusus Monastery

How to Get There

Car: From Jerusalem, it is a 30 minute drive to Solomon Pools. Drive out of Jerusalem through the so-called Tunnels CP over Road 60; after the Tunnels CP, continue straight for 3.6km (2.2 mi.) until the first turn-off to your L to the Efrata (north) settlement and al-Khader village. Take this turn-off and turn L again at the roundabout: drive onto the main road connecting al-Khader to Bethlehem. Take the second turn-off to the R to the Solomon Pools. This road is located 700m (0.43 mi.) from the previous roundabout. Road signs are poor here but watch out for signs to Irtas, Bethlehem Convention Center or Solomon Pools. From Ramallah, drive to Bethlehem via Beit Sahour. In Bethlehem, pass through the city center to get onto Hebron

Grapes at the Hortus

Road towards al-Khader. Towards the end of this road Solomon Pools are located to the L. A short-cut can also be made on smaller roads from Beit Sahour via Artas village.

Public transportation: via Bethlehem or Beit Jala.

Where to Park

Parking space is available either on the quiet road parallel to the pools or at the parking of the Convention Center.

Eat, Drink, Relax

There are no restaurants in Artas but the Folklore Center can prepare traditional Palestinian meals for guests (advance notice required). Close by, Bethlehem, Beit Jalla and Beit Sahour are prime tourist hubs with a wide range of restaurants.

Overnight

For overnights closeby consider one of the many hotels in Bethlehem, Beit Sahour or Beit Jalla.

Places to Go, People to Meet

The 3 day **Artas Lettuce Festival** is held every spring (April or May) featuring music, traditional dance, poetry, short and long hiking tours and, of course, lots of lettuce. Contact the Artas Folklore Center for more information. Other places worth to visit are **Solomon Pools**, the **Artas Hortus Conclusus Monastery**, the **Artas Folklore Center** and the nearby **al-Khader Monastery**. Nearby Bethlehem is the West Bank's main tourist hub; check out the city's Visitor Information Center on Manger Square for an overview of the many things to see and do (see link below).

On the Web

www.palestine-vic.ps

مار سابا Mar Saba: Desert Monasteries

For more than fifteen centuries monks have inhabited the uninhabitable. From Mar Saba to Hyrcania, you walk the desert where they sought to get closer to God. Mar Saba is among the most ancient and wondrous desert monasteries in the Holy Land, continuously in service since its foundation in the 5th century. Surviving natural disasters, pillaging armies and the currents of numerous empires, the Monastery appears less ancient than it is from the outside: following an earthquake, the monastic complex was restored to its present state in 1893. The large jagged wall around it was originally built after a 7th century Persian invasion and has kept out intruders ever since; that includes women who have been generally barred from entering Mar Saba's gates since its foundation. Over a dozen monks presently live in Mar Saba; they still practice Byzantine time in which the day ends the moment the sun sets.

If you think Mar Saba is an isolated place, consider the ruins of Hyrcania—also known as *Khirbet Mird*—where this walk will lead you. Mar Saba's founder, St Sabas, established a second monastery there. Prior to that the hill served as one of Herod the Great's many fortresses and it was an execution place for the king's many enemies. The trail between the sites of the two monasteries makes you wonder about the efforts it took to build such outlets so far out into the wild. The walk takes you right through the desert where hardly anything grows, a desolate landscape with increasingly spectacular views as the walk progresses.

Once the desert was a city

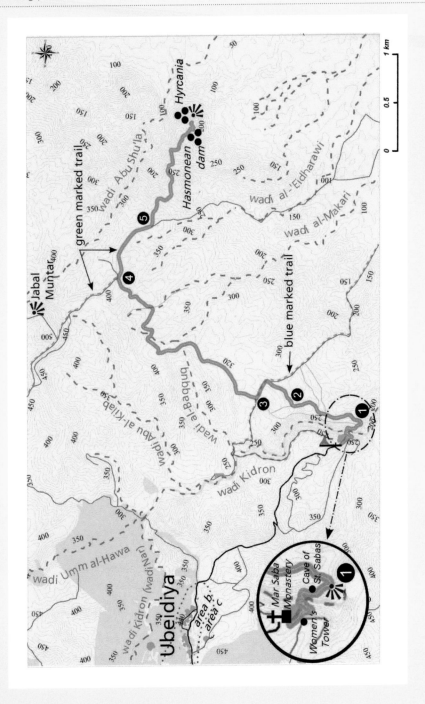

22. Byzantium Now and Then: Mar Saba to Hyrcania (*Khirbet Mird*)

Given the desert surroundings, this should be a very quiet walk. On Saturdays and during holidays, however, the odds are that you will encounter some motor bikes or quad bikes along the way but not in any great numbers. Otherwise, this route will be entirely deserted save for a Bedouin herder or two that you might meet. Note that the overall distance of this walk is nearly 14km (8.6 mi.) through the desert. The steepest ups and downs are at the start and end of the walk and at Hyrcania in the middle. There is no shade along the trail; make sure you bring more water than average, something to cover your head, sunscreen and some food.

Trail: Mar Saba to Hyrcania

Grade: Moderate

Surface: Dirt roads and one steep scramble

Marked: Partially (first and last 4.5km/2.7 mi. unmarked)

Distance and Duration: 13.8 kms/8.5 miles; 4–5.5 hrs

Elevation Change: 550m ascent and 550m descent

Start Coordinates: N31 42.293 E35 19.826

[0-550m/0-0.34 mi.] From the front of Mar Saba walk up the stairs to the R side of the monastery. You pass underneath the women's tower from where there are excellent views over the monastic complex. From here start your descent past Mar Saba's exterior walls and into Wadi Kidron 330 steps down. As the stairs zigzag down you pass old hermit cells and parts of the ancient complex that are now ruins. On the other side of the wadi you see more cells spread across the rock surface. When you get to the bottom of the wadi, towards the small bridge crossing the stream you will see (and probably smell) the waste floating down through the Kidron stream (it comes mostly from East Jerusalem areas that have no proper sewage systems). From the bridge walk up the stairs—they are mostly carved out of the rock surface here—and continue on the small path that passes right underneath St. Sabas' cave

Mar Saba at dawn

(decorated by a white fence with a cross and the initials A and C, meaning St. Sabas). Continue on the path as it passes more caves and then crosses over a small natural rock bridge. !! From here, scramble up onto the hill slopes L and all the way to the top of the ridge 35m (114 ft.) above (a small single track footpath runs to the L directly below the ridge; it offers an alternative but steep route to the blue marked junction mentioned below). You've arrived at a wonderful 360 degree viewpoint (**❶**). Here you can take in the full scale of the Mar Saba complex, the multitude of cave cells spread around the Wadi Kidron and another monastic tower built in the middle of the wadi's slopes to the S.

Hermits in the Desert

After five years of living in solitude in a cave above Wadi Kidron, the monk and hermit Sabas founded Mar Saba in 483 AD. He then encouraged other monks to settle there. The population soon spiraled to over a hundred and the desert monastery—or lavra as the Greek Orthodox call it—was expanded to include a bakery, a hospital, water reservoirs and a large church. Sabas (now St. Sabas) was a leader in a popular movement of monks who left the cities and villages behind to settle in the most barren and isolated regions of the desert. Their purpose? To better nourish the soul, get far away from the material world and ever closer to God. The movement was a reaction to a watershed change affecting Christians since the 4th century. The conversion of the Roman Emperor Constantine to Christianity in 312 AD meant the end of three centuries of persecution for Christians. Their faith had become a safe and respect-able religion in the Holy Land and across the Roman empire. With the ultimate sacrifice of martyrdom now much less evident, new questions were posed on what kind of religious life was fitting in this new and more comfortable world. Many monks opted for a lifestyle of solitude and soberness, close to nature and with both physical as well as spiritual challenges. They found it in the desert.

Between the 4th and 6th century AD, as many as 150 monasteries are estimated to have flourished across the deserts of the Holy Land. Entire monastic cities arose in the heart of the desert: Mar Saba in its heydays served hundreds of hermits (some sources speak of as much as 700). Such numbers suggest enough souls to keep one another distracted from a truly meditative life but a desert monastery was no place for social camping: most monks did not live inside its protective walls but led a hermit life in the cluster of cells and caves spread around it, subsisting on little else than bread and water during the week and only gathering at the church for communal prayer on Saturdays and Sundays. Their economic survival was organized through the weaving of baskets. Isolated as it may have been, Mar Saba was not ignored by the outside world. In 614 AD Persian forces raided the monastery and murdered all the monks they could find. As in St. George Monastery in Wadi Qelt the hundreds of skulls are still preserved inside one of the churches. Despite these dramatic events, Mar Saba recovered and apart from a few weeks after the Persian raid, it has been a continuously living community for over 1500 years.

[550m-1.8km/0.34-1.1 mi.] From the viewpoint, walk towards a dirt road some 50m (54 yards) to your L and follow this road as it runs over the ridge parallel to the wadi and with another great view over the Monastery. Having left Mar Saba behind you, the road splits a few times: !! keep to the L junction at the first two splits (the road keeps climbing gradually). After the road begins to descend you reach a small dry side steam that flows towards Wadi Kidron: the road splits again (for the 3rd time) immediately after crossing this stream (❷): go R here following the stream upwards. 450m (0.27 mi.) further you come across a blue marked dirt road.

[1.8-4.6km/1.1-2.8 mi.] Go L on the dirt road and follow the blue markers for 220m (0.13 mi.) until you meet a 3-way junction (❸): turn R here and leave the blue markers (which continue straight). You are now on your main dirt road towards Hyrcania. Continue to follow this wide road as it meanders in NE direction. The desert landscapes become ever more barren and desolate as you follow the road meandering up and down for a number of km. After 4.3km (2.6 mi.) into the walk, you arrive at an unmarked 4-way junction; continue straight (going down) and after another 350m (0.21 mi.) you come across a second 4-way junction (❹). Here a green trail (only vaguely marked) crosses your path: to the L you will see Jabal Muntar (524m/1,719 ft.) rising above everything else. Here yet another desert monastery was founded (Monastery of Scholarius) in the 6th century AD although very little remains can be seen today. The 360 degrees panorama views from Jabal Muntar are spectacular (Bethlehem, Jerusalem, Jericho and the Judean Desert) but note that including a diversion to this site and back will prolong the walk to Hyrcania by at least 1.5 hours.

Through the barren desert to Hyrcania

A desert panorama

[4.6-6.9km/2.8-4.2 mi.] To continue to Hyrcania, take the green marked trail to your R and continue to follow the green markers on this wide road. At 5.4km (3.3 mi.) into the walk, the green trail splits away to the L from the main road (❺). Continue to follow the green markers as they start meandering gradually down the hills. The trail veers L around a steep hill and then turns into a smaller footpath. Continue to follow this footpath (still green marked) as the landscape turns more dramatic with jagged rock formations and steeper drop-offs. After having circled around a few hills you will see the large and impressive Hasmonean dam below with ancient water reservoirs on both sides. Pass the

Mar Saba: maze on
the cliffs

dam to walk the zigzagged foothpath up to Hyrcania
(248m/813 ft.). The most impressive feature of the site
is the spectacular views over the Jordan Valley, the Dead
Sea and the mountains of the Jordanian side of the valley. The site is a great location for a picnic and you can
stroll around exploring the ruins of the Monastery with
some walls, cisterns, tomb-chambers and a patch of
Byzantine mosaics still visible.

[return] To go back to Mar Saba, retrace your footsteps.
Pay attention to your route as turn-offs can look a lot
like one another in the desert. Follow back the green
marked trail to the 4-way crossing near Jabal Muntar.
Turn L here and follow this road until after several km
you meet the blue marked 3-way crossing: turn L here
again. After just 220m (0.13 mi.) on the blue marked
road, turn R at the first junction to find your way back
to Wadi Kidron and Mar Saba. For a safe descent back
to the Monastery choose the same path by walking
past the monastic complex for some 100m (109 yards)
before turning R and starting your descent.

Logistics and Guides

Walks and tours in the desert can be organized by
a variety of organizations, among which **Siraj** (02-
2748590) and **ATG** (02-2772151). Ahmad Abu Haniya
(0597-903500) organizes camping in the desert near
Ubeidiya (see below) and can also arrange guides for
walking tours.

How to Get There

Car: from Jerusalem/Ramallah, it is a 40/60 minute
drive to Mar Saba. From Jerusalem, on the road S
towards Bethlehem (Hebron road) take a L turn towards
the settlement of Har Homa. Once you reach the main
junction close to the actual settlement, take a L onto
Rd 356 that passes around Har Homa towards the CP
of Mazmouria. Pass the CP, and continue on Road 356
until you drive over an overpass; immediately after the
overpass, turn L and take a R (E) on the road below.
You are now on the road coming from Beit Sahour to
Ubeidiya. Continue through the town of Ubeidiya on
a long winding road that eventually passes the Greek

Orthodox St. Theodosius Monastery (where the three wise men supposedly rested after visiting baby Jesus). The road first widens and 300m (0.18 mi.) after the Monastery the road splits at a police station: the L leg descends sharply towards Container CP and Abu Dis; the R leg goes further into the village and towards the E. Take the R leg and continue to follow the main road as its winds further E; after a few km you will leave the last houses of Ubeidiya behind and drive on a lone asphalted road with breathtaking views of the desert. You pass a garbage dump before circling sharply down the hill towards the Monastery. From Ramallah, drive towards Bethlehem via the Container CP. Once up the hill after Container, take a sharp L to follow the village of Ubeidiya in E direction and follow the directions above.

Public transportation: there is no public transportation to the Monastery. Take a private taxi from Beit Sahour or Ubeidiya and agree your return pick-up with the same driver (bargain and settle on the price beforehand).

Where to Park

You can park at the Mar Saba Monastery.

Eat, Drink, Relax

Surprise surprise: there are no restaurants in the desert. Your best bet on your way back from Mar Saba are the various places near the Shepherd's Fields in Beit Sahour (E of Bethlehem). To get there, continue straight on the rd from Ubeidiya into Beit Sahour and follow the signs to Shepherd's Fields.

Desert vegetation

Overnight

Unless you are a pilgrim and have arranged an overnight in Mar Saba, there are no options at the Monastery. A nearby place to enjoy the desert at night and camp Bedouin style is **Tal al-Qamar** (Hill of the

Moon): located at a wonderfully scenic location S of
Ubeidiya, this place is great for sleeping under the
stars, or (if it is too cold) under the cover of a tent.
The site is fitted with a basic kitchen, toilets and (cold)
showers. A night of camping, including an evening
barbeque and breakfast the next day, costs around 120
NIS pppn. The owner, Ahmad Abu Haniya, can also
arrange for walks across the desert to places such as
Herodion or Rashayda, another location where camping out is possible. Contact: alkarmel48@hotmail.
com and 0597-903500. If you don't fancy sleeping in
the great outdoors, more regular overnight options
can be found in the town of Beit Sahour.

Mosaics amidst the ruins
of Hyrcania

The desert as a moon landscape

Places to Go, People to Meet

A visit to **Mar Saba Monastery** is a fascinating experience but not always easy to arrange. It is normally not open to tourists and if you are not a pilgrim arriving unannounced could leave you stranded outside (you can, of course, always try a spontaneous knock on the door). To arrange a visit beforehand contact the Greek Patriarchate in Jerusalem (02-6285901). The Monastery holds great views over Wadi Kidron and, because of its structure, over itself: it contains a maze of cells, stairs, hallways and churches literally wrapped around its central courtyard. The two churches are the **Church of the Annunciation of Virgin Mary** where the relic of the body of St. Sabas is kept since it was returned from Venice in 1965 (mischievous Crusaders had stolen it a few centuries earlier) and the **St. Nicolas Church**, built inside the cave from where St. Sabas founded the Lavra and now holding the skulls of monks martyred in the past 15 centuries. Between the churches is a small domed temple holding the tomb of St. Sabas where he was originally buried (before being whisked away by Crusaders). Women have not been allowed into Mar Saba for 15 centuries and will have to make do with a peek over its exterior walls (which can be done from a hill on the R side of the Monastery). According to local legend, a woman once tried to enter Mar Saba dressed up as a man; however, the earth started shaking and so the priests found out about this imposter.

Not on the Web

The web has not nearly caught up with the fascinating set of books that describe the origins, history and fate of desert monastries and their monks across the Middle East. My favorite? William Dalrymple's *From the Holy Mountain*.

بتير Battir: Hugging the Green Line

A circle of concrete is closing in upon the ancient springs, canals and terraces of Battir. Yet the village's intriguing history holds inspiration for the future. In Ottoman and British mandate times, Battir used to be part of a long string of small villages tied in closely with Jerusalem. Yet its connection to Jerusalem was cut partially in 1949, more fully in 1967 and almost completely in the last two decades. Battir and other nearby villages find themselves increasingly hemmed in between large Israeli settlements, various by-pass roads and the construction of the separation barrier. This should however not deter a visit to Battir's beautiful historic wadis which contain a unique human heritage going back some 4000 years.

Battir and the railway that determines its fate

The village's more recent history holds cause for both hope and anxiety. Settlement and barrier expansion, urban sprawl and the gradual abandonment of cultivated farmland are threatening Battir's heritage. Yet the village has not stood idly by, with prize-winning projects to preserve its unique landscape. The starting location for both walks is the so-called **Court of the Seven Widows**, which lies at the heart of Battir's efforts to rejuvenate historic buildings in its village center. For some impressive views prior to the start of either walk, ask for access to one of the roof terraces. From there, you have excellent views over the historic **Wadi Battir** and the historic railway line connecting Jerusalem to Jafa. Located below Battir village, the railway is on the Israeli side of the Green Line.

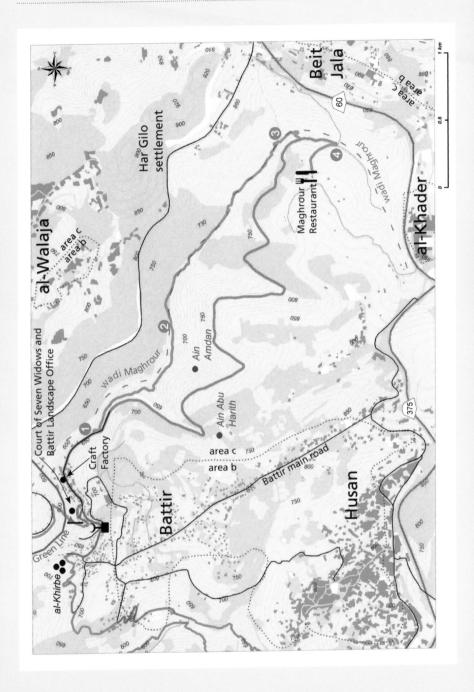

23. Tombs and Terraces: Battir to Wadi Maghrour

This circular walk will start from the Court of Seven Widows and takes you through the bed of the beautiful Wadi Maghrour E of Battir and towards Beit Jala after which it runs back over the slopes of the same wadi with pretty views over the surrounding landscape. In the middle of the hike, lunch at **Maghrour Restaurant** is highly recommended. Close to the start of the walk, another site to explore is the impressive and centuries' old network of springs, terraces and canals directly below the village center.

Trail: Battir > Wadi Maghrour > Battir

Grade: Moderate

Surface: Predominantly dirt road and single track; some off-road inside Wadi Maghrour and a minor section on paved road.

Marked: Planned (red)

Distance and Duration: 11.0 kms / 6.8 miles; 3–4 hrs

Elevation Change: 400m ascent / 400m descent

Start Coordinates: N31 43.719 E35 08.391

[0-800m/0-0.5 mi.] From the Court of the Seven Widows, walk back up the stairs towards the main road where car parking was advised. On the main road go L. Pass the Battir Craft Factory—handmade gifts, Muslim and Christian souvenirs and antiques on sale—and continue straight. !! Continue to follow the main road as it leaves the last houses of Battir behind and Wadi Maghrour lies to your L below. 125m (136 yards) after leaving the last houses behind, you come across a large electricity pole located to the L side of the road: another 140m (153 yards) after passing this pole, and just 60m (65 yards) before the road bends L, you find your single track path that veers off to the L side (❶). This path gradually descends into the wadi.

[800m-2.0km/0.5-1.2 mi.] Take this single track path and follow it downwards as it skirts large rock formations and slowly descends into the wadi for the next km. To the R side of the path you will notice tombs carved into the rocks from the Byzantine/Roman age. The path splits on a number of occasions forcing you

243

Wadi Maghrour olive groves

to choose between a L leg (going down into the wadi) and a R leg (keeping straight or going up): choose the R leg at splits where the L legs descend into the wadi in the direction opposite to your walking direction; similarly, choose the L leg, where the option to R would take you back up the terraces. With some minor ups, the trail will continue to gradually go down towards the wadi bed.

[2.0-4.1km/1.2-2.5 mi.] At 2km (1.2 mi.) into the hike you approach the wadi bed. You will pass a huge rock dropped in the center of the wadi bed (❷) with a hole to one of its sides, appearing to be another rock tomb. It may also be an old water cistern turned 90 degrees as the rock broke off from the rock bed above the wadi. Shortly after having passed the large rock, the path crosses the wadi bed and continues on its L flank. For the next 2km (1.2 mi.) the path crosses the wadi bed a number of times. Depending on the season, the path might disappear briefly in an olive grove or other field that has been plowed but following the right direction is easy from here: simply continue to follow the wadi bed in the direction of Beit Jala (SE) and look for the best path on either side of the wadi bed (usually, the best path runs on the "wider" side of the wadi bed where most of the terraces and fields are cultivated).

[4.1-4.3km/2.5-2.6 mi.] As you approach Beit Jala and Rd 60 (located 100m/328 ft. above), you will notice more and more *qasrs* overseeing the terraces of Wadi Maghrour. !! Just as the wadi makes a slow bend to the R (S), the path splits with one leg veering up to the L side towards Beit Jala and a leg to the R (❸) continuing in the wadi bed. Make sure you continue to follow the wadi bed to the R until after about 100m (109 yards) you hit a stone wall blocking the wadi. At this point,

turn R following the path as it climbs the slope of the
wadi to its R side. The path leaves the wadi bed and
starts zigzagging upwards. Continue to follow it until
you reach a wide road, some 20m (21 yards) above the
wadi bed. At the time of writing, this was a dirt road in
Area C but there are plans to pave this road subject to
Israeli approval.

[4.3-4.9km/2.6-3 mi.] Once on the wide road, there
are two choices: follow the route back immediately or
make a small detour to first visit Beit Jala's best kept
secret: the Maghrour Restaurant. This is a wonderful
spot to rest your legs under the shade of old fig trees
and enjoy the pleasure of a fresh juice, a *nargilleh* or
an excellent meal; make sure you do not miss the delicious *Baba Ghanoush* (eggplant dish). An afternoon
hike might even tempt you to try the list of various
alcoholic beverages. To get to Maghrour Restaurant,
turn L once you have reached the wide road described
above and R at the first junction (❹) with a paved road
running up the hill. It is located 400m (0.24 mi.)
from this junction.

[4.9-11.0km/3-6.8 mi.] To get back to Battir, from the
restaurant retrace your steps back to the junction
with the wide road described above. From here, follow the road W as its winds back to Battir overlooking Wadi Maghrour and giving expansive views over
Israel's Jerusalem Forest beyond the Green Line. The
road back, while longer in distance will take you less
time than the path through the wadi because of the
quality of the road. Halfway back you will see the
upper part of Battir on the hill to the NW as well the
edge of Battir's center (boys' school) at the lower end
of Wadi Maghrour. At the time of writing, the last
1.5km (0.9 mi.) section of the road leading back into
Battir had been paved.

Along ancient canals in
Wadi Jama

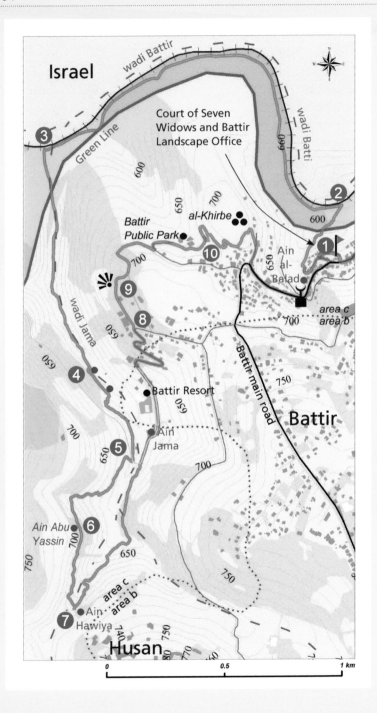

24 Eggplants Along the Railway: Battir to Wadi Jama

This circular walk also starts from the Court of the Seven Widows. The trail takes you along the centuries' old Battir water system over the terraces towards Wadi Battir with its turbulent history of the railway connecting Jerusalem to the coast. The walk then turns into Wadi Jama to the S of Battir where it passes a number of springs near the village of Husan. Before turning back to its starting point, the hike passes the Battir Public Park and the archeological site located above the village center.

There are quite some sections in this trail where the path might be momentarily unclear and some occasional scrambling over rocky patches will be necessary. It is important to be aware of the direction of the trail in order to retrace the path should it become unclear. The majority of the trail is on dirt roads and single track paths with some trail near the end on paved road.

Trail: Battir > Wadi Jama > Battir

Grade: Moderate

Surface: Predominantly dirt road and single track; minor sections on paved road.

Marked: Planned (blue)

Distance and Duration: 8.5 kms / 5.2 miles; 2.5–3.5 hrs

Elevation Change: 350m ascent / 350m descent

Start Coordinates:
N31 43.719 E35 08.391

[0-550m/0-0.34 mi.] The trail starts inside the Court of the Seven Widows, near the Hassan Mustafa Cultural Center (❶). At the end of the court, turn L walk up the stairs to your R. You reach a paved road; turn R here and continue for 100m (109 yards) passing the Battir Basic Girls School run by UNWRA (the school is spread over several buildings). You get to another paved road at the corner of one of the school buildings: turn R here and walk down the stairs where you encounter the centuries' old water system that supplies the terraces of Battir. Follow the main canal as it passes to the R of the terraces and underneath a cliff. The canal then passes the Islamic Shrine of Abu Yazeed Al Bustami. After this, the path becomes

Terraces below Battir's old city

unpaved. Continue to follow it as it descends into the valley and towards the railway line and passes a large variety of crops among which peppers, pumpkins and the famous Battir eggplant (*baitinjaan battiri*). In the past, a special festival was even devoted to Battir's yearly eggplant harvest in October. Approaching the railway, you now are in the unique position of walking both inside Israel as well as in the middle of Battir's agricultural land which is located on both sides of the railway. The location seems a perfect spot to just cross the railway and walk into Israel's Jerusalem Forest unnoticed; don't try, as crossing here is only allowed for farmers who work their land on the other side. If you do, Israel's security folk will come down the hill for you faster than you can say "*baitinjaan battiri.*"

[550m-2.4km/0.34-1.4 mi.] At the railway line (❷), turn L onto the dirt road that runs parallel to it. After a while the road starts to climb while continuing to run alongside Wadi Battir. On the other side of the wadi you look at the Jerusalem Forest, a haven for hikers and mountainbikers in Israel. Continue to follow the road until, after 2.5km (1.5 mi.) into the walk, the road descends

back towards the railway which crosses Wadi Jama over a small overpass. Turn L here into Wadi Jama (❸).

[2.4-3.6km/1.4-2.2 mi.] Follow the trail into the wadi bed. The dirt road turns into a footpath. The first km into this wadi bed, the path is small but easily traversed as it crosses in and out of the wadi bed. At 3.3km (2 mi.) into the hike the wadi bed becomes more narrow and deep with stone walls on both sides. Continue for another 100m (109 yards) until you spot an old stone water reservoir (pool) elevated a few m above the wadi bed to your R. Turn R here (❹) on a small path that climbs up behind the pool and then runs parallel 6m (19 ft.) above the wadi bed. At this point you have to climb onto the canal and walk between it and the stone wall (this is exciting but be careful as the trail is very narrow at this point). 10m (11 yards) after you pass a second pool and the open canal you walked on becomes a covered canal, turn R onto a small path that zigzags further up the hill.

[3.6- 4.6km/2.2-2.8 mi.] Climb up the hill until the small path meets a broader footpath running parallel to the wadi. Follow this path above the wadi's terraces

The Village and the Railway

With water springs and public buildings named after him, writer and journalist Hassan Mustafa (1914-1961) is Battir's hero. During the 1948 war, while nearly all of the village had fled, Mustafa kept up the appearance that it was still fully inhabited and protected: he lit candles in deserted homes and let animals into their yards. His act of deception worked: when a ceasefire was agreed between Israel and Jordan, the Israelis had not succeeded in conquering Battir despite its key strategic importance. Yet, in April 1949 the village was nearly lost after all as the details of the agreements put the famous Green Line exactly through the village.

When the Israelis came to demarcate their side of the border, Hassan Mustafa went out to meet them at the railway, protesting the location of the freshly agreed border. Israeli military officials, led by general Moshe Dayan, insisted that Israel's only con-cern was that the Jerusalem-Jaffa railway could operate undisturbed. An agreement was struck between Hassan Mustafa and the Israeli military, later ratified in official documents, in which Israel committed to full access for Battir's residents to both their village and their land. In exchange, Mustafa committed Battir village not to interfere with the operation of the Israeli run railway. After more than six decades, it is one of the few agreements from those days that still holds today: Battir farmers still cross the railway to access their lands on the other side.

With the building of the separation barrier since 2003, many West Bank villages close to the route of the barrier have been cut off from their farmland. Not yet built at the time of writing, the barrier is officially planned to encircle Battir and its neighboring villages in their entirety, leaving only one underground exit passage for access to Bethlehem. Battir has received notice that the barrier will also be built along the railway, thus cutting off farmers from their lands and damaging much of Battir's ancient landscape. The plans have meanwhile led a diverse coalition of Palestinian and Israeli human rights and environmental activists to protest the planned route.

If despite this opposition the barrier is built, the 1949 agreement would become meaningless. The special case of Battir and its long-standing accord on a friendly boundary might still inspire more imaginative solutions on borders than those made up of concrete slabs, barbed wire and land confiscation. Time will tell if Hassan Mustafa and Moshe Dayan were ahead of their times.

Red peppers in Wadi Jama

for 280m (0.17 mi.) until—just before you reach the curve of a wide dirt road—the trail veers up to the R, crosses the dirt road and then steeply ascends the hill above on a small single track path (❺). After the first steep incline, follow the path upwards to the L (the path follows the direction of the wadi; do not climb straight up the hill). The path continues to zigzag upwards over the hill to the L, climbing up between wild vegetation, then stoned terraces and ultimately onto natural rocks until it reaches Ain Abu Yassin at 4.6km (2.8 mi.) into the walk (❻). From the spring, you have an excellent view over Wadi Jama, the myriad water canals streaming through the cultivated terraces below and onto the outskirts of Husan village on the hills directly across.

[4.6-4.8km/2.8-2.9 mi.] From the spring, start descending in the direction of the next one: Ain Hawiya, which can be seen to the R on the other side of the wadi. Tread carefully as the decline is on a small path that is fairly steep and includes rocks that can be slippery. At junctions in this path, keep L. On the last stretch to Ain Hawiya (❼) you follow the canal until you

The trail just below Battir's old city

reach the spring which is an excellent spot for a break and a snack. While *hawiya* means ID in colloquial Arabic—a word much in use in Palestine—the name of the spring stems from classical Arabic meaning infinity. The spring was named so because its source in the caves (up to 2.5m high) behind the pool of the spring has never been traced and it produces water all year round. You can enter the caves but not with dry feet.

[4.8- 6.5km/2.9-4.0 mi.] From Ain Hawiya the trail returns to Battir following the canals as they gradually wind down the terraces on the R side of the wadi bed. The canal splits once at the end of a plateau: here, follow the L branch which begins with some crude downward steps. After this, continue to follow the canal on the R side of the wadi as the trail curls further down for 800m (0.5 mi.) until it reaches the same paved road it crossed earlier. Keep R here and follow it as it passes the largest spring of the wadi, Ain Jama. Subsequently, the road becomes paved and passes the Battir Resort (swimming pool, ice cream and food to order; open April-September), a mosque and starts curling up to the center of the village. Climb along the paved road for the first 4 sharp curves but at the 5th one (**8**) leave the paved road for a smaller road running to the L.

[6.5-7.2km/4.0-4.4 mi.] After 230m (0.14 mi.) you have a wonderful view over Wadi Battir. At the first pine tree (**9**), follow the trail R and up the slope until you reconnect with a dirt road above. Turn L here as the road winds down and around newly built terraces. Once you reach the paved road coming from the village, turn L and descend towards Battir's Public Park, a nice place for a picnic or a short break.

[7.2-8.5km/4.4-5.2 mi.] From the park continue on the dirt road that runs behind the park towards a

PEOPLE & PLACES

"What shapes the face of Battir is the close dialogue between humanity and nature. The trail means a lot to me because it collects the heritage of my community and a lifetime of memories. It traces the immortal footprints of all the people that crossed this land throughout history, coming from all over the world, searching in the end for the same thing."

—Hassan Mouamer, Guide, Battir

freestanding house (⑩). The path passing the house closely on the L side was there before the house was built and passersby still have the right to pass over it. On top of the hill behind this house lies Battir's archeological site, dubbed Khirbet al-Yahood (Jewish ruins) by Israeli sources and just *al-Khirbe* by Palestinians. (The ruins were excavated once by Israeli archeologists in search for remains of the Jewish Bar Kochba revolt; no firm conclusions were drawn on the veracity of their findings, but the site exposed did reveal a large fortified site with origins dating back to the Middle Bronze age and Roman periods). !! To get there, pass the house on the L side and curve around it between the stone walls 30m (32 yards) to its L and then pass

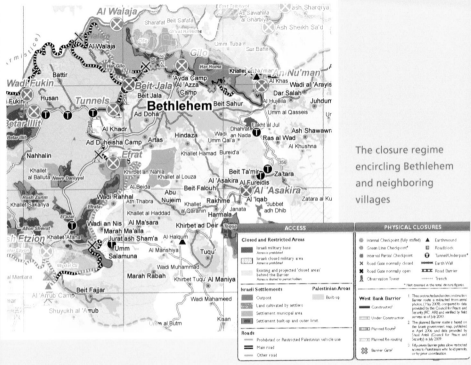

The closure regime encircling Bethlehem and neighboring villages

Mind the Map

Few things in the Middle East are so contentious as maps. Yet when traveling without them, you miss out on a lot of information on how the different sides look at the same piece of land (and a small detail: you might get lost). Despite the wealth of a shared Holy Land for tourism, public institutions on either side frequently ignore the other on the maps they publish. One key map considered indispensable for all expats working in the international community is the *West Bank & Gaza Strip Closure Maps* produced by the UN Office for the Coordination of Humanitarian Affairs, or: OCHA. The maps detail the location of around 500 movement obstacles that Palestinians face across the West Bank: checkpoints, earth mounds, gates, crossings and trenches. It also provides updates on the routing and rerouting of the 721km long separation barrier. The map above depicts part of the Bethlehem area including Battir. OCHA maps are available free of charge on their website (www.ochaopt.org) and are updated regularly.

over a set of large rocks leading to a single track path right behind the house. After 80m (87 yards) leave the path to climb further up the hill to the L until you reach the ruins at the top. Behind the site a short dirt road leads R towards the Battir main road. Follow this dirt road and as you reach the main road, turn L to go down to the village center. Pass the Battir Mosque and after 230m (0.14 mi.) turn L to return to the starting point inside the Court of the Seven Widows.

Logistics and Guides

For guided walks you can contact the **Battir Landscape Office**: 02-2763509; or call Hassan Muamer: 052-5897437. Guiding fees were around 50 NIS pp at the time of writing but were still subject to change prior to the opening of Battir's Eco Museum.

How to Get There

Car: From Jerusalem/Ramallah, it is a 40/90 minute drive to Battir. From Jerusalem, drive S through the Tunnels CP over Rd 60; after the CP, take the first junction to your R towards Beit Shemesh, and at the roundabout immediately following this junction take R again onto the parallel road towards Husan. This road winds towards Husan and Battir: after 1.2km (0.74 mi.), take the first large junction to your R: this is the road leading straight (down) into Battir village. Follow the main road for 2.5km (1.5 mi.) when it curves back towards the center of town and you pass the Battir Mosque (to your R); 230m (0.14 mi.) further down the main road you find the entry to the Court of Seven Widows on the L side next to a few cypress trees and opposite a small supermarket: the entrance (not signposted) to the Court of Seven Widows is by means of a wide set of stairs going down. From Ramallah, you can reach Battir via Bethlehem and al-Khader village.

Public transportation: via Bethlehem.

Battir's centuries' old irrigation system

Battir's Public Park

Where to Park

You can park on the main road near the entrance to the Court of Seven Widows. Walk down the stairs; the court runs down to the L. You find the Hassan Mustafa Cultural Center in one of the last houses on the R side. Battir's new Eco Museum, the start of both walking trails, was planned for in another set of historical buildings located next to the Cultural Center.

Eat, Drink, Relax

On the Wadi Maghrour walk, a stop at the **Maghrour Restaurant** (052-2877515) is highly recommended. For the Wadi Jama walk, it is recommended to bring a picnic. At the time of writing, there were no restaurants in Battir.

Overnight

No accomodation was available at the time of writing but a guesthouse was being planned as part of a larger project to further revive Battir's historic center. Nearby options for accomodation can also be found in Beit Jalla, Bethlehem and Beit Sahour.

Places to Go, People to Meet

The Battir Resort (Muntaza Battir) has a swimming pool and a shop for snacks and is located just above Wadi Jama and next to Ain Jama. It is open between April and September. The **Battir Public Park** is on the Wadi Jama trail and a nice stopover for a picnic. **Battir's Craft Factory** sells local crafts and is located on the main road at the start of the Maghrour trail. As the cradle of Christianity, nearby Bethlehem is the West Bank's main tourist hub; check out the city's Visitor Information Center on Manger Square for an overview of the many things to see and do (see link below).

On the Web

www.palestine-vic.ps

My Favorite Walk

What is it that confers the noblest delight? What is that which swells a man's breast with pride above that which any other experience can bring to him? Discovery! To know that you are walking where none others have walked (. . .)

Mark Twain wrote this in *Innocents Abroad* as he passed through Rome, and on his way to Palestine. He pressed upon his readers his grand disappointment with the fact that everything he saw on his journey had already been discovered and described by others before him. Twain was not referring to being literally the first man to put his footprint somewhere, but to actually experiencing a place in a fresh way and without the deep flaws of travel guides. By informing the reader on what is there and why it is special, guides inevitably are spoilers as much as they are helpers. This book is no exception. It could have made do with just one phrase: Walk Palestine. Yet few would have gone.

Another flaw of travel books is the false claim of comprehensive coverage. Somewhat belatedly, in this last chapter, this book hereby claims incomprehensive coverage. It provides the mere first steps with some 250km of Palestinian walking trail. And so there remain hundreds of villages, wadis and hills outside the scope of this book. From the terraces around Deir Ghassaneh to the vineyards of Hebron and the long shores of Gaza.

25 From Palestine to Palestine

[1-8km/0.62-4.9 mi.] My favorite walk has always been discovering a new trail: exploring new areas, meeting new people, hearing new stories. Beyond the limited number of walks in this book, I would encourage others to do the same. If you go on a new walk, take the practical advice provided at the start of this book to heart.

[9-16km/5.5-9.9 mi.] There is not one right way to plan new walks. You can go by local knowledge, or consult books and websites. However much you can discover online, a good hard copy map remains essential to actually explore new walking routes. At the time of writing there was no Palestinian-made map with sufficent detail available for the West Bank as a whole. The Israeli maps produced by the Society for the Protection of Nature in Israel (SPNI) provide a good practical alternative. Although place names are indicated in Hebrew only, with an English road atlas to the side these can be easily converted to English or Arabic for non-Hebrew speakers. Google Earth and Google Maps are an excellent online tool for planning walks and for measuring their distance and elevation change. As with paper maps, however, images are often outdated; beautiful wadi trails can turn into paved roads and hillside terraces into apartment blocks. Going into the field is the only way to find your way.

[16-25km/9.9-15.5 mi.] Virtual communities provide superb means to share ideas and information. It is no different for exploring Palestine's ancient walking paths. If you would like to learn from others and share your ideas, pictures or GPS coordinates about trails, villages, ancient sites and places to enjoy the outdoors, walk on online: www.walkingpalestine.org.

Trail: *Min ay mahal la ay mahal* (from somewhere to elsewhere)

Grade: Possibly easy, probably moderate, maybe hard

Surface: Dirt roads, single track paths, off-road scrambles and some sections of paved road

Marked: No

Distance and Duration: Various km and several hours

Elevation Change: Yes

Start Coordinates: www.walkingpalestine.org

Digging Palestine

If you are keen to dig deeper into historic Palestine, there is one source unrivalled in its comprehensiveness, unparalleled in its detail. Almost immediately after its founding in 1867, the British Palestine Exploration Fund undertook what has remained its most renowned project up to today: the *Survey of Western Palestine*. The work was undertaken between 1871 and 1878 by a team of British academics and army lieutenants quietly exploring a Palestine then ruled by the Ottomans. The work resulted in over 3000 pages of documentation on Palestine's geographic and ethnic composition, including unique drawings, and a detailed set of maps. Walkers keen to dig down some 140 years can find information on the smallest of Palestinian villages that straddle the walking trails in this book, and much of the landscape described. As for the original survey, alas, it is only available for those with deep pockets: the complete volumes cost around US$ 7000 in the better antique book stores. Yet parts of the work have been reprinted in more affordable copies and much is available online (www.archive.org).

Fortunately, since the 1870s a few more recent initiatives to share a wealth of information on Palestine have been undertaken. Salman Abu Sitta moved mountains to painstakingly put together a wealth of historic information in his 600+ pages *Atlas of Palestine 1917-1966* (Palestine Land Society, London). Under the guidance of US academics from the University of Southern California (USC) and the University of California, Los Angeles (UCLA), a group of Israeli and Palestinian archeologists managed to do what public officials and politicians have been unable to achieve: they painstakingly put together a database of all Israeli surveys of West Bank and East Jerusalem sites since 1967. The database, searchable through a Google Maps interface, includes information such as site names, their major components, historic periods, GIS location, and relevant publications. Publically available, the database helps correct a large asymmetry of information that existed previously when much of the research records on the West Bank were available in Hebrew only, and in records kept at Israeli institutions. So if before or after a walk in the West Bank you are keen to track down the history of the ruins, caves, tombs, cisterns, and occasional shreds of pottery you come across, navigate the database at: http://digitallibrary.usc.edu/wbarc/.

Heritage in Sebastia

Fording Your Way Around: Palestinian Public Transportation

When you travel, if you want to get to know a people, use their public transportation. If you look for optimal comfort, minimum hassle and a lot of privacy, the Palestinian commute is not for you. But if you relish a truly local experience and consider it a part of your West Bank expedition, public transportation is a good option. Essentially, what you need is enough time on your hands. And yes, a small amount of money: to the budget conscious, using public transportation will cost only a fraction of car rental or taxis and helps save you money for better things to come.

The most important difference with other transportation such as car hire or tourist buses is that an immersion in Palestinian public transportation will subject you to the same systemic uncertainty that Palestinians face when they travel. Inside the West Bank, more often than not, a journey will be smooth and the time difference between bus and private car is often negligible—in particular as most bus drivers tend to step on it whenever they can. However, Palestinian buses (like Palestinian cars) can also be stopped and held up at Israeli checkpoints inside the West Bank. If it is your unlucky day, hold-ups can be long. Another difference is that while public transportation runs frequently throughout the day, in the evening hours there are few options with none at all from some locations.

Inside the West Bank

With their random alignment of conspicuously identical yellow vans, bus stations in any Palestinian city seem to reflect a higher order of chaos. Appearances deceive however: there is a system at work here and one that is not too complex to understand for an outsider if you make the effort. In fact, Palestinian public transportation is not much different than it

Organized chaos in Ramallah

Slow wheels in Sebastia

is elsewhere around the world. Veteran back-packers might be even positively surprised as the extreme crowdedness you find elsewhere is not the standard in Palestine. Regular large and mid-sized buses (*basaat*) operate between some of the big cities and to and from Jerusalem but the bulk of Palestinian public transportation is made up of the smaller yellow service taxis called *servis* or ford (plural: *fordaat*), so named after the 9 seater Ford Transit vans

that are mostly used.

Fordaat cost slightly more than the bigger buses but they leave more frequently and take less time (in part, it should be said, because of more hazardous driving). The *fordaat* do not have set times but leave when they are full or nearly full. In the main cities, *fordaat* leave very often, especially towards other major cities. Stops can conveniently be requested anywhere along the route (fellow passengers will help

you when in doubt) and prices are fixed. Your secret to decoding a bus station full of unnumbered anonymous *fordaat* is to open your mouth. Just ask around and you will quickly find your way to the right bus, knowing what to pay and where to get out. At a bus station (*karaj al-basaat*) you will not have much trouble finding a Palestinian who speaks English and can help you. Keep in mind that *fordaat* are small and packed so it is best to keep your own luggage to a minimum.

To get around in the West Bank to the locations described in this book, there are basically three main hubs. Ramallah is the West Bank's central hub with direct connections to nearly all Palestinian cities. If the direct connection is not leaving any time soon when you arrive at the station, you might be better off with a ford going in your direction and changing later on. Bethlehem is the main hub for traffic going south and Nablus for traffic going further north.

From Jerusalem

There are two Palestinian bus stations in Jerusalem, both close to Damascus Gate and only a few hundred meters from one another. Buses for Ramallah and the northern Jerusalem suburbs such as Beit Hanina and Shufat leave from the northern station (*Karaj Nables*) whereas buses to southern Jerusalem and Bethlehem leave from the southern station (*Karaj Baab al-Amoud*). Bethlehem connects to the southern West Bank and Ramallah to virtually all other West Bank destinations. Travel to Jericho is via the village of al-Azzariya. From and to Jerusalem, the buses are numbered: 18 to Ramallah (white-green) and 21 and 124 to Bethlehem (white-blue). Bus 124 runs only to the so-called Rachel Tomb (or 300) checkpoint at the northern end of Bethlehem after which you have to cross on foot and take a taxi on the other end. Bus 21 runs via Beit Jalla.

You will normally not be checked leaving Jerusalem for Ramallah or Bethlehem. On the way back, it is a different story. Passengers have to disembark and walk through a pedestrian crossings for airport style x-raying of belongings and a quick identity card check (always take your passport with you). In contrast to airports though, no effort has been made to beautify or comfort the experience of crossing: concrete blocks, steel-barred rotating doors and crossing guards that wished they were somewhere else set the mood. The crossings can be crowded, especially in the morning hours and late afternoons. Remember that if you wish for a local Palestinian experience, you might get both the honey and the vinegar.

Rent a ford

If you are a fairly large group traveling inside the West Bank, consider renting a local ford to your destination. It will be faster, easier and can be cheaper than organizing public transportation with transfers for lots of people. While some drivers have fixed routes that they have to drive, others are free to take groups and serve as inexpensive taxi buses. Ask around the bus station to know which drivers would be available for this.

Prices and duration

Prices for public transportation are reasonable, and especially low compared to hiring a car or private taxis. A commute from Jerusalem to either Ramallah or Bethlehem (around 40 minutes) costs around 7 NIS. From Ramallah to Bethlehem (90 minutes) around 20 NIS, and Ramallah-Nablus (60 minutes) should set you back around 16 NIS. Nablus to Jenin (40 minutes) costs around 15 NIS.

Walking Civil Society: Ecotourism in Palestine

The number of visitors to Palestine has been on a steep rise in the last few years. While pilgrimage to world renowned religious sites such as Bethlehem's Nativity Church remains the largest segment, eco-tourism and tourism focusing on heritage, history, local communities, and culture has been booming as well; a new hybrid of all these forms is so-called solidarity tourism, which often involves voluntary work in addition to sightseeing. Local tourism inside the West Bank has also increased, leading to an additional boost of new restaurants, pools and resorts, guest houses and hotels.

The following section gives an overview of some of the public, private and civil society organizations that together make up much of the Palestinian tourism and hospitality sector, or are involved through their work on heritage, wildlife and conservation.

Palestinian NGOs in ecotourism, wildlife and heritage conservation

Lacking a few basic features that are normally considered fairly essential for any tourism destination—an airport for example, or these things called borders—Palestinians make up for this through their unabated energy in creating civil society organizations for virtually every possible cause. In tourism, there are quite a few and the following is a list of organizations working to promote eco-tourism, wildlife and heritage conservation. Many of these NGOs have been important resources in supporting the work done for this book and can be approached to assist with guided walks or multi-day tours. They are presented in alphabetical order.

The Alternative Tourism Group (ATG) is the only NGO in this list that focuses solely on tourism to Palestine, hosting groups of regular tourists, pilgrims, academia, journalists, foreign NGOs and political organizations on a wide variety of tours. They organize walking tours on the Nativity Trail with Siraj (see below). ATG is based in Beit Sahour. www.atg.ps; info@atg.ps; and 02-2772151.

The Applied Research Institute of Jerusalem (ARIJ) is devoted to sustainable development and carries out economic, social, environmental and agricultural research across occupied Palestinian territory. ARIJ is also Palestine's state of the art mapping center with maps developed across a wide range of political, social, economic and environmental themes.

They are the first institution to have developed hiking maps for the West Bank area. ARIJ is based in Bethlehem, Ramallah and Tubas. www.arij.org; pmaster@arij.org; and 02-2741889.

Friends of the Earth Middle East (FOEME) is a regional NGO consisting of Palestinian, Israeli and Jordanian environmentalists aiming to protect their shared environmental heritage. FOEME has worked on so-called "Neighbors Trails" which contain walking routes along Israeli, Palestinian and Jordanian villages facing specific water issues. www.foeme.org; info@foeme.org; and 02-2747948 (Bethlehem), 03-5605383 (Tel Aviv), +962 6-5866602 (Amman).

The Hakoura Center is a Jenin based project providing a platform for a wide variety of local NGOs providing activities for young people and families around Jenin in areas such as education, IT, language classes, fair trade products and tourism. Hakoura,—meaning "small garden"—offers tours on history, archeology and life in Palestinian communities to groups or individuals that visit Jenin city and its surrounding villages; it can also organize walking tours. www.hakoura-jenin.ps; center@hakoura-jenin.ps; and 04-2504773.

The Jericho Mosaic Center is a training center for young craftsmen and women in mosaic production and conservation. It also aims to promote local awareness about Palestinian cultural heritage and works with local communities in linking Palestinian heritage to tourism opportunities. Their main office, shop and workshop is in Jericho but they also do work in Sebastia. www.mosaiccentre-jericho.com; info@mosaiccentre-jericho.com; and 02-326342.

The Palestinian Association for Cultural Exchange (PACE) is based in Ramallah (al-Bireh) and promotes Palestinian culture through education, preservation work, research and exchange programmes. It has specialized among others in running tours for foreign visitors to the lesser known Palestinian cities such as Hebron, Nablus, Jenin and the vicinity of Ramallah. It has also done work on stimulating rural tourism to the Jenin area. www.pace.ps; pace@p-ol.com; and 02-2407611.

The mission of **The Palestinian Wildlife Society** (PWLS) is to conserve and enhance Palestinian biodiversity. It has developed activities in research, education, and eco-tourism for a local and international audience. Most trails in this book include excellent spots for watching birds and the PWLS gladly offers professional guidance (and equipment) to help you spot them (keep in mind that if birdlife is your focus, walking a trail with PWLS will take longer than indicated in this book). PWLS is a partner in Birdlife International and is based in Beit Sahour. www.wildlife-pal.org; pwls@wildlife-pal.org; and 02-2774373.

Riwaq focuses on the understanding, protection and rehabilitation of Palestinian cultural heritage. Its survey work of historic buildings in 420 Palestinian villages in the West Bank, Gaza Strip and Jerusalem culminated in a National Register of Historic Buildings. Riwaq is based in Ramallah. www.riwaq.

org; info@riwaq.org; and 02-2406887.

The Rozana Association is a Birzeit based NGO working on agro-cultural tourism in the Birzeit area. Rozana organizes tours in Birzeit and other Palestinian villages such as Deir Ghassaneh, Deir Ammar and Taybeh. It is also partnering in the rehabilitation of the Birzeit's old city. www.rozana.ps; and 02819850.

The Siraj Center for Holy Land Studies aims to create links between Palestinians and people elsewhere through educational tourism, interfaith dialogue, and youth exchange programs. Siraj is based in Beit Sahour and organizes multiday walking tours on the Nativity Trail from Nazareth to Bethlehem (with ATG) and is a co-founder of the Abraham Path Initiative (*Masar Ibrahim al-Khalil*). www.sirajcenter.org and www.abrahampath.org/palestine.php; info@sirajcenter.org; and 02-2748590.

Celebrating Palestine: Festival Calendar

Apart from a long list of feasts and celebrations surrounding religious holidays, the following are some of the Palestinian festivals taking place in the West Bank and Jerusalem. Festivals usually take place around the same period every year, but dates tend to vary, especially when Ramadan is near. Check the links below for more information.

February	**The Jericho Winter Festival** a multi-venue, multi-activity outdoor festival organized by the Jericho Municipality. www.jericho-city.org/english.php
March/April	**Artas Lettuce Festival** celebrating the Palestinian peasant with food, dance and folklore. Artas Folklore Center: 0599-992509 or artasfcenter@gmail.com.
May	**Jifna Apricot Festival** enjoying the apricot season with food and music. First half of May.
June	**Beit Jala Apricot Festival** yet another celebration of apricots, this time in the pretty town of Beit Jala. **Fakkus Festival**, **Beit Sahour** famous for its special *Fakkus* brand of cucumber, Beit Sahour residents organize festivities in its honor.
July	**Jerusalem Festival** 10 days of music and dance from renowned international and Palestinian artists, staged at the ancient Tombs of the Kings in Jerusalem in the second half of July. www.yabous.org **Sounding Jerusalem Festival** chamber music festival organized on scenic locations in East and West Jerusalem and in the West Bank. www.soundingjerusalem.com **Palestine International Festival for Dance and Music** a wide variety of Palestinian and foreign artists performing in Ramallah, across the West Bank and elsewhere. www.popularartcentre.org

July/August	**Sebastia Festival** putting the spotlight on Sebastia's heritage with three days of events among its Roman ruins and at al-Najah University in Nablus. **Battir Festival** a folk celebration around the results of the yearly *tawjihi*, the local school exams. Check the Battir Landscape Office for dates: 02-2763509.
September	**Al-Khader Grape Festival** long live al-Khader grapes, especially with folk songs, dance and poetry at their side. Organized by the al-Khader municipality.
September/October	**Taybeh Oktoberfest** innovative micro makeover of München's grand beergardens and supported by a potpourri of Palestinian and foreign music and dance groups. www.taybehmunicipality.org
October	**Olive Oil Festival, Bethlehem** sounds, sights and tastes of traditional Bethlehem at Manger square. www.visitpalestine.ps
November	**Olive Harvest Festival, Jenin** Palestine's largest celebration of the olive harvest, includes food tasting, music, dance and poetry. Organized the first Friday of November. www.palestinefairtrade.org **Wine Festival, Beit Jalla** tasting the one and only Palestinian wine at the Cremisan Monastery. www.cremisan.org

A good overview is also provided by the Ministry of Tourism's web portal: www.travelpalestine.ps/site/Events-Celebrations.php.

Tafaddal! Arabic on the Trail

Arabic is no easy language, but learning a few basics goes a long way in making contact and finding your way around.

There is no standard form to write Arabic in transliteration. In the other chapters of this book, Arabic words and place names have been transliterated in the forms most frequently used in Palestine. In contrast, the words and phrases below have been written in such a way that they come closest phonetically to English. Most but not all Arabic letters correspond directly to letters in the Latin alphabet. Below an attempt is made to introduce some of the ones that do not.

The letter *khaa* (خ, depicted below as *kh*) is pronounced as *ch* in the Scottish loch. The *'ain* (ع, ') sounds somewhat as a strangulated *ah* sound (but you are likely to be understood even if you mispronounce it). The *qaaf* (ق, *q*) sounds like a *k* but pronounced softer and in the back of the throat. The *ghayn* (غ, *gh*) is a non-existent sound in English; it comes close to the sound people make when gargling, and also resembles closely the throaty *r* in the French word rue.

Double vowels in the list below: *ee* as in the English word deer; *ii* as the long vowel in knee; *aa* as a prolonged *a* in arm; *oo* as in moon; and *oa* as in road.

BASICS	TRANSLITERATION	ARABIC SCRIPT
Hello	*marhaba*	مرحبا
Hello (peace be upon you)	*a-salaamu 'alaykum*	السلام عليكم
response: and onto you	*wa 'alaykum a-salaam*	وعليكم السلام
Good morning	*sabah il-kheer*	صباح الخير
Good evening	*masa il-kheer*	مسا الخير
Welcome	*ahlan wa sahlan*	أهلاً وسهلاً
How are you?	*kiif haalak? (m) / kiif haalek? (f)*	كيف حالك/ كيف حالك
Response: fine, thanks to god	*al-hamdulila*	الحمد لله
Nice to meet you	*tsharafna*	تشرفنا
Bye (go in peace)	*ma' asalaame*	مع السلامة
See you later	*bashufak*	بشوفك
Yes	*aiwa*	أيوة
No	*laa*	لا
Maybe	*mumken*	ممكن
Thank you	*shukran*	شكراً
Excuse me	*aasef (m) / aasfe (f)*	آسف/ اسفة
Please / you are welcome	*tafaddal (m) / tafaddali (f)*	تفَضّل/ تفْضلّي

INTRODUCTION	TRANSLITERATION	ARABIC SCRIPT
What's your name?	*shu ismak? (m) shu ismek? (f)*	شو اسمك – شو اسمك
My name is . . .	*ismii*	اسمَي
Where are you from?	*inte min wain?*	أنت من وين
I am from . . .	*ana min . . .*	أنا من
America	*amriika*	أميركا
Europe	*europa*	أوروبا
Germany	*almaania*	ألمانيا
France	*faransa*	فرنسا
Britain	*britania*	بريطانيا
Spain	*espania*	إسبانيا
Italy	*italia*	إيطاليا
Netherlands	*holanda*	هولندا
Israel	*israiil*	إسرائيل

DIRECTIONS

I walk from . . . to . . .	*bamshi min . . . la . . .*	بمَشي من ...لَ
Where are you going?	*wain raayeh?*	وين رايح؟
Where is . . . ?	*wain . . . ?*	وين
Is there . . . ?	*fii . . . ?*	في
How many minutes/hours to . . .	*akam daqiiqa/saa'a la . . . ?*	أكم دَقيقة / ساعة لـ...؟
Straight	*dughri*	دغري
Left	*shmaal*	شمال
Right	*yamiin*	يمين
Up	*foaq*	فوق
Down	*tahet*	تحت
North	*shamaal*	شمال
South	*janoob*	جنوب
East	*sharq*	شرق
West	*ghrarb*	غرب
Here	*hoan*	هون
There	*hunaak*	هناك

TRAIL SPECIFICS

Path	*masaar*	مسار
Way/road/trail	*tariiq*	طريق
Map	*kharta*	خارطة
Village	*qariiya*	قرية
City	*madiine*	مدينة
Wadi	*wadi*	وادي

Valley	*marj*	مرج
Hill	*tal*	تل
Mountain	*jabal*	جبل
Cave	*m-ghrara*	مغارة
Spring	*'ain*	عين
Ruins	*khirbe*	خربة
Church	*kniisa*	كنيسة
Mosque	*jaame'*	جامع
Large	*kbiir*	كبير
Small	*z-ghriir*	صغير

TRANSPORT/ ACCOMODATION

Car	*sayaara*	سيّارة
Taxi	*taxi*	تكسي
Service taxi	*serviis / ford*	سرفيس / فورد
Bus	*baas*	باص
Bus station	*karaj*	كَرَاج
Checkpoint	*makhsom (Hebrew)*	محسوم
Crossing	*ma'abar*	معبر
ID	*hawiiye*	هويّة
Passport	*jawaaz safar*	جواز سفر
Hotel	*funduq*	فندق
Room	*ghurfe*	غرفة

WEATHER

Rain	*matar*	مطر
Sun	*shams*	شمس
Wind	*hawa*	هوا
Warm	*shoab*	شوب
Cold	*bard*	برد

FOOD

Water	*maye*	ميّ
Market	*sooq*	سوق
Bread	*khubez*	خبز
Fruit	*fawake*	فواكه
Vegetable	*khudra*	خضرا
Coffee	*qahwe*	قهوة
Tea	*shai*	شاي

Glossary   Walking terminology used in this book

Dirt road unpaved road—usually an agricultural road—wide enough for tractors

Ford yellow mini buses used for public transportation in the West Bank

Gully a small natural water channel running down a hill slope (formed by streams of rainwater flowing down to the wadi bed)

Single track footpath wide enough for walkers but too narrow for vehicles of any kind

Slab less than vertical cliff

Trail walking route as provided in the description and on the map, either marked or unmarked

Trail markers paint signs on stone or other surfaces indicating the direction of the trail

!! Attention to route

ARABIC WORDS

Ain	spring
Beit	house
Burj	tower
Deer	monastery or convent
Dunam	unit of land measure with 1 dunam being 1000 m² (10 dunam is 1 hectare)
Jabal	mountain
Khirbe(t)	ruins
Maqam	shrine/holy place
Nabi	prophet
Qasr	castle or palace
Souk	market
Tel	hill
Wadi	seasonal river bed (usually dry except during hard rains)

ABBREVIATIONS

Rd	Road
R	right
L	left
N	north
S	south
E	east
W	west
m	meter
km	kilometer
CP	checkpoint
pp	per person (price)
pppn	per person per night (price)

CPSIA information can be obtained at www.ICGtesting.com
Printed in the USA
LVIW01n2116020718
582502LV00007B/80